Head Case

A Very Painful Healing Journey

Herbert Stepherson

Joshua Tree
Publishing

• Chicago •

Head Case
A Very Painful Healing Journey
Herbert Stepherson

Published by
Joshua Tree Publishing
• Chicago •
JoshuaTreePublishing.com

13-Digit ISBN: 978-1-956823-55-4
Cover Artwork Credits: Front © jiris Adobe Stock
Back © Rawf8 Adobe Stock

Disclaimer:
This book is designed to provide information about the subject matter covered. The opinions and information expressed in this book are those of the author, not the publisher. Every effort has been made to make this book as complete and as accurate as possible. However, there may be mistakes both typographical and in content. Therefore, this text should be used only as a general guide and not as the ultimate source of information. The author and publisher of this book shall have neither liability nor responsibility to any person or entity with respect to any loss or damage caused or alleged to be caused directly or indirectly by the information contained in this book.

Printed in the United States of America

Dedication

This book is dedicated to everyone out there who suffers from mental health and substance abuse issues. It is dedicated to all those who are the front lines in the treatment industry, working tirelessly and selflessly to help those who suffer. This book is dedicated to the families of loved ones who suffer. It is for those who suffer in silence, feeling like there is no one to talk to, and that no one understands. I understand brothers and sisters! This book is dedicated to each and every one of you who has suffered traumas that no one knows about. I pray that the pages of this book can and will inspire you to find the courage to finally get vulnerable and open up to some professional help so you can finally heal those wounded places. And that you find peace.

This book is dedicated to the "Outcasts," the "Lost Ones," and those who have been bullied, beaten, neglected, and hurt. This book is for the "Have-nots," the "nobodies," the "Underdogs," and for all those who are fighting silent internal battles.

This book is for all who love people like this.

For I am with you because I am you. I believe in each and every one of you! You are mighty warriors and survivors! Do not ever give up! Tomorrow is better with you in it! I truly believe in you with my whole heart!

This book is also dedicated to my family: my wife Tiffany, and our children Jamie, Logan, Connor, and Luke. It is dedicated to my Dad and step-mother Gail. To my brothers Joshua and Lucas.

Thank you so very much for believing in me and for never giving up on me! I love you all with my whole entire heart.

Table of Contents

My Diagram of PTSD

Post Traumatic Stress Disorder (PTSD)

PTSD: Exposure to actual or threatened death, serious injury, or sexual violence in one (or more) of the following ways:

- Directly experiencing the traumatic event(s).

- Witnessing, in person, the event(s) as it occurred to others.

- Presence of one (or more) of the following intrusion symptoms associated with the traumatic event(s), beginning after the traumatic event(s) occurred:
    - Intense or prolonged psychological distress at exposure to internal or external cues that symbolize or resemble an aspect of the traumatic event(s).
    - Marked physiological reactions to internal or external cues that symbolize or resemble an aspect of the traumatic event(s).

- Persistent avoidance of stimuli associated with the traumatic event(s), beginning after the traumatic event(s) occurred, as evidenced by one or both of the following:
    - Avoidance of or efforts to avoid distressing memories, thoughts, or feelings about or closely associated with the traumatic event(s).
    - Avoidance of or efforts to avoid external reminders (people, places, conversations, activities, objects, situations) that arouse distressing memories, thoughts, or feelings about or closely associated with the traumatic event(s).

- Negative alterations in cognitions and mood associated with the traumatic event(s), beginning or worsening after the traumatic event(s) occurred, as evidenced by two (or more) of the following:
  - Inability to remember an important aspect of the traumatic event(s) (typically due to dissociative amnesia and not to other factors such as head injury, alcohol, or drugs).
  - Persistent and exaggerated negative beliefs or expectations about oneself, others, or the world (e.g., "I am bad," "No one can be trusted," "The world is completely dangerous," "My whole nervous system is permanently ruined").
  - Persistent, distorted cognitions about the cause or consequences of the traumatic event(s) that lead the individual to blame himself/herself or others.
  - Persistent negative emotional state (e.g., fear, horror, anger, guilt, or shame).
  - Markedly diminished interest or participation in significant activities.
  - Feelings of detachment or estrangement from others.

- Persistent inability to experience positive emotions (e.g., inability to experience happiness, satisfaction, or loving feelings).
  - Marked alterations in arousal and reactivity associated with the traumatic event(s), beginning or worsening after the traumatic event(s) occurred, as evidenced by two (or more) of the following:
  - Irritable behavior and angry outbursts (with little or no provocation) typically expressed as verbal or physical aggression toward people or objects.
  - Reckless or self-destructive behavior.
  - Hypervigilance.
  - Exaggerated startle response.
  - Problems with concentration.
  - Duration of the disturbance is more than one month.
  - The disturbance causes clinically significant distress or impairment in social, occupational, or other important areas of functioning.

- The disturbance is not attributable to the physiological effects of a substance (e.g., medication, alcohol) or another medical condition.

Borderline Personality Disorder (BPD)

Borderline Personality Disorder (BPD: A pervasive pattern of instability of interpersonal relationships, self-image, and affects, and marked impulsivity, beginning by early adulthood and present in a variety of contexts, as indicated by five (or more) of the following:

- Frantic efforts to avoid real or imagined abandonment.
- A pattern of unstable and intense interpersonal relationships characterized by alternating between extremes of idealization and devaluation.
- Identity disturbance: markedly and persistently unstable self-image or sense of self.
- Impulsivity in at least two areas that are potentially self-damaging (e.g., spending, sex, substance abuse, reckless driving, binge eating).
- Recurrent suicidal behavior, gestures, or threats, or self-mutilating behavior.
- Affective instability due to a marked reactivity of mood (e.g., intense episodic dysphoria, irritability, or anxiety usually lasting a few hours and only rarely more than a few days).
- Chronic feelings of emptiness.
- Inappropriate, intense anger or difficulty controlling anger (e.g., frequent displays of temper, constant anger, recurrent physical fights).
- Transient, stress-related paranoid ideation or severe dissociative symptoms.

Space Shuttle

Recently, there was an event that led me to a monumental upheaval in my life and in my mind. Or was it just an event? Or was it not, as always, a culmination of both recent and not so recent, unhealed parts of myself coming to the surface?

I find myself sitting in front of another therapist, finally willing to look at parts of my life . . . difficult, ugly, and fragile portions of me . . . that I had tried so hard not to acknowledge for many, many years. I don't even know if I possess the ability to try and explain all of these swirling thoughts in my heart and in my mind. But I owe it to myself, and to my readers, to try.

I was instructed to download/order a book by my therapist. A book which would help me better understand why I am the way that I am. Why my mind fires the way that it does. The premise is to "Recognize Patterns, Heal from the Past, Create Yourself."

Heal from my past?

But I thought that I had already done that? Is that not what step work, confession, meetings, sponsorship, fellowship, etc. is all about? It is, but what I have realized recently is that there are parts of me, parts of my past, that I hid, even from myself if that even sounds possible.

What is Trauma?

Have you ever experienced trauma? How do you know that it was indeed trauma, by definition? I personally never really fully understood the meaning of trauma until recently. I was just so used to saying things like, "I've been through a lot" or "I've had it rough for a long time." I hadn't ever really put two and two together until I was finally able and willing to speak some really ugly, shameful truths about my life overall.

I suppose that I was so accustomed to chaos, and to surviving trauma, that in my recent years I kind of developed a crack pot theory that went something like: "I believe that, for some, the simple and basic process of merely growing up and living life is traumatic." And that is true, I believe, to an extent.

My therapist said something like, "Just think about it. The event of simply being born is trauma for some. Going from 'sleep' inside your mother's womb, in the dark, comfort and warmth, to then seemingly out of nowhere, BOOM. You're thrust into these blinding lights, and your life here on earth has begun."

I can certainly get with that, but what do we as new-born babies really process? Or is it mostly shock and awe that we first experience?

It's very interesting to me how these ideas and memories have seemingly been unlocked in my brain recently. I suppose that I have adapted to so much over my young 36.5 years here on earth that I have figured out how to protect myself through disassociation and compartmentalization.

What's equally interesting to me, is the way that I have adapted certain "responses" in my repertoire without even designing them— they just sort of happened.

They say that we are products of our environment, which I agree with to some extent, but we also must find a way to not be. We also must find a way to heal and overcome the things that we were born into. But for some, that is much easier said than done.

For me, I didn't even realize until recently, that some of the things that I needed to overcome and heal from even affected me. I guess, I was just continuing with my life as if I had been healed from them, like some type of arrogant survivor of great battles; but the truth is, I never even acknowledged them. I was doing the exact same thing, as I was conditioned to do, that I had always done my entire life. I was stuffing things deep down inside, hoping that nothing would ever "prick" those memories, self-medicating myself, and hiding from it all. But those of us who do not learn or heal from the past, are doomed to repeat it.

The last time I was in therapy was some years ago, and the wonderful lady that I was seeing for my sessions kept using the term, "Trauma Repetition."

At the time, and during the sessions when this buzz word would come up, I would nod my head in agreement as if I actually had any sort of deep understanding of what this meant. I didn't, but I think that I am starting to understand it now.

Those of us who are familiar with recovering addicts/ alcoholics—or have been around anyone who struggles with mental health or substance abuse—have probably heard them say something along the lines of, "Oh, I'm really good at bouncing back. I can 'come up' with the best of 'em."

But what is that really saying? Is it saying, "All I know is the constant cycle of chaos/destruction/trauma, and how to burn things to the ground as a result, then compartmentalize it, dust myself off, and only bounce back as far as my repetition cycle will allow me to . . . only to go and do it all over again?"

I hope that makes sense because I can see it in my mind. And that's what I've known and done for pretty much all of my life.

Trauma Repetition.

The idea that I am only truly "Comfortable" in the turmoil, in the chaos, and in the "rebuilding" from said turmoil in some self-preserving facade to "prove" (delude) myself that I have actually made progress, when in fact, nothing deep down inside has actually ever been addressed—because I have never been spurred to actually go deep, go back, and open up those old dusty boxes buried inside my mind.

And what I am starting to realize lately, is that if I/we do not confront those unhealed parts of our childhood, or those painful parts of our adolescence, then our current life and current relationships are the ones who are going to pay the price for that. I think this is what they mean when they say, "If we don't heal from our past wounds, then we will bleed on people who never cut us."

We will bring our maladapted minds and existing internal wounds into our current lives, and we will still operate on the mechanisms they bring about as today's traumas happen right before our eyes in real time. Even if it is twenty years later.

So, if I still possess abandonment trauma, I may live in the fear that my partner is going to leave me. Then I act out in various fear-based ways, like being jealous, suspicious, or accusatory. Then when they have finally had enough and end up leaving me over my delusional ways, I can say: "HA! I KNEW IT! I knew they were just gonna leave anyway, because I am unlovable, and no one wants me." Thus, reinforcing that trauma cycle and repetition all over again. Interesting.

The traumas that I endured seem to have shaped my mind and influenced my perspective on things. They very much influenced my ideas of people and of the world. And somehow stripped away my sense of self—my individuality.

I suppose because I always felt so invisible and unheard, that I became a traumatized, violated, voiceless, and formless young man whose only real model of adult behavior was that of addicted, untreated, unhealthy, codependent humans. I had no idea what healthy communication and processing was. I had never experienced real trust and bonding before.

The only thing I knew about love was that if I love someone, then there's a very real chance that the person I love is going to leave me—and probably very soon. Trauma touched and shaped everything about me. Every single relationship I have ever had, even the relationship with myself has been viewed through my trauma lens. I had trust issues, major fears of abandonment and betrayal, and felt truly ashamed most of the time. Like, somehow all of the things that I had experienced had happened because of me, not to me. And so, because of all of this, and having zero ways to actually cope with all of it, I possessed zero processing skills. I had little choice but to find relief somehow.

I believe that from a very early age, I began disassociating as a way to escape what was going on around me. Checking out. Like hopping into a little mini-sized Space Shuttle, made for a little boy and flying away to a faraway land. A land that was actually inside of me.

I had to somehow find a safe place, even if that place didn't exist. I had to create one. I began the lifelong practice of compartmentalizing and disassociating in early elementary school. How very sad.

Any time a very high stress event, moment, or season would happen upon me, I would hop into my space shuttle and off I would go.

Disassociation.

1985

Trauma (noun): A deeply distressing or disturbing experience. A personal trauma like the death of a child.

Post-traumatic Stress Disorder (PTSD) and **Traumatic Stress**: An anxiety disorder that develops in reaction to physical injury or severe mental or emotional distress, such as military combat, violent assault, natural disaster, or other life-threatening events.

L ife truly is an interesting experience. It's funny how things can change, just by changing the way we look at them. For the longest time, I would share my story to whoever was listening, and I would say things like, "Yeah, I had a pretty normal childhood." Or, as one of my blurbs from the first book put it, "Herb spent his life like most kids in Georgia, riding bikes and playing baseball." And though that second one is true, it isn't completely. It lacks so very much.

I recently got out of treatment. I had a very steep and dramatic decline in my mental health and was turning to alcohol, India Pale Ale (IPAs) more specifically as a way to cope and deal with all of the symptoms that came along with such an ugly spiral.

Fear, Rumination, Isolation, Suicidal thoughts, Angry outbursts, etc. And it's interesting to me, the whole "The past ain't changin'" school of thought. Because, for me, it absolutely did. I went to treatment "for alcohol, and mental health" and came out with a brand-new perspective on the story of my life. And in order to accurately try and explain it all, I suppose we should start at the very beginning.

July 12, 1985. Foreigner, Skynyrd, and ACDC blast on the sound system of a local bowling alley in Clayton County, Georgia. The sound of pins smashing against each other can be heard from end to end of the building. Pool balls splash as local pool sharks, hustlers, and guppies sip Pabst Blue Ribbon (PBR) beers and smoke Marlboro Reds. The whole place smells like cigarette smoke and cheap hair spray.

High fives go up as a team probably called "The Gutterballs" battles a team probably called "7's and 10's" for the league championship, a $25.00 gift card each and shitty plastic trophy. On lane number 9, a small group has gathered for a Friday night out. Wings, beer, shots of Jack, and more than likely, some key bumps of cocaine in the bathroom. Or Crank. It's the '80s, who the hell knows. An Atlanta Braves game drones on mute on nearby TVs, and some unaccompanied kids run amuck, only stopping by their parent's lane to ask for more money to play in the arcade on the other side of the alley.

It's a normal, hot, and sticky summer night in central Georgia. The crowd is average size and average looking for this particular moment in human history and place on the map. Lots of mustaches, big hair, denim, and motorcycles out front. A small circle of people is gathered around the hood of a muscle car smoking some shitty '80s weed out of a metal pipe while "Freebird" blares through the speakers. Giant yellow moths dart back and forth around the streetlights and the lights above the batting cages.

Inside a group from the lanes bops up to the bar for a couple pitchers of Budweiser and a couple shots of whisky, as one of them throws a five dollar bill into the jukebox and another five into a cigarette machine. The sound of a strike fills the air, followed by the "woooos" and "booms" of celebration as a team takes the lead over the other.

The group from lane number nine is having the best night ever. And they have their own stories to tell. It's been such a journey for them already, and they are just out enjoying the night together. A man and his wife, her brother and his wife, and some friends. They talk about everything under the sun all the time, but tonight it's just having fun. Just enjoying being alive.

The women from the group all make a trip to the lady's room and enjoy a couple bumps of cocaine in the restroom, maybe checking their makeup and scrunching their hair so it looks fresh and extra big, nice and "Aqua Net-y." They laugh and crack jokes about the men in their group, and how they "woulda beat that bitch's ass if she would have kept goin' earlier."

The men in the group decide to take advantage of the women's absence by heading out to smoke a joint and have a cigarette in the parking lot. All is going really well. They are having the best Friday night out in a while. Work's good, spouses are good, life is good. It's a beautiful and warm summer night in Georgia, and no one has any complaints.

The crew reconvenes on their lane, and the night marches on! Pitcher after pitcher, key bump after key bump. Open frame after spare after strike. High fives around. Karaoke breaks out in the bar room, and once their game is over, it's off to hit those notes! The women sing in a group to "Like a Virgin," and the men sing in a group to "Take on Me" as the crowd cheers and yells for an encore. Pull tabs are purchased and played, the losing tabs being discarded into large metal pails. The ashtrays grow increasingly full. The men in the group decide to challenge the women in the group to some team 8-ball with the losing team buying shots for the winners. Life is going incredibly well. Another joint in the parking lot. Another pack of smokes from the machine inside the bar. The men beat the women four games to two, in their little best of seven tournament—and back to Karaoke they go!

This time the women sing a Stevie Nicks' song, and the men sing an ACDC song. Everyone is having the best night ever. It feels so good for them all, to be out and about with zero responsibilities and finally be able to blow off some steam and let the pressures of life wait until Monday morning. After all, they have earned this. Life has been a crazy journey for each and every one of them, and tonight they're just gonna cut loose and seize the night!

The night continues to grow later and later. Blurrier and blurrier. Another key bump in the bathroom will set the world's new slant back to normal, and for the mean time it does!

"Late night Bowl" begins, and the lanes are darkened overhead. The pins become illuminated with various colors and smoke. Now the sound system is taken over by the likes of The Bee Gees, ELO, and Bob Seeger. The night is picking back up, and the crew decides to hop back in for a few more games before they head back to one of their homes for some continued partying and eventually, some food. The place is electric with boogie music, cigarette smoke, cocaine, and acid-washed denim. This is truly a high point in Americana in the mid eighties. Hanging out, getting loaded at a bowling alley, with your friends and family. Hugs are shared, funny stories are told, sexual glances are exchanged between partners, dance moves are busted, songs are sung.

Our little bowling crew is enjoying one of their best nights in a long time, when the girls head off to the bathroom and "powder their noses." Once more the men order up one more round of shots and two more pitchers of beer. The night is drawing to an end—well, this portion anyway. The crew had made plans to reconvene at one of the couple's houses, just after this game ends, and there are only a few frames left.

The men raise their shot glasses in salute, cheering to a successful night and toasting to their friendships. Simultaneously, as the shots hit their stomachs, and the glasses hit the table, one of the men feels a tap on his shoulder from behind. He turns his head around to see who was calling for his attention, and he sees his wife standing just behind him. There is a stagger to her stance from all of the chemicals pumping through her bloodstream. She pulls him in close with her arms around his neck, and on his shoulders. She leans in as if to kiss him and slides her face around to the side of his head, as if to tell him a secret in the dark, disco-lit, late night bowl,

"I think my water just broke," she says to him in a very hushed tone.

Just a couple hours later, a baby was born. A baby was brought into this world drunk and with cocaine in his little system.

On July 12th 1985, a baby was born into chaos and turmoil in Clayton County, Georgia. The baby was me, the couple at the bowling alley that night were my parents.

My first breaths on this planet wouldn't pass a breathalyzer.

My first moments on earth were spent with alcohol and drugs in my system, and my first moments on earth were spent experiencing the first of many, many traumas to come.

The year was 1985.

Snuggles and Popples

*"You know, it's funny, how some things you can
remember and some things you can't?"*
Tom Hanks in *Forrest Gump*

I remember somehow, being told that I was going to be a big brother. And it's weird because I was only like four-years-old at the time, I think. Obviously, it came out of nowhere, but I somehow remember being told that I was going to have a little brother. Now, I can't exactly tell you the outside details of this, like where we were living, or what day or month it was, but it was a big deal to me, which I believe is why I am able to recall it.

My parents had told me they were expecting a baby, and that it was going to be a little boy, and that they had already named him Lucas. And I was so happy! I vividly remember asking my mom very regularly if the baby was ready yet. I was obsessed! It was all I could think about. I would touch my mother's belly all the time and feel little Lucas kick and move around. I would even talk to him and lay on mom's belly to nap with my little brother. I was so excited to have my own little brother. I already had a big brother, Josh, and he was awesome too. I just knew that now having a third, and a little brother too, would just complete everything! I was so happy and proud. Even though I had not met the little guy yet, I just knew he was gonna be my best friend for life!

I suppose my parents had told me that they were expecting a few to several months into the pregnancy, and that's how they already knew the gender of the baby and what they were naming him. So, I can only calculate that at the time, there was only so many months to go, until he was here with us. But man did it feel like forever! I couldn't wait to meet him. I would sit on my mom's lap all the time and ask silly questions about what he was doing in there, how could he breathe, and all of the innocent child questions in preparation of the delivery of my new lifelong friend.

Mom's belly grew and grew! I remember being astonished at how big it got, and a little grossed out at my mom's belly button. LOL. But that's one of the many things that was so fascinating about how my mother's body was changing to accommodate the little human that was growing inside her. I remember just feeling so many emotions. Everything from curiosity to pride, from excitement and anticipation to frustration that he wasn't "ready" yet. It seems like every day I asked her or my dad if the baby was coming soon. I am more than sure I got on their very last nerve. But I am sure that they understood. I was a little one myself, and this was my very first experience with new life, and the process of it. And this was definitely my first experience with having a new brother. I thought about all of the things we would do together as we grew up. I couldn't wait to hold him and kiss him and feed him and protect him. I was gonna be the best big brother ever!

The months dragged on, mom's belly continued to balloon out. As Lucas got bigger and bigger, my excitement grew right along with it! I remember for Christmas that year my parents got a bunch of baby stuff for Lucas and I got a "Snuggles" stuffed teddy bear in the mail from my Gramma, and a "Popples" stuffed toy from my parents. I was so excited to have gotten them both and remember wanting to "share" the stuffed animals with my new little brother when he came. He was all I could think about. I already loved him so much.

I held on to that damn Snuggles bear until I was like twelve-years-old. It actually makes me a little sad to think about right now, but I wonder whatever happened to that stuffed bear of mine. Not in any kind of unhealthy way, but it sure would be nice to have him back, as an heirloom of my childhood to pass on to Lil Luke now. But he's been gone for a long time.

Ah, yes, "Little Luke." You see I love my little brother so much that I named my only biological son after him. But that's a whole other tale.

Anyway, time marched on through the holidays, and I could tell that the baby was going to be coming soon! I could tell by the way people were acting, the way they were talking, and the new crib in our bedroom! I just couldn't take it any longer! I was so excited.

The days absolutely dragged on like molasses, but I did my best to remain as patient as I could. I knew it couldn't possibly be much longer. I remember listening in on the adults' conversations, specifically as it pertained to Lucas coming. And I could tell it was going to be literally any day now. I remember the adults joking about what to do if Lucas was born on the 29th of February. It was Leap Year that year, and there was a real chance he would be born on that day, so what would everyone do about his birthday each year?

Looking back, it is obvious that they would just celebrate him on either the 28th or the 1st, but I clearly remember being so awe stricken that he would be such a "magical" baby right off the bat. I mean he would only have a birthday every four years! He will never grow old! He was gonna get to be with me forever! I was blown away by this concept. The day simply could not get any faster! I made him a card and everything! I drew him a picture of chicken scratch, showing him all the wonderful things we were gonna do and all the cool stuff I was gonna show him!

And then the day finally came! I don't know how it all got started, but I assume it was much like when every other baby in the world has ever been born. Mom's water broke, or she could just tell it was time.

But I do remember all the commotion of the day. The hustle and bustle. Mom and Dad taking off in the car and heading to the hospital. It was a lot to take in, and one of the interesting parts of the memory of it all, is I don't remember who took me to the hospital later, or if it was even that same day. I don't recall the exact timeline, but I think that's because it was just all so much to process and take in. But I do know that it was not a very long time in between. Maybe twelve to twenty-four hours tops. But I will never forget what took place after this. I was still a short little guy, and once I got up into the hospital room area finally about to meet my new little brother, my dad scooped me up to take a look at him. And in my eyes, he was absolutely perfect! This tiny little red-looking, wrinkly little guy. Arms up at his sides, little bitty diaper on him, belly button bandaged up. Just sleeping in heavenly peace. And I remember just being in such awe and loving him so much and just wanting to pick him up and hold him.

I put my own little hand up on the glass, as if he could actually feel my presence, and in that moment, he could. And I just wanted him to know that I was here and that I loved him and always would. And as the weight of the moment lessened and the scope of it all broadened, I was able to take it all in. And I finally noticed that he was in a clear looking tent thing, and that there were tubes and stuff connected to him. And doctors were paying very close attention to him. And even though I was only a little guy myself, I could just feel in my heart that something was very wrong.

"Is he sick dad? Please tell me he's okay."

This was what I can literally feel myself asking my dad, even right now as I write this entry. This moment is so very much branded onto my heart. But in my four, almost five-year-old vocabulary, it probably sounded something like, "what's wong wit him. Lukie sick?"

But I remember the overwhelming feeling. I remember the fear and the heartbreak so very well. My eyes mist just recalling all of this. I just couldn't understand how all of this was happening.

Did I do something wrong? Did I touch Mom's belly too much? Not enough? Does he not want to stay with us?

I remember being so scared and confused by all of this, and almost paralyzed. And what I am able to process about all of this now, and with the help of a therapist, is that this was my first traumatic event. Perhaps that's why some of the details leading up, during, and after are so vivid—and some are non-existent or blacked out. I was experiencing overwhelming traumatic stress for the very first time at the age of almost five, and I just didn't possess the faculties to process it all. It all came together as paralyzing shock.

In the days to come, my parents and I stayed right there in the hospital loving Lucas and being there for him and with him. I remember at one point my grandmother, my mom's mom, coming to try and take me out of there. To take me home to get me some rest and give my parents a break, and I went absolutely ape shit. I think I bit and kicked her. And I am sorry for that, but I was a little guy, and there wasn't anyone about to separate me from Lucas. He needed me to be there, and I was his big brother—I was staying. I didn't care who you were or what you tried; I was not leaving that hospital.

After pitching such a fit and going crazy on my grandma, they let me stay. And I stayed in that hospital with my parents every second that they did. I believe from what I am told that I ended up staying there with them, even overnight, for a total of about two weeks as Lucas battled pneumonia. He had somehow ended up with a very serious case and was clinging to life inside that tent. The tent and the tubes were taking care of him, and there were a few times when things looked grim. But in true Stepherson fashion, he wasn't going out without a serious fight, and he would go on to overcome it! And I was there when they finally took him off everything, removed him from the tent, and put him in swaddling, and brought him out to us. I just knew he was gonna make it, and I am so happy that I was there to protect him through it all!

I finally got to hold my little brother with the help of my parents, and we just stared into each other's eyes. I cried and was so happy! I showed him Snuggles and Popples, and I told Lucas that it was us three, me and the stuffed animals he had to thank for being able to get better. We had his back, and he was gonna be safe as long as he had us three and Josh!

I remember such a peace and ease and joy and happiness coming into the world as we were finally able to take him home. The car ride back to the house, all I could do was talk to little Lucas, and tell him everything! It was one of the best days of my life. But what I didn't know then, or up until recently, is that all of this little glimpse of my life, all of this happening, this event, and everything building up to it, was my very first trauma. Even though it had a happy ending, all the ins and outs of it were very much traumatic for me, and for many I am sure.

But that was okay in the moment. Lucas was coming home, and he had me, Snuggles, and Popples to protect him.

Big Bird

My parents worked a lot—or at least that's the narrative that was shared with me. Now, please forgive me ahead of time if some of my timelines don't always add up 100%. I am trying to put all of this together as best I can as things occurred as I am told. I remind you all that the blacking out of time is common when we are talking about trauma. So, I am doing my best to piece all of this together so that it flows and hopefully it comes out like watching a movie. But anyway, I was told a lot of stories throughout my life by the adults around me, to the point to where I am still not sure to this day what was true and what was made up to "protect" me and my brothers. But looking back and watching the movie of my life in my mind—a lot of things did not make sense.

Another form of trauma, that I would like to point out here, is abandonment trauma. I believe that this is probably the one that actually ended up affecting me the most throughout my life. I remember being very little, and I am not sure exactly how old, maybe "pre-kindergarten" age. I do know that I was able to comprehend something: that for some reason my dad was not there. He was not around and had not been for some time. To be honest with you, I still don't know why. The family has been so fractured over the years, and many are gone now. And it was so long ago now, I doubt if anyone would even remember what I'm talking about. But I know. I remember it very well.

I remember waking up each day and actively looking for my dad. He was nowhere to be found and didn't return home for a very long time. Or, a very long time as my mind could comprehend it. I do remember talking to him on the phone a few times during this period, and the only explanation I was offered at the time was always "Daddy is at work." But I was just old enough to start actually computing things, and my very young senses told me that if he was really at work, he certainly should have come home by now. I mean, he's gotta come home to eat and to shower and to sleep once in a while, right? Well, that was not happening, and it was really starting to weigh on me.

I remember, probably daily, asking my mom if daddy was coming home today. And I also remember the sadness and frustration in my mom's voice every time she would respond with something like, "No, Stevie, not today baby. Soon though, I promise."

I was always very bonded to my dad. I am not exactly sure why, and I don't regret it, but typically, or so I thought, younger littles tend to bond with mom more so than dad early on. But for me, I was always stuck to my dad's hip. He and I did everything together. He, Lucas, and I were inseparable. We always called ourselves the Three Musketeers later on life—all for one, one for all. That was our motto. Dad even took me to work on many, many occasions, when he was working at the cable company. He almost killed us both in a bulldozer one night while we were burning a bunch of trees and old tires working midnights for Peachtree City, but that's a whole other story altogether. The point is that we were always tight. I think it was because I was his first-born son. Josh, although he loved him very much, was fathered by my mom's first husband so Lucas and I were his only biological sons.

Apparently this particular separation really impacted me at the time, because it sticks out in my trauma bank and memories like a sore thumb. I remember literally bugging my mom daily about when my dad was coming home. Throwing tantrums over it, I was screaming and bawling saying things like "I want daddy."

And on one particular evening, when I had been watching cartoons, I remember vividly looking up at this old picture we had of my dad up on the wall. In the picture, he was wearing this PCDC tee shirt (PCDC is Peachtree City Development Corporation). He had a mustache as always, and was kind of looking of at something over the photo taker's shoulder . . . and I absolutely lost it!

I was freaking out so badly that my mom had to call my Aunt Laureen over with her son, so he could come over and play with me. I just knew that I was being lied to, even at that age. Not with any kind of ill intent of course, but because to the adults around me, there was no way that I could possibly comprehend the fact of where my dad really was for that time. I know this may not sound like a truly deep and historical trauma in my life, but remember this one, because it will make a little bit more sense later on.

But it's interesting to me looking back on all of this, because I can see and feel it all as if it were happening right now. And in that time, while I am losing it over the picture on the wall, I finally realized that I am being lied to. That dad is not coming home and is not at work like they say he is. Finally blowing a gasket, it was fully confirmed to me when my aunt and cousin came in the door to help soothe me. My god the immense stress my poor mother must have been feeling at that time. And that's when it really hit me that he was gone somewhere else . . . not to work and not returning any time soon. I don't even recall the timeline that followed, and I don't even remember him finally returning home. But I do remember that when he did come home, he brought me a giant Big Bird stuffed animal. So interesting. How my mind works.

So what's the point? I don't know. But I am trying my best to share with you what all, I believe, went into the making of my trauma brain. And I believe this season was part of it.

Another thing is that this story may not strike you as something overly traumatic, and that's okay. You have a right to feel that way. But just because something like this may or may not have impacted you the same way, doesn't mean it didn't me.

Empathy. Don't lose it. Just because "you/I/we" have suffered worse than someone else, doesn't mean that the other person's pain is invalid.

I still think about where the hell he was during all that time.

Monty

When I was about kindergarten age, we lived in a very diverse apartment complex in Peachtree City, Georgia. I was just like any other kid. I just wanted to play with friends, ride my bike, and be a little boy. I had made a friend about two buildings down, a black boy about my age, who's name escapes me, but I want to say that it was Monty. We played together every single day after school. We were best buddies. We would ride bikes together, swing on the swings, and just run around the complex catching bugs and exploring life.

Well, one day I rode my bike down to Monty's door and knocked as I always did. I was prepared to ask my routine question, "Can Monty come out and play?"

When the door pulled open, I saw a couple of "big kids" standing there. So, I asked, but I immediately remember feeling fear and started to kind of tread backwards, in retreat. The two big kids, who I still don't know who they are to this day, came outside on to the stoop, and started pushing me around, picking on me, and saying really mean things to me.

"Oh, this that little honky boy Monty always talkin' bout, yeah we heard about you—Stevie. Nah we done heard that Monty been runnin' around with you and you need to get ya little pink ass up outta here."

They pushed me to the ground and kicked me in the face. They slapped me, they spit on me, and every time I tried getting up, they would push me down again. I remember being scared, like really scared for the first time.

One of the big kids went inside, grabbed a broom, and then proceeded to beat me repeatedly with it while the other boy absolutely destroyed my little bike and threw it down into a culvert. Finally, Monty came running out trying to help me but was carried back inside crying about what was being done to his buddy. Eventually, a neighbor heard the ruckus, came out to break it all up, and helped me back home. I was bloodied, scraped, crying, and my feelings were so hurt.

When the neighbor finally got me back home and inside to explain what had just happened, it got even worse. My mother threw on her shoes, walked down the sidewalk, and knocked on the very door where all of this just happened. Now I couldn't hear what was being said, but I could see that mom was very angry.

I think my Dad was holding me back, as I didn't want to see any more violence or anyone to get hurt.

The mother of the big kids, who just did this to me, emerged from the apartment, and a confrontation ensued. Out of nowhere the lady went to grab or push my mom, but then she got dealt a brutal right cross that sent blood, spit, and teeth flying out into the grass. I believe this lady was asleep before she even hit the ground. As soon as she did hit the ground, my mom proceeded to stomp her guts out, kicking her in the face, and stomping her head. Once she was satisfied with the revenge that was just dealt, she came back to the apartment, and helped my dad wash all of the blood, snot, and tears off my face. She then sat down and smoked a Marlboro Red 100.

* * *

This was the type of shit that I was exposed to regularly. I used to excuse it as, "It was Georgia in the 90s. It was a really crazy time," but the fact of the matter is no child should have to experience this. And it didn't stop.

Shortly after this, my parents, and Monty's parents made us fight each other, and neither one of us wanted it to happen.

"Beat his ass or I'll beat your ass, boy."

They pushed us at each other, and I refused, but Monty did not. It was very horrible and scary to not throw a single punch and to get the crap kicked out of me by my best friend. All because a little white boy wanted to be friends with a little black boy. This was my first experience with racism. I didn't even know that Monty and I were different at all. I just knew that he was my friend, and now I am being forced to fight him because we have different shades of skin—by our parents of all people! The very people who are supposed to be protecting us from this very type of situation are thrusting us into it! It's disgusting, and it breaks my heart.

Shortly after that, Monty and I found a way to sneak down to the park and play. His older cousin, Travis, caught us swinging on the swings. He tried to play nice like he wasn't bothered at all and had asked us if we wanted to see the new golf club he had just found in the dumpster of the apartment complex. So, being kindergarten naive kids, we said something like "oh yeah, AWESOME!"

Well, Travis used that iron to split my head open from the top of my eyebrow-backwards and then had the soulless audacity to drag me up from the park and knock on a neighbors door asking for help—he got away with it too. I was taken by ambulance, and the cops left because he convinced them all that it was an accident—that we were just playing around.

It breaks my heart that someone could do something like this to a little boy.

I never spoke to Monty again. We would see each other on the bus, or at recess, but we never spoke another word to one another again. I hope he didn't turn out like his predecessors.

Babysitters' Club

I believe the year was probably about 1992. I am not sure if this was before my parents and Monty's parents made us fight each other or not. I feel like it was shortly after. Maybe like a year or so.

We were either still, or again, living in the Woodsmill Apartments in Peachtree City, Georgia. But what I do know is that this is where it took place. We moved a lot, so it is kind of difficult to keep the timeline together.

During the summer, I imagine that this was particularly challenging for my parents as we were not in school, and they, I assume, could not afford full-time day care for us. Sometimes, when our parents, aunts, and uncles would all go out, or have poker night, Josh, my older brother, and/or one or more older cousins would come sit with us and spend the night. We would have pillow fights and watch movies and stuff so that was always nice. Usually though, it was just basically whoever was available to watch us, and it was pretty much a roll of the dice.

This one time, I am not sure who the actual sitter was from memory, but later in life, I learned it was one of my Mom's friends who was watching us during the day. I guess during this time in her life she was a big-time stoner and was pretty much always high. Well, the day was pretty normal I suppose. Cartoons, snacks, playing in the yard, and playing with toys. I remember some time going by, and I had decided to go up into my brother Josh's room and find a book to "read."

I was still quite young and my reading skills very undeveloped. I remember that I loved those children's books, with all the pictures and stuff. I began making my way upstairs to find myself a book to read. My babysitter on this day, as I am told, was out back smoking a joint and unaware that I had left my spot on the living room floor where I had previously been before she stepped outside. So, I am completely unattended in my current journey up the stairs, but that's ok. I'm a big boy. And I am just going upstairs to read a book.

I remember making entry into my brother's room and sitting right in front of his large bookshelf with all of the books, baseball cards, etc. My plan was to find myself a nice picture book to enjoy, sit and rock in the chair, and enjoy my imagination with the Bernstein Bears, or whoever else filled the pages of my selection.

So, I began to make my way towards the shelf. But the books were just a little bit out of reach, so I had to step up onto the seat of a rocking chair, lean up high, and grab myself a piece of childhood literature. And that I did. Standing way up on my tip toes, I was able to lean forward and upward just enough so the rocking chair leaned into the shelf, and I grabbed myself a book.

I carefully slinked my way down the same way I had gone up. From the pads of my feet onto the back of my heels, I was able to ease the rocker back to a more flat and stable resting place. I sat myself down and cracked the book open to begin my journey through Bernstein Bears land.

What I didn't know, or realize at the time, was that this was one of those big ol' two-piece bookshelves where the top portion actually sits on top of the bottom portion, connected by those little pegs— thin wooden pegs that slide into the holes. All of the pegs were in fact broken, and my body weight leaning against the bookshelf caused it to start to separate and cave in toward me, ever so slowly. The top half was leaning toward me little by little. What I didn't realize was that at the top of the bookshelf, literally sitting on top of the whole damn thing, was a fifty-plus pound porcelain sculpture of a bulldog. Like a real officially licensed souvenir one. Super heavy duty.

My brother loved the Georgia Bulldogs and had this one on top of the shelf. It was really cool. It had a little red sweater on and everything. Well, it was now making its way toward me.

As I cracked open the book, the whole shelf started tumbling down toward me, as I sat rocking. I think I had gotten about three words into the book and KABOOM! Night Night.

The entire shelf fell on me, and the very first things that collided was the bulldog sculpture on the back of my skull. I was knocked completely unconscious and laid pinned, bleeding profusely from the back of the head until my babysitter finished her joint—and came looking for me. I remember coming to in the back of an ambulance on the way to the hospital, completely covered in my own blood. I still have a pretty gnarly scar on the back of my head to this day.

* * *

Another babysitter of mine from this exact section of time and apartments was a girl who lived a few buildings down. Now, I don't really know a whole lot about her. I believe that my trauma has blacked a little bit of this out, but what I can tell you is that I never wanted to go to her house. That much I know. I am pretty sure that she was like the last option for my parents, because of how much I hated to go there.

You know it's so weird how we can look back on our lives and see things for what they really were. I remember her being so over the top nice to my mom when it came to her being paid cash money to watch me, and yet, she wasn't ever really not "nice" to me.

She was always really pleasant to everyone in the neighborhood, but what she was was a child molester. And every single time I was over there, some weird shit happened.

I remember one time she walked me into her apartment and immediately wedged some kind of kitchen tool into the corner of the wall and door, so that the door wouldn't open. We lived in those Section 8/low income government subsidy places. They had those massive hinges and doors on the apartments, and if you wedged something behind the hinge, it would prohibit the door from opening. Well, she did this so I couldn't open the door and get out. And then she proceeded to put some kind of porn video tapes into the VCR and made me sit there and watch it with her.

I was like seven-years old, maybe eight. Was this normal? Of course, it isn't. It's disgusting and vile, which I know now. But at the time, I was so young and innocent and impressionable that I couldn't discern what was right and what was wrong. Plus my mother entrusted me into this woman's care, so how would I know? I was still developing my moral compass and learning life as I went. And I am being exposed to trauma more and more, so what did I really have to judge my life against?

It's truly disgusting what people do to children behind closed doors. She would make weird little comments about what I was watching and ask me questions about it. I didn't know what I was watching. I just knew at the time that it was shameful, and that the adults in the videos were doing stuff to each other that involved their private parts.

It made me really uncomfortable. But I was maybe eight years old? I couldn't even articulate what I was feeling, or really identify it quite frankly. It felt weird, gross, and scary. Was this normal?

I mean your parents don't pay a late teenage woman money to babysit you and she forces you to watch adults screw each other and use their mouths on each other while she asks you questions like, "Do you like what you're seeing?" and "Do you think you could do that?"

No? Just me? Gotcha. okay.

I hated going to her house. She made me uncomfortable. Sure, sometimes she would take me down to the park, and we would play on the jungle gym, swing on swings, and play with sidewalk chalk. But that didn't ever truly matter to me. I was able to block out the other stuff at times, which was a skill I learned right about this time and carried with me for decades. This is what I refer to as "getting into my space shuttle"—total disassociation. And the "Time Capsule"—total compartmentalization. Burying it. Hiding it. Stuffing it down as far as I could.

As if the videos weren't bad enough, it wasn't long until she started showing her body to me.

My mom would struggle to find a sitter, and as last resort, she was always there to take my mom's money. She would come down and take me by the hand while I pleaded with my mother not to make me go. I was a child and couldn't speak up for myself as to what was happening down there. I didn't know how to. Would anyone even believe me? Who knows.

She would take me by the hand, and I would put my head down in shame, or maybe not. Sometimes I would walk down with her willingly and happily—the times that she would bribe me by showing up with a toy and without words convince me that today was gonna be one of the fun trips where we were gonna have fun and play together.

And sure as shit, as soon as we would get inside, she would block the hinge, and take her top and bra off. She would walk around in her panties and smoke cigs while on the phone for hours. Sometimes with porn on the TV, and sometimes she would put cartoons on.

One day, in an attempt I'm sure to "break the barrier" so to speak, she kept insisting that I needed a bath. So she took me upstairs to bathe me. She was topless and had her boobs fully exposed as she did so and spent a lot of time touching me in very strange and uncomfortable places.

Once she got me out of the tub, she wrapped me in a towel and sat me on the toilet while I had to watch her shower and play with herself. She was fucking sick. She even made me "model" for her one time. I suppose she was some kind of aspiring artist of sorts and made me stand in the living room fully naked while she drew very up close and very detailed sketches of my privates. She did all of this totally naked. It was very uncomfortable for me. I began to fully realize that this was absolutely not supposed to be happening. And it was wrong.

I devised a plan. Not to tell on her, because I didn't know how to, who to tell, what to say, or if they would even believe me. But to run away. The next time I was gonna find a way to escape.

I waited until she was well into her topless phone conversation on the phone one day. And made a B-line for the back door, which was not wedged shut. I probably would have gotten away with just being a silly kid and wanting to "run outside to play" but I made the mistake of shouting over my shoulder as I ran, "I'm tellin on you!"

She proceeded to snatch me up by the arm just before I got to the door and pulled me back into the kitchen, and then the living room. Now I am terrified. She began screaming and scolding me as she put her clothes on and hung up the phone.

The next couple minutes are a bit blurry, because I was in full blown survival mode at eight-years old, but I must have said something to make her mad. The next thing I know is that she is throwing me against the couch in the living room and spraying some kind of mist in my face. I had no idea at the time, but all I remember was that it burned and hurt like nothing I had ever experienced in my life. Like tiny little needles all over my face and all over my body. My eyes felt like they were on fire and like I was being stung by thousands of tiny little bees.

My babysitter. A young adult woman from my neighborhood. A woman, who was not only entrusted with me but paid to take good care of me, was spraying me directly in the face with mace because I was about to run away and tell someone that she was molesting me.

I believe something came over her, and she may have realized what she had just done. And that this was not a small deal. Because then she began to panic. I remember laying there squirming and bawling and wretching in pain. Not knowing what just happened or what I could possibly do about this, I just tried to escape, but she forcibly stopped me. So what was I to do? I had never felt so helpless and defenseless, and vulnerable and scared in all of my life. I was truly beside myself in paralyzing fear.

Why is life like this? What had I done to deserve such treatment?

I peed myself. I cried. Everything was a blur. The next thing I knew I was surrounded by EMTs and paramedics. They were washing my little face off, and the neighbors were outside. There was commotion and panic everywhere. Especially inside of me. My parents finally came driving up, as I am sure someone called them and had them come home. I remember them finally getting me into their arms. I felt safe again. I had never experienced such shock and fear.

And the thing that makes the whole thing particularly sick, is that the babysitter had fucking evil in her heart. She had the audacity to turn around and blame the whole thing on me. She told the EMTs and police and my parents that I had gotten my hands on her keys which contained the mace canister and accidentally sprayed myself in the face with it, thinking it was perfume. And they believed her.

The only thing I could muster from my little mouth was, "No I didn't, no I didn't, no I didn't." But it didn't matter. I was eight and she was like eighteen. They took her word over mine.

Thank God that my parents saw the mace thing as a reason to never use her as a babysitter again. God only knows what would have happened.

Be careful with your kids. Listen to what they're not telling you. Ask questions.

Sometimes trauma looks like a toy and a trip to the park. We never really know what is going on behind closed doors.

Rumble

I stood leaning against a wall in the hallway of our home on Scatterfoot Drive in Peachtree City, Georgia. We lived in a white ranch style house with an attached garage on the right as you look up the big hill on which it sat.

Inside this home lived a lot of people, at any given time. My grandma and grandpa, uncle, great uncle, mom, dad, both of my brothers, and a cousin of mine, plus myself. We seemed to live with relatives off and on. Running down the internal middle of this house was a long L-shaped hallway. At a ninety-degree corner of the hallway, I leaned against the wall and crouched down. It was the summer between first and second grade, and we had moved out of the apartments where the molesting and fights had taken place, and in with my maternal relatives, for reasons unknown.

My parents had been really going at it recently. This evening was no different. They had been fighting a lot lately. And being that we were living in my mother's family's home, I heard a lot of blame shifting, a lot of side-taking, and a lot of resentment, bitterness, judgement and conviction from both sides. This is something that really led me to feeling torn and jaded later on in life.

Kids hear, see, and feel a lot more than most adults may know when there is conflict in the home and amongst family. I certainly did. The fighting scared me. The name calling hurt me. I would say from the time I was about four until the time I was about thirty-seven I pretty much lived my life very much "on edge." I would suppose this is because from the time I was a child, my emotional and nervous system dysregulation began. My "fight, flight, freeze, or fawn" mechanisms began to develop and take control of how I interacted with the world. We are shaped so much more than we know, by how we are taught, groomed, and shown how to process and deal with life at an early age. Everything in my life was reactive. I reacted to everything. There was so much stress and turmoil going on all the time that it kept me in a state of essentially shock, I guess. I was constantly on guard, watching for continuous and ongoing threats, perceived or real. I was always reacting.

* * *

So here I was, leaning against this wall, silently sobbing, listening to all this. All the vulgar language, all the personal attacks, the judgement, the ugly, the threats. I just couldn't handle what all was happening right then, or all I was hearing.

My mom was leaving my dad for the first time. And to the best of my trauma brain's recollection, it was for another man. This is also what I was told later on in life. She was so steadfast and selfishly leaving us—even though she was leaving us to live in her family's house on Scatterfoot Drive. Like that's not gonna be an awkward breakfast in the morning. She was packing her bags while she and my dad screamed and fought, spewing wreckage verbally into my life from the other room. She was serious. And I wasn't having it anymore.

At the age of maybe eight or nine, I was gonna handle this situation myself. I was gonna fight back against all of this. It was time to make a stand. I had prepared for this moment. I snuck into my older brother's room, rooted through his closet, found his boxing gloves that he used for backyard boxing with my cousins, and strapped the massively oversized red Everlast gloves on to my tiny hands. I fastened the velcro wrists bands on as tightly as I could and assumed the attack position.

With tears rolling down my face, I was ready. This wasn't happening. Not today. I was not about to let my family fall apart, not here and not now. I had no choice. This was the only thing I knew how to do to potentially make myself heard and seen. I had long since felt invisible and brushed aside by everyone in my life, especially the adults who were supposed to protect and teach me. I did not know how to speak up concisely for myself. I did not know how to interpret what I was feeling. I did not know how to communicate maturely with adults, but I did understand taking a stand. That's exactly what

I was about to do.

I heard the suitcases hit the floor, assumingly from on top of the bed where my mom was loading it up. I heard the steps begin making their way down the hall. Four feet were now in motion toward me, mom in front. My dad was right behind, alternating between begging her not to leave and threatening her if she did. I tensed up. Ready to make my stand. Big breaths in, big breaths out.

This was my chance to save my family. Right here and right now. What had been happening in my life, in our lives, was wrong— and my little heart knew it, even if I couldn't articulate it. The time was coming.

They inched closer and closer. Seconds passed like minutes as I waited. Finally, mom emerged around the corner of the hallway, large suitcase in tow, and a bag slung over her shoulder. I pounced! I punched her in the legs, thighs, butt, and hips. I let those boxing gloves go on her as best I could. You see, I had put the boxing gloves on because I didn't actually want to hurt her, even if I was capable of doing so, but I just wanted to get her attention. I wasn't actually capable of hurting anyone. I was too soft hearted. But boy did I want to get my point across. And I did, I think. I let those gloves walk all over as best I could. Left jab, right jab, push, slap, tears running down my face, high-pitched squeals coming out. A child's fury and heart break exploding all over the corner of this hallway.

"If you leave right now, you're not my mom anymore!!!"

I finished delivering my message and ran bawling into the bathroom. I closed the door behind me, locked it, jumped into the bath tub, and closed the curtain. I laid on the floor of the bathtub, balled up and cried my little eyes out. Still wearing the boxing gloves, I sobbed and sobbed over the background noise of them still fighting and packing bags. Silently repeating to myself, "Please don't go mom. Please let that have worked."

It didn't. The yelling and cussing continued. Probably for another half an hour. She didn't even try and talk to me. She didn't even knock on the door. I heard the final trip of suitcases and cussing make its way down the hall, and the screen door slam behind her, then the car start. I knew she was leaving. I unlocked the bathroom door and made my way to the bay window in front of the house. As she backed down the big hill of the driveway and out of our lives, I sobbed silently with my boxing gloves on and mustered a wave as she put the car in drive to start her journey to wherever she was going.

"I love you mom. I hate you," was all I could muster as my voice cracked and tears flowed.

She was gone.

Butterflies

Not more than a couple days after the boxing gloves battle royale with mom, it became very clear to me that we were not going to be staying in that house anymore. It was more awkward and uncomfortable than ever. There was a lot of tension. I didn't even know what the word tension meant at the time. I wasn't even in second grade yet. But I knew that what I was feeling inside myself, that house, and within the family, was definitely not good. It was clear and obvious to me that we were not going to be staying with any of my mom's family.

Once mom took off, her side of the family, at least the ones we shared a roof with currently, had no use or desire for my dad, Lucas, or me. This was just bad.

Where in the world would we be going now and when? What was going to happen now?

I couldn't take it anymore. I knew something was coming, and it was not gonna be awesome. It was gonna be soon. I could just feel it. Plus I had learned the patterns by now, so it was only a matter of time, after a blowout like this, that something was about to happen.

And I was right. Again. Here we go.

* * *

I am not certain how many days had passed since the incident when my mom left, but it wasn't many. The day finally came when Dad told Lucas and me that we were gonna be leaving. Lucas could barely talk, or communicate, but I understood him perfectly. It's weird how that connection happens amongst little siblings. I remember vividly, countless times when the adults and older cousins would have to ask me, "What's Lukie saying?" But anyway, I could talk just fine. And I was perfectly up to speed with what just happened, and what was happening now.

The packing of our things began. Dad got as much of our stuff together as he could. I gathered the essentials. Snuggles, Popples, and this white blanket with little pandas on it. I loved that blanket. It had pandas holding little pots of gold with rainbows shooting out patterned all over it.

The packing seemed to go by very quickly. Like in the blink of an eye. But there was also a lot of bickering and name calling between my dad and grandmother. They did not seem to like each other very much. She, along with others in the family, blamed my dad for everything.

We got the last of our stuff loaded up in the red Ford Grenada with the white top and backed out of the driveway. As we pulled out, dad rolled the window down and made some kind of hand gesture out the window and said something like, "fuck y'all motherfuckers." Whatever that meant. I had absolutely no idea where we were going, but at least the three musketeers were gonna stick together. That I was almost always certain of, until I wasn't. But we had some snacks in the car and some toys in the back seat with us. And off we drove, into certain uncertainty.

* * *

Now usually when were moving, it typically was to the other side of town. Or from this apartment to uncle so and so's house. Or to grandma's. The drive usually only takes about twenty to thirty minutes. This one was taking an unusual amount of time, and I was starting to notice.

Ugh. Where in the world were we going?

I don't think I had ever been in a car this long in my entire life. I didn't even know that the world went on this far. We had to be reaching the edge of the world by now. Would we circle right back to where we came from? It was nighttime now. Like really nighttime. The incredibly tall highway signs for Waffle House and truck stops would illuminate the back seat as we trekked on through what I now know as the mountainous and hilly terrain of northern Georgia and southeast Tennessee. We would pull over from time to time for gas, snacks, and to use the restroom.

As we merged back on to the highway, somewhere in the middle of nowhere Tennessee I suppose, at about 3:00 a.m. I wake up from one of my many naps in the back seat.

"Where are we going, Dad?"

"Well, Stevie, I am taking you and your brother to my sister's in Tennessee for now. And then I am going to find your mom."

"Oh," I thought. Somehow, in my little mind I knew it was going to be an answer like this. I cried myself to sleep in the back of the car, hugging Snuggles, saturating the stuffed bear in salt and snot on the final leg to northwest Tennessee.

We spent the night, the three of us, at my Aunt and Uncle's house in Martin, Tennessee. At first it was kind of awkward because I didn't really know any of these people. I think I had met them before, but I didn't actually know any of them. They lived on a really big farm with lots of animals, which I thought was absolutely awesome!

I had four big cousins there who were always really good to me. My cousin Simone became my best friend. I think she knew how screwed up everything had been for us and so she had empathy. We did everything together, she and I, and Lucas.

I believe we moved there in the summer, so we had lots of time to play! I spent that whole summer exploring nature at the farm and being Lucas's translator for my relatives.

"What's he sayin Stevie," I would be asked multiple times daily, and I was happy to oblige. It made me feel important. I had a job to do, not only as his protector, but as his translator. Someone had to let the world know what my kid brother was saying.

Sometimes, I would get really sad. I would miss Josh really bad. He was the best big brother, and when Mom took off, Josh stayed in Georgia. He stayed with my grandma and the others. His dad who we called "Uncle Bob," lived there too, so I guess I understand why he stayed. Grandma and them always seemed to favor him over us. I guess it was because there was so much animosity between grandma and my dad, that when she saw Lucas and me, she saw dad. And she let that resentment be made very clear. They were nice to us, sure. And they let us stay with them a lot. I have no doubt that they loved us very much, but I could always just feel this unspoken tension from her.

It's okay. I am not judging. I loved her and grandpa too. I wish

I had gotten to bond with them more. But it is what it is.

Other times I got sad were when I would catch myself wondering where Mom and Dad were. I would wonder if they were coming back at all, or if this was gonna be our new family. And then I would think about that option, which didn't actually seem so bad. We had the best times there! We chased the cows around the pasture and played with the baby chicks. We even learned how to can vegetables and make homemade wine!

I know, I know, children making wine? It sounds bad, but we never drank it. They just let us help in the process. They had these big long Muscadine vines in their yard, and we would pick the grapes, load buckets full, and then stomp them with our bare feet! Lucas and I thought it was just the coolest thing ever.

* * *

One morning, Simone came and woke me up at what seemed to be much earlier than normal.

"Stevie, get up. I wanna show you something."

I was instantly up and excited. She was really nice to me. Very "Tom-boyish" at the time, so she was into a lot of the stuff I was into too. This was exciting! What was she gonna show me. I knew it was gonna be something cool, and I trusted her completely! It was like an adventure, as we padded around through the old farm house and clod hopped our bare foot asses right out the front door, off the deck, and down toward the barnyard.

We kept on walking right up to the gate of the barnyard, where all the chickens hung out and did their chicken thing. There were these big long broad leaf vines hanging down. Intertwined all throughout the chain link fence were vines crawling and stretching in every direction. I thought this was what she wanted me to see, and this alone was really cool! I was so happy she woke me up to show me such a cool plant growing in such a cool way!

"No, Stevie, come closer, come look."

She lifted up a couple of the big broad leaves to reveal hundreds, if not thousands, of those big gnarly green, yellow, and white caterpillars crawling all over the leaves and chewing them to bits. I was in awe. They were so cool looking! We would pick them up and let them crawl all over us—and even let them crawl on our heads! It was such a cool moment for me.

"You know what were gonna do, Stevie? We're gonna come out here every day, and we're gonna check on them, cause these little guys, guess what, they're gonna turn into butterflies! And we get to watch the whole thing!"

NO WAY! This was the coolest thing ever. I just had to tell Lucas. So I got him up and showed him too. And we checked those leaves and the progress being made by the caterpillars every day that summer. All the way until they turned into big and bright butterflies, and flew away. It was one of the coolest experiences of my childhood. Simone was a good friend.

The summer flew by! I think my relatives did the best they could to keep our little minds occupied so that we weren't constantly thinking about our parents and where they could be. I got to "drive" the tractor while my uncle plowed the fields. We chased the chickens, we chased the cows, we played all summer long. It was a lot of fun.

Although I was having a lot of fun on the farm, I still somehow knew that I was in the space shuttle, meaning that I was still "away" from my thoughts about my parents and brother Josh.

Looking back on things, I was pretty disassociated most of the time and had developed the "skill" of jumping in and out of the shuttle as need be. I could secretly tell deep inside how much time had passed, and that Mom and Dad were still gone. I cried myself to sleep a lot of the time and did my best to protect Lucas. I would read him books, and lay with him until he fell asleep.

More nights than not, I would wait till all of the relatives were asleep, and I would sneak out into the living room and hop up on the couch in front of the picture window. Knees on the cushions, and my little torso against the back of the couch, I would just stare outside. It was a very rural and remote little town, so seldom did a car pass by. But every single time one did, I would lock onto the headlights way off in the distance, and say to myself "please, please, please, please," only to see each and every one pass by. It was never them. I cried a lot of tears on that couch that no one knew about.

One night, my aunt had gotten up to get something to drink and caught me sitting there looking out the window crying. It had to be at least midnight. I can still hear her voice, in her southern twang, "Whatcha doin hun?"

And I lost it. "They're not coming back are they?"

She was the most gentle and loving lady. She was exactly who I needed at the time, and she just floated right on over to me and held me as I cried. She rocked me and "shhhhhhhh-shhhhhhhhhhh-shhhhhhhhh'd" me and did her best to ease my pain. She did everything she could to make me feel better

Then she did something that I don't think she fully understands just how profoundly it impacted me to this day. She taught me how to pray. She talked to me about God. She told me about the power of prayer and what it had done in her own life.

Right there, in almost second grade, I offered my heart to Jesus. I didn't know who He was or why He was so important, but I trusted my aunt. She sure seemed to think this was very important, so I followed her prompted prayers right along word for word. It didn't seem to make a difference at the time for me, but trust me, it would later. I am eternally grateful for her selfless love and guidance for me. She loved me very much. And we just sat there, me on her lap, and she hummed me songs. Sometimes there were words, sometimes there were tears. But I trusted her, and somehow I knew, that someday, everything was gonna be okay. I did not know that that day would not come until I was thirty-seven and a half years old, but I knew it would come.

* * *

Summer was coming to a close. Simone, Lucas, and I did our best to maximize the time. It had been communicated to us that we were gonna be going to school this year in Martin with them, which I had kinda figured by now. Our parents were still gone, and I had just kind of accepted the fact that they may not be coming back. But I knew how to talk to God now, so I did that every single night.

One night, toward the end of the summer, the three of us were playing in some mud across the street where they were building the new high school. We had found a spot that we could jump from and land in a big puddle that was about knee deep and made a big splash! We were about to wrap up the evening hours and head in for dinner, but we decided to all jump in one more time. Simone went, and then it was my turn. I went for the big splash! I jumped off the manhole yet to be installed into the puddle and made the biggest splash I could! As I did, I felt a really sharp pinch on my right heel.

"Owwwwww!!!"

I quickly hopped up onto the street from the ditch to find that my entire right foot from my heel to my Achilles tendon was wide open and deep-rich purple blood was pulsing out with every heartbeat! The three of us looked at it and took off toward the house.

Simone scooped up Lucas as I did my best to hobble as fast as I could toward the lights pouring out through the kitchen door window. I knew this was bad, and they were gonna be so worried. I was losing a lot of blood, and remember getting dizzier with every step. It seemed like a mile to the house but was really only about one hundred yards. I had to cross a full blown rocky gravel driveway, barefoot on basically bare bone, and torn open flesh. I gritted through it with all I could muster and slammed the door open.

"Help!" I screamed in agony as I made my entry into the kitchen area.

My aunt and uncle took one look at my foot and looked at each other. The looks on their faces said it all. This was really bad.

"Call 911, I need to go to the hospital!"

But apparently that was not an option, and this needed to be dealt with now. The nearest hospital was a long way away, and it would take forever for an ambulance to get there. So the good ol' country relatives of mine did what good ol' country relatives do. They handled it themselves.

My aunt threw me into the big wash tub sink in the laundry room, butt ass naked and scrubbed all of the mud and filth off of me as fast as she could, while my uncle got a bunch of stuff out of a cabinet above. He then cleared a table off in movie style fashion with one arm and took his belt off. My aunt flopped me down on the table on my belly and shoved the belt folded up in my mouth while uncle prepared a needle and some kind of thread.

"Stevie, baby, I need you to bite this belt as hard as you can."

I can still taste the leather.

"This is gonna burn really, really bad, okay?"

I was squirming and flopping all over the table, and my aunt leaned her entire body weight on me to pin me down, as my uncle poured some kind of alcohol all over my heel, and then iodine. He wrestled my flailing leg into his grasp, pinned it to the table, and began sewing away. I passed out and woke up laying in bed, fully clothed with my foot wrapped in towels and elevated on some pillows that were wrapped in trash bags.

I had just experienced some good ol' fashioned country medical work. They probably saved my life honestly, as bad as I was bleeding. And whatever it was in the mud that cut me so badly, just happened to miss my Achilles tendon by like half an inch. God was looking out for me that day. I still cannot believe to this day what a good job they did repairing my foot like that. I am very grateful.

* * *

The summer finally wrapped up and school was beginning. I was attending Martin Elementary school, and my teacher was Miss Jackson. I think that my aunt may have filled her in on what was going on in our lives, because she was really nice to me from the start. I remember she gave me a book called, *A Pocket for Corduroy*. She even signed it and everything. I must have read that book to Lucas a hundred times. We loved that one. I think I still somehow have that book too, packed away somewhere with all of my trophies and stuff.

School really made time go by fast! It kept me busy and occupied. I would come home and watch *Goof Troop* and *Darkwing Duck* every day with my cousin. We would play in the pastures after school once I could run around again, and I was just pretty much accustomed to my new life now. I hadn't sat at the window for awhile and had kind of just accepted life as it was now. A few months had gone by into the school year, and I would read Lucas books at night.

One night I found myself really sad, missing my parents, and crying silently in bed. I remembered the prayer that my aunt had taught me, so I was using it and talking to God. But I just couldn't shake this feeling that I had, like something was up. I cried and prayed, tossed and turned. Why was this happening? It had been such a good stretch of life lately, and things were going smoothly. I prayed and I cried, but I just could not seem to shake this anxious and sad feeling I had.

I decided to go look out the window. It was about oh, I would guess about ten, maybe eleven o'clock at night. The whole house was asleep, and I just sat there on the couch, knees on the cushions, torso against the back of the couch, silently crying and talking to God.

A set of headlights appeared up the county road. I latched on to those damn headlights with all of my will, and with all my might and strength.

"Please, please, please, please, please . . ."

As the headlights drew closer and closer, the approaching car passed underneath a far off street light overhead, and the white top of the Ford Grenada shone in the country road. It was them! They had finally made it back! I watched as the car drew nearer and nearer, only to pass the house!

Then brake lights! The car began to reverse backwards, back past the driveway again. And then lurch forward and finally settle into the driveway.

Dad was back! He had just missed the house. But he was back! I ran to the kitchen door and looked out through the window. They were both back! He had found mom!

Oh thank God! The prayers worked! We were finally going home!

Shiloh

Shortly after returning home to Georgia, the four of us—Mom, Dad, Lucas, and me—settled into a trailer home in Peachtree City, Georgia. Peachtree City was, and I believe still is, a very economically diverse city. In some places there are homes that run in the millions of dollars, and in others, there are Section 8 homes and trailer parks. Kids can be incredibly cruel when it comes to knowing where everyone stands in the socioeconomic scope of things. I never really had any major issues with the rich kids, as I pretty much got along with everyone. But even though I never had any direct conflict with anyone from school, I heard the term "Trailer Trash" a lot. I knew that's how many felt about people who came from where I came from. So it applied to me too, and it really hurt my feelings.

I did, however, have a lot of conflict with kids from the trailer park. It was wild. Some days were just as easy and fun as could be. We built jumps for our bikes, forts, and spent time playing in the creek and catching critters. Other days, seemingly for no reason at all, I was being challenged and bullied by a kid who just yesterday was my friend. I think, looking back, a large majority of us came from really damaged homes and families. The instabilities we showed and projected on to one another were a direct reflection of the instabilities and brokenness going on in each of our homes.

I get a very type of bittersweet nostalgia from the ending of the movie *The Sandlot*. When I think back about these times, I wonder what happened to a lot of the kids I once called friends, once called enemies, and then called friends again.

* * *

I don't know if it's just my experience in life, or if most kids have experiences similar to mine. Is it normal at one point on a weekend day to be practicing your skills on the homemade dirt jump at the end of the road, and then later that day be over at a group of some older kids' trailer and being forced into the "Fight or Fuck Room?"

I'm guessing probably not. It was all very confusing to me. Why would one of the older kids in the park come over, knock on our door, and ask if I could come out to play and ride bikes, only to lure me into their trailer and force me to either fight a much older and larger kid, who would easily beat the shit out of me, or watch the trailer park floozie blow one of the boys?

Is this "playing?" Is this what "normal" was? I don't know. But it made me afraid. It made me afraid to hang out and play with anyone. It made me disassociate even more. I felt like if I just hopped into my space shuttle again, it would all be over soon. It was traumatic for me.

Who could I tell? Would anyone even believe me? If I did tell, the bigger kids would surely kick my ass. I know this because they told me so. So I just bottled it up. Every single time it happened.

Now, I don't know why, but the whole trailer park seemed to be full of weirdos . . . and not just the kids. A lot of the adults were creeps too.

One of the more "normal" kids I liked to play with and trade *Goosebumps* books had a dad who was weird as shit. I cannot begin to tell you how many times I saw this man naked. It was bizarre. We would be over playing Nintendo in their front room, in the middle of a weekend day, and this man would come out and talk to us, or yell at my friend, or get something out of the kitchen, butt ass naked. Sometimes we could hear his parents having sex very loudly, and the dad would come out afterward and describe in pretty specific detail what he had just done sexually to their mother. It was gross man! I always felt really bad for my friend and his little brother. They both got bullied badly at school too. I wonder what ever happened to him.

Another group which were particularly sick was this family at another end of the trailer park. A mother, father, and three boys— two who were much older, like junior high and high school The youngest was about my age. I have no idea what could have possibly gone on in their family, but looking back, I would venture to guess that there was a lot of drug use and sexual abuse going on.

I remember one day going down to the creek with a couple

friends to catch critters. As we made the bend at the trail, we came across an opening into the woods where the two older of the three brothers were both leaning against a tree, while a girl not much older than us was on her knees in front of both of them at the same time. Shocked and afraid, my friends and I tried to turn around and hide. We knew if they saw us, we could be in big trouble.

"HEY!" one of them yelled.

Oh shit, I am sure we all thought!

The oldest of the two ran over and corralled us, cutting us off from the path, forcing our trajectory back over to the girl and the other brother.

Why were people like this? These two big bullies with a knack for pedophilia just couldn't let us go about our business, could they?

No, they had to threaten to beat our asses if we told, or if we didn't stay close by and watch while they finished what they were doing. It made me so scared and sad. Each and every time an incident like this occurred, it planted this deep, deep shame inside of me. I felt so helpless and violated.

This wasn't the last I had heard of these three sickos. There were numerous weird run-ins with this trio. But I think the weirdest thing that I experienced with this family, was a day when a group of us had gone over to knock on the youngest brother's door. We were trying to assemble a football game, and we needed some players. Each one of our little friend's group were all gathered in the middle of the street with our bikes and a football. We were a few guys short, so we would need to go knock on doors and round up some players. The so-called leader of the group assigned one of us to go round up kids. Wouldn't you know it. I got assigned to go knock on the door of the pedophile brothers!

"Come in!" a voice from the other side of the door responded to my third or fourth grade fist knocking on the door.

So I did as requested. I mean, certainly they wouldn't yell to come in, not knowing who was on the other side of the door if they were up to no good, would they?

"Oh, hey, Stevie, you looking for _____?" I heard from a man sitting on a couch in the living room?

"Yes," I replied.

"He's back there in his room," the man said, as he put his hand on top of a woman's head who was sitting on her knees blowing him.

Another man, who was also naked, was sitting on the end of the couch and took a hit off of some kind of glass smoking pipe. He was also getting blown by another woman who was kneeling in front of him. Was this fucking real life? These four adults were all naked, smoking what I can only assume was meth, with porn on the TV, while a child is walking right past them. They just yelled for me to come in like what they were doing was 100% normal. It 100% was not.

More shame. More violation. More fear. I got my friend as fast as I could, and we boogied out of there to play football. Neither of us spoke of what just happened to the other. I think he knew it was shameful too. I hope he didn't become as corrupted as his brothers did. But I am sure that he did. I've encountered a lot of sick people in my life. It makes me wonder how things would have turned out much different for me had I not. But there's nothing I can do about that now.

And then there was the "Wrestling Coach" who lived on one of the end streets of the trailer park. Now this dude was fucking sick. We used to always play soccer in the street. The street had speed bumps sporadically throughout the community, and we would designate one side of the yellow perforated (split down the middle) speed bumps as a goal, and the game would only run one way. We operated the game kind of like "21" in basketball.

If the goalie made a stop, you had to "take it back" and begin momentum back toward the speed bump, as we only had one speed bump about every quarter mile. We made do with what little we had. Anyway, the speed bump we often utilized just so happened to be in front of the "wrestling coach's" house. Everyone called this guy the wrestling coach because he always asked the kids in the neighborhood if they wanted to come over and learn how to wrestle. This was a grown man. Like in his thirties or forties. We were all so naive that we didn't know what to make of this guy. Some of the kids even called him "coach" for short. I guess that was his approach. His guise or design to lure kids in.

I didn't know about any of this shit until later on, when I found myself getting a "lesson" from him. He seemed like a pretty normal guy. Not at all like the other blatant weirdos in the trailer park. He came off as very polite and regular. One day I was having a hard time finding friends to come out and play. I was kind of just riding my bike around by myself when "Coach" called my name.

"Hey, Stevie, do you have time for a quick lesson?"

He caught me completely unaware and unguarded. Without even thinking, I was dropping my bike in front of his trailer deck and walking through his front door. He shut the door behind me as I walked in, and locked the dead bolt. Immediately he took his clothes off right in front of me! Now, he did leave his underwear on, but it was still weird. I remember telling him that I wasn't comfortable doing the same, but he ensured me that this was what all the great wrestlers did.

If I was going to do anything, I wanted to be the best at it, so I took off my t-shirt , kicked my shoes off, and began to take my pants off. Literally, swear to God, the second my pants came off, the door was kicked completely in, busting the dead bolt right through the wall, and slamming off the counter behind it.

"No I don't fucking think so Mother Fucker!" yelled the voice of my older brother Josh. He had seen my bike out front of this guy's trailer and knew I definitely should not have been inside this pervert's house.

"I, I, I, was just showing him some wrestling moves," stammered Coach.

"Nah you ain't either, not with my little brother you fucking pervert! I'm about to let everyone know about you, dog," Josh tells the guy in his southern twang.

Then he grabbed me up in my underwear, scooped my clothes up off the floor, picked my bike up with the other hand, and began walking me back toward our trailer. (For context here, Josh lived in a trailer with grandma and grandpa on Wagon Wheel Way, and Mom, Dad, Lucas, and I lived on Buffalo Road. "Coach" lived on Shiloh Drive, which was visible from Grandma, Grandpa, and Josh's trailer.)

He must have noticed my bike over there and came over to get me. Josh very well may have just saved me from a very traumatic experience. It could not have happened with any more impeccable timing. My middle school brother had just saved me from probably being raped. At first it kind of seemed like an overreaction, in my little mind.

But a few days later, "Coach" had packed up and just moved out of the trailer park. No one saw or heard from him again. He was just gone.

It's crazy how one heroic act can have such a profound lasting effect, in ripples. I wonder how many of us trailer park kids were spared, simply because my brother was paying attention? Josh was always there for me.

* * *

One of the more difficult days for me in the trailer park did not involve any kind of sexual predators or weirdos, though. It was actually a rather normal and fun day for me, until it wasn't.

My friends and I had been riding bikes and playing at the park pretty much all day. I remember there was this big concrete slab, used for setting trailers up, and it was vacant. The slab had about three feet of drop off at the back end of it, as this was a lot that was on a hill. We used this as a bike jump. We would speed up to the end of the slab, pull up on our handle bars, and see who could get the most air! It was fun. Sweaty, dirty, adventurous kids, having good clean fun.

Out of nowhere I heard mom's whistle. She could use her fingers, press them into her mouth, and whistle like nothing you ever heard. It was so loud. And the rule was, any time mom would whistle, it meant to come home. Usually the whistle occurred just as the street lights came on. But this was the middle of the day.

Hmmmm. "Gotta go guys."

And then I hit one more sweet jump off the back of the slab and made my way back to Buffalo Road. As I came up to our trailer, I could see that mom and dad were arguing about something—and it was very heated. My little brother was inside watching TV as I made my way up to the house. I parked my bike underneath the raised deck and boogied inside. My parents followed and utter chaos ensued. Screaming, name calling, accusations. Mom threw a bowl at my dad. He ducked, and it hit the cabinet and shattered. I gathered Lucas up and headed back to our bedroom and shut the door.

The fighting continued until I heard something about dad leaving. I hurried out the bedroom door and shut it behind me, just as he was walking out the front door. He was much taller and faster than I was. I followed, pleading with him not to leave.

"Dad, don't go, please stop. Come back."

I could feel in my little bones that something serious was going on, and this might not be good. So I had to do my best to save the day here. But dad was not listening.

"Go home Stevie," he yelled back over his shoulder and continued his trek. He went all the way up Buffalo Road, made a left on to the main drag of the trailer park, and headed toward the exit.

I did my best to follow him. I huffed and puffed, ran and walked. I cried, pleaded, and begged. I couldn't keep up and I couldn't get him to stop.

"Son, I told you to go home."

I wouldn't listen. I was following him. This was NOT happening. Not today. On we walked. All the way to the front entrance of the trailer park, which is Highway 54. Dad walked out to cross the traffic and stood in the median of the crossway traffic. Being so young I was afraid to do the same, so I stood watching and crying, pleading with him not to do this.

"Please don't Dad!"

He stuck his thumb out right there in the grass of the median of the highway. A pickup truck slowed to a stop just past him. My dad stuck his head in the window, and a short talk took place.

"I told you to go home, Stevie. I will be back son. I am not leaving you."

But he was. He jumped in the front seat of the truck. And they sped off.

I sat there on the side of the highway and the main entrance to Shiloh Trailer Park, buried my face in my hands, and bawled my eyes out. I was in elementary school.

Why is life like this?

Shortly after, my mother pulled up in the Ford Grenada and put me in the car. I would again be spending some nights looking out the windows for dad to return.

It wasn't too terribly long this time though . . . maybe a week or so until dad returned. He and mom seemed to be really codependent and toxic with one another. But God did they love one another. That much I know. Even though they had their fights, and would split up from time to time, they always found their way back together.

Fear of abandonment.

Perhaps the single most fucked up thing I witnessed during my days in the trailer park took place not long after dad returned home. Things had settled back down and seemed to be going pretty well. Sure, there were times when I had to walk across the street and borrow water from the neighbors because ours was cut off. This was actually more common than you might think in those days. Everyone in the park struggled from time to time. There were times when a bunch of families would pitch in to pay power bills for others and buy groceries. It was common. We didn't all live here because we were high on the hog, that's for sure.

One evening we were just hanging out and finishing up the evening playing at "The Wall," which was this white cinder block wall, about three blocks long that bent around the corner of intersecting roads and under a sign. It was damn near dark out, and the street lights had come on, but I hadn't heard the whistle, so I was in the clear for a little bit longer. Giant moths darted around the street lights, and one by one, each of us received our signals from our parents to come home. One parent would yell, another parent would bang on a large kettle pot, until it was just one other childhood friend of mine and me, sitting on the wall talking about life. Eventually, I believe we both just decided to call it a day, and head our respective ways.

"Ok, man, see you tomorrow!" we said and off we headed. He in one direction, and me in my own.

Living in the trailer park was an experience unlike anything else. We saw and heard all kinds of crazy shit back then, so it wasn't really a shocker to me when I saw this lady come running out of her trailer screaming her head off. Well, it wasn't at first anyway.

Being so used to all the crazy shit we heard and saw on almost a daily basis, I wasn't really all that worried when the lady in the white robe came running out of her trailer screaming hysterically, cordless phone in hand—until I was able to make out what exactly she was actually screaming.

"He's fucking killing himself, somebody help me!"

I pushed the pedals on my bike backward to activate the brakes and see what the hell was going on. The lady kept running by several trailers and made a sharp cut through a yard, up a deck and into a front door!

What the heck was going on! This was crazy. I guess she must have known whoever's house she just run into.

This was wild. Hmm I thought to myself, as I went to restart my journey back home.

Kicking myself up on to my seat with my left leg to get momentum going, I steadied my bike to head home, only to be startled again by a man coming out of the same trailer as the lady in the white robe. He looked drunk and wobbly. He was trying to say something to me and raised his hands out to me like some kind of crazy zombie. He shuffled and staggered toward me, and as the overhead street lights caught him, I could see that he was absolutely gushing blood from both of his wrists and forearms. He made it about five more steps in my direction before he collapsed onto the blacktop road, smashing his face into the pavement as he did so. Seconds later, a group of people poured out of the trailer the lady had run into. About five of them came rushing toward the man and me. I inched up to kind of check on him. I had no idea what was actually taking place.

"Get the fuck home, Stevie. My son is killing himself, and the ambulance is coming!" she screamed at me.

Well now I knew. *Holy shit!* I pedaled faster and harder than I ever had in my life. I had just witnessed a suicide attempt.

I was in elementary school.

In Control

L ife was really hectic, scary, and confusing for a very long time for me. I am sure that is pretty evident just by what I have outlined thus far. What is very interesting about this thing called life is that up until recently, like the last couple years, I actually thought that some of the things I experienced were just a normal part of life.

Now I don't want any of my readers to think that I am sharing these stories for any other reasons other than my own catharsis, and to try to portray and explain what I believe to a be very real and direct link: Trauma and Addiction.

I am not sharing these stories from my life for your sympathy, and I am not sharing them to play some kind of victim role. I am also not sharing them to make my parents or relatives look bad. Aren't we all, mostly products of our environment? But if we are going to play the blame game, then we might as well take it all the way back to Adam. To blame the parents is to blame their parents, is to blame their parents, is to blame their parents. Make sense? The more I learn and understand myself, the more I am able to understand that everyone is doing the best they can with what they have and with who they have and the circumstances that they were born and raised into.

We all live life pretty much according to our last mistake, and life is a constantly on going learning experience. I am simply doing my best to shed some light on how the experiences that we have shape us, from very early on especially. Hopefully, by my sharing such intimate details of my own traumas, I might inspire at least one person out there to get vulnerable with their own—and perhaps take that courageous step and finally commit to therapy, or treatment, or recovery: to finally open up about some of the things that they experienced themselves. Because, one thing that I have learned in my thirty-seven and a half years here on earth, is that recovery and healing both demand exposure. We don't have to tell everything to everyone, but I believe that we all need someone that we can tell everything to.

Trauma is a living and active thing. They say, "What we resist, persists." If we cannot peel our layers back, expose the pains, and lean in to our secret places, over time, those dark and ugly parts of us will ultimately end up consuming us. By learning about ourselves, and re-processing our pasts, we gain new perspectives on our lives with trusted individuals. Really getting "naked" with someone who can point out things that we cannot see—that's how we can learn to know ourselves. That's how we can fully audit our lives, and take an honest and objective look at who we really are. We cannot change what we refuse to confront. I learned this the hard way.

One of the many things that I have come to learn about my own traumas is that it kind of happened (in a very abbreviated way) like this:

> Isolated incident, isolated incident, isolated
> incident and the impact that is left on me.
> The world is bad, people can't be trusted, love
> isn't real, and people will only hurt you and
> let you down. It's best to just keep my walls
> up, stay in the space shuttle, and push people
> away before they hurt me.

But what is also very interesting, is that because I operated on this mechanism, I am the one who ultimately ended up suffering the most. I stayed lonely, isolated, fear-driven, on edge, and relied on ego and control to get me through my life. The ego came from my shame and fear. My self-esteem, self-worth, and feelings of invisibility and helplessness also helped to create my over inflated sense of self, ego, as a way to protect myself from vulnerabilities. The absolute need for control came from all of the inner turmoil, grief, and helplessness I felt going on inside of me. The less control I felt on the inside, the more control I would TRY to have on the outside, seeking and using external sources for internal validation; and doing my best to arrange, design, manipulate, and control the world and its people.

* * *

Interestingly, I never had control. I never had control of really anything. I had zero control over having to go to six different elementary schools in six different years. I had zero control over having to ask my teachers to buy me lunch at those schools because I was starving. I had zero control over being left at one of those schools until 3 o'clock in the morning.

I had been in one of those after school programs, where we would play kickball and stuff like that until the parents got off of work and would come pick us up, one by one. Typically I would be in the last percentage of kids to be picked up, because often times my parents worked later than most.

Well, on this particular day, something must have happened because I was sitting there in the cafeteria of my school with one of the volunteers until 3 a.m. This was obviously before the time of the cell phone, so we were at the mercy of whatever was going on. I remember rather well, the volunteers and teachers repeatedly referring to calling Child Protective Services, and the police, because no one had ever just left their child like this. I was totally abandoned at my elementary school, and no one could find my parents.

I begged and pleaded with them every time they mentioned calling the authorities, "No! Don't! They'll be here, I promise! They're just working!" And they actually listened to me, for the time being. And didn'tcall them.

This one sweet old lady just sat there with me, and we colored, played with clay, and walked around the hallways of the school. Finally she ended up finding some of those mats that the kindergartners used for nap time, stacked a couple on top of each other right there in the cafeteria, and covered me up. I went to sleep.

I remember being woken up as my dad was scooping me up off the mats, grabbing my stuff, and casually thanking the lady for staying with me for so long. Like it was just a regular old day.

I also had zero control over the fact that Child Protective Services knocked on the door of our trailer the next day, and my parents wouldn't answer the door until they had coached us on what to say to them to make sure that they got out of this. And we did. We did as we were instructed, and we told the ladies who came exactly what we were supposed to say to them. They came and went, and things resumed right back to normal.

You see, all of these incidents that took place in my life left a mark. They left an impact. They helped shape my sense of reality, of self, and of the world and its people. All of the uncertainty, the fear, the broken trust, the lack of protection, the abandonment—shaped my mind to believe that nothing is consistent:

> I need to constantly be afraid. No one can be trusted. I must find a way to protect myself, and everyone is just going to leave me anyway, so why get close? The world is violent and full of people who want to violate me, so I best really hone my ability to disassociate or learn how to violently fight back.

But I didn't really possess the heart to hurt another person, so to disassociate was my only plausible option. So I continued to improve my space shuttle.

The less in control my life was and the more chaos I was subjected to, the less control I felt on the inside. The less control I felt on the inside, as I grew older, the more I would try and control on the outside.

> "Though I am not without weakness
> I will define what lies ahead;
> I'm not out of control."
> "In Control" by Greensky Bluegrass

Fudge

It wasn't long after witnessing the suicide attempt that we loaded up the U-Haul, and off we went. This time, we were moving back into the house on Scatterfoot, where "Rumble" took place. I believe the house was pretty much just my uncle and cousin at the time. My older brother and grandparents were living in the trailer over in Shiloh. At least that would be good, not as much commotion this time. Less people meant less personalities, and less opinions, and less fighting. So that was good.

We had a dog. A chocolate labrador named Fudge. He was my buddy.

One regular ol' day, I was hanging out, probably watching cartoons when out of nowhere mom started freaking out! She was rushing all through the house, screaming, crying, and panicked. It took me a little bit to fully understand what was taking place, but when I did, I too was very concerned.

My little brother had somehow gotten out of everyone's sight, and presumably slipped outside without anyone knowing. I think he was in like first grade maybe. Just a little guy. Now, this wouldn't have been such a big deal if he had just gone out the backslider and into the fenced in backyard to play. He had not. I could tell by all the commotion and excitement that extensive efforts had been made to locate him all over the property, and all throughout the house. He was nowhere to be found.

Dad took off in the car and was driving all over the neighborhood looking for him. Very loud screams for "LUCAAASSSSSS," could be heard all the way back at the house as he drove all over searching and screaming for his return. Nothing.

It wasn't too terribly long until the police got involved. Lots of them. I was terrified. Officers coming and going, writing stuff down. I was in actual shock.

What had happened to my little brother? How did he slip off so easily? Why didn't he tell me he was going outside?

I was scared. I was worried sick about my little brother, and there was basically nothing I could do about the situation. I remember feeling really helpless but also wanting to offer any kind of advice and support that I could. But what could I possibly offer that would be of use?

Time dragged on. The police searched and searched. Nothing, no sign of him. It had to have been at least a couple hours since my dad took off looking for him when the cops arrived—and still no sign of him. Relatives had arrived, aiding in the effort. Mom was hysterical. People were crying, and there was nothing I could do. I sat on the couch in the living room as my mother bawled her eyes out. I remember very vividly kind of locking eyes with Fudge and having this *moment*. Maybe it was my imagination, or child-like wonder, but something came over me. I knew what my idea was going to be.

"Mom, let Fudge out, he will find Lukie, I know He will."

I could tell that mom thought this was both sweet and ridiculous. Minutes went by, the telephone would ring, someone would answer, "No, nothing yet," and hang up. Mom would cry. Cops were driving to and from our house with no news. This was bad.

So I just took it upon myself. I nonchalantly slipped off the couch, holding Fudge's collar and walked him toward the front door. I remember him looking up at me and then back out the front door. I quietly pushed the screen door open, and yelled, "Okay, Fudge, go get him boy! Go find Lukie!"

My mom was absolutely pissed off! Not only was Lucas missing and this was one of the most stressful experiences of her life, but now the dog was on the loose and probably gone forever! Fudge absolutely bolted down the hill, around the corner and out of sight.

"I'm sorry mom, but if anyone is gonna find him, it's Fudge, I just know it."

I knew I was going to be in big trouble as soon as all this was over, but I I had to try something.

Mom picked me up and sat me down on the couch. I resumed whatever it was that I had been watching on the TV. More phone calls. More comings and goings. More cops knocking on the door.

More commotion. No news. Minutes dragged on like hours I am sure, although to me it was all one big blur. It seemed to have happened at all once. I was so overwhelmed by it all. It was one of the scariest days of my family's lives I have no doubt. This was becoming more and more serious by the minute. Everyone was absolutely beside themselves.

I remember that it had been about three or four hours since dad took off and the cops came. Night was fast approaching, and everyone was worried about being able to find him in the dark, when headlights panned the back wall, indicating that a car was pulling up the driveway. It was a police car, and when mom saw it, I could tell she was thinking and fearing the worst. You could just sense it.

The cop car slowed to a stop right before the garage, and a uniformed man got out. He turned toward the back of the car and opened the back door. Out poured Fudge and Lucas. I cannot make this up. Fudge came running right up to the door and inside, and Lucas followed him. We still to this day do not know where Fudge found him, but the officer spotted the two walking up a golf cart path, between two houses, heading back toward home. It had actually worked. Fudge went out and did what none of the humans could do. He found my little brother and had brought him safely home. I could not believe it, but at the same time, I had no doubt. Something was telling me to let Fudge go look, and I am glad I listened. This was probably my proudest moment in life up until that point.

Looking back, it is one of the coolest experiences I have ever had. That dog literally saved my brother's life.

Heimlich Maneuver

I think I must have been in about fifth grade, and at the school where we did the hand prints on the wall. Yes, that is correct, because I remember that my teacher had taking a "liking" to me. And I use the quotes over the word liking, because what I really mean is that I believe she could tell I was going through a lot, and she felt sorry for me.

For the life of me, I cannot recall why we were staying with grandma and grandpa in their trailer. Given everything that had gone on up to this point, any reason was possible. I just can't recall it. I was pretty much fully checked out most of the time. But anyway, I think that we would go to school from our trailer and then go to our grandparents' trailer after school until our parents got home from work.

There had been a pretty decent stretch of consecutive days where I didn't have money for lunch at school. At first I was able to kind of shrug it off like my parents and grandparents forgot to send money. I don't know who was responsible, or at fault, but someone was. Then I was able to get by, by borrowing an item of food from one of the kids who took their lunch to school. Then I was able to get by just not eating. I would just sit there while the rest of the kids ate their lunches.

I am not exactly sure how long this went on. It wasn't a very long time, but it was long enough to matter that the teacher started to notice. I remember one day, when I was sitting at the lunch table with nothing in front of me, my teacher approached me and pulled me aside in the cafeteria. I thought I was in trouble at first, but she was concerned that I hadn't been having lunch lately.

Upon her initial inquiries about my food and lunch money

situation, I did my best to play it off. I think I said something like, "I'm not really hungry, so I didn't get a lunch."

Another time she asked it was something like, "I was gonna bring my lunch, but I forgot it on the table."

Another time it was, "I don't really eat a lot, so I'm not really hungry."

Finally, one day, she held me back in the classroom to ask me what was really going on, as the other kids spilled out into the hallway and headed to the cafeteria. And this time, I didn't utter much in explanation. I just kind of did my go-to when the heat turned up—checked out and stared at my shoes. She did the best she could to get information out of me, but I was not going to give her any. I had been down this road, or a very similar one before, and I knew that if I volunteered a lot of information to her, then Child Protective Services would come knocking on the door, so I just stayed quiet.

I think she was able to discern that something was really off, and that I wasn't going to talk, so she did what the mother in her told her to do. She got into her pocketbook, pulled out a five dollar bill, and gave it to me. What happened next told her everything she needed to know. I wrapped my arms around her, gave her a big squeeze, and said thank you. Then I made a very quick beeline toward the door and cafeteria. I was starving.

And wouldn't you know it? Just my luck. I was so damn hungry that when I sat down I started devouring my food like a hostage would eat. I finished up the main stuff and unpeeled an orange. I wolfed that thing down as fast as I could. A little too damn fast apparently, because it got stuck in my throat. I was choking, like really choking. I flailed my arms and made really strange noises as I attempted to gulp in air. I got those sketchy butterflies in my stomach. This was terrifying. I couldn't breathe, I couldn't get it out.

One of the kids sitting by me noticed and was like, "Are you okay, Stevie?" And yelled for help. And guess who ran to my aid? Yep, my teacher. She ran over to me, wrapped her arms around me from behind, and gave me a tight squeeze of her own. With two fists wrapped into each other, she applied pressure into my chest and out popped a nasty ball of half chewed orange, some peel, and a seed. She had quite possibly just saved my life. I was so embarrassed. What a crazy turn of events.

When I got back to my grandparents' house and they asked

how school was, I told them about what had happened, and they were happy I was okay. But they were very unhappy about my teacher buying me lunch. Apparently I was in trouble for this. Or someone was, but they were not happy, I could tell. I don't know if they were mad at me for exposing my family or what, but it was made very clear to me that this was not to happen again.

So. when I was again at school with no lunch, and my teacher again pulled me aside, I had to tell her that she wasn't allowed to buy me lunch anymore because I was in trouble for it. So she didn't. She packed me a lunch every day. On days that I had lunch money, which was rare during this stretch, I got my own. On days I didn't, she handed me a brown paper bag with a sandwich, fruit, some crackers, and a chocolate milk, every single time. This must have happened more times than I can recall, and it must have happened so many times that apparently she had seen enough of it. Now, I cannot confirm or deny if it was in fact she who called, but someone did. Someone called the authorities and called my grandparents directly. I don't know who was on the other line when the call came in, but I was sitting right in front of grandpa's big ol' wooden framed turn-knob TV when it did.

The conversation was relatively short and heated.

"Didn't I tell you NOT to be gettin' lunches from your teacher, Stevie?" grandma asked me.

And grandpa, a man of few words chimed in, for me to go out back and pick a switch off the tree in the yard. "And if it ain't thick enough, I'm gonna use something else!"

Well, apparently it was not thick enough, because next thing I knew, I am being held by both my grandma and grandpa, with all their might, while I did my best to squirm and fight to get away, while they absolutely blasted me all over my back, ass, legs, and arms with an extension cord! I must have taken about twenty licks all over me. I was squirming and screaming and scared. White hot blast, after white hot blast. My skin was on fire, and the feel of being hit with a glowing piece of wire was absolutely horrible. I was bawling and screeching and squirming. I had never been beaten like this before.

When it finally stopped, I was told to go to Josh's room and not come out—or I would get it again. When I got back with my parents, they were told of the incident and I was then scolded by them too, for taking lunch from my teacher and getting the authorities called on everyone. I had never felt so voiceless and powerless in my life. Life sucked. I was just hungry.

After the savage beating from my grandparents with the extension cord, I had to wear jeans and long sleeves to school for about a week to cover up the welts so no one would see them. But at least no one forgot to make sure I had lunch every day from then on, so that was a win.

I didn't feel safe anywhere. Anytime I did get to experience safety, I knew it was only a matter of time before it was ripped away from me.

Knock Knock

Even though the story about Fudge finding my little brother had a happy ending, it was still incredibly traumatic for me, and for many I am sure. It was "isolated events" like that that led me to constantly feeling on edge. It was almost like I lived in a state of hypervigilance, always tensed up, waiting for the next horrible and scary thing to happen.

I always knew that there was something lurking just around the corner that I would need the space ship for—and I was never wrong. I had become so accustomed to tragedy and trauma that I expected it. It's kind of like I had bad days with some good sprinkled in.

Now, as I continue to heal and grow, practicing self-awareness, I have good days with some bad sprinkled in. I had been so morbidly shaped by all of the events and on-going stress of my childhood and the traumas that came along with it, that it had actually made me quite depressed at times.

I remember sitting in my neighbor friend's car one night. I was spending the night with him, and we made a trip with his mom to Kroger for snacks and stuff to watch movies. On our way back, for no particular reason, I decided to tell him and his mother,"I don't really see a point in this whole life thing. I don't really have a reason to live."

Think about that. An elementary school child, who is supposed to be so full of wonder and imagination, with so much excitement and innocence actually thinking that he has no reason to live. How truly sad. But I suppose that is what happens when we as children have our innocence taken from us. I was subject to so much emotional upheaval, so many adult problems, so many devastating blows to my spirit that had occurred at such an early age, I didn't really see a point. I mean, who would?

If what I had seen, experienced, and been a part of was how life went, what was the point? More suffering? No thanks.

Like I said though, there were some good times sprinkled in. They were just few and far between. I remember that we were still at the Scatterfoot house when school had finished up for the day. We had literally just started the new school year. I had just had the honor of feeling recognized when my fifth grade class got to put our hand prints on the walls all throughout the inside walls of Kedron Elementary School. We were the very first "graduates" of the brand new school, and as a way to commemorate the occasion, all of the students had our palms rolled with either purple or green paint, the school colors, and we had our hand prints placed on the walls for all of time. Then we had a big graduation ceremony in which we got to walk up to a microphone, say our name, and what we were going to be when we grew up.

"My name is Stevie Stepherson, and when I grow up I am going to be a professional baseball player," was what I went with. Oh to be so young and naive. But anyway, that was last year, and this was now.

I had just started at J. C. Booth Middle School, and I think we were about two weeks in. We had finished up with school for the day, and we, our family, had actually been having a really nice streak lately. No major blow outs, no fights, no ugly events. Life actually seemed to be somewhat settled down, which was nice. My guard was finally starting to come down a bit, and I was starting to relax and trust again. It felt good.

I was laughing and joking with my neighborhood friends on the bus as we made our way toward our respective stops at the end of a long day of learning. We, as friends, were making plans to play for the afternoon, probably football out back in the soccer fields, or kickball, or something. We were a really active, sports centered bunch. It was gonna be a nice afternoon.

A kid got off the bus, and then another, and then another. My stop was approaching, and I was preparing to stand up and make my way to the yellow line. As we bend the corner of the large loop or circle that Scatterfoot Drive is, I could see that there was a large white truck in the driveway. It was parked with the front of it facing away from the house and down the hill. I went around the front of the Blue Bird and could see that it was another U-Haul.

Ugh. Not again. Where in the world were we going now?

At least this time, I was not super worried because I was at Booth Middle School, which covered a great deal of the city, so I was pretty confident that I wouldn't have to be changing schools. And truth be told, I was actually kind of excited. I thought that maybe finally, we were gonna be moving out of Uncle's house, and getting a place of our own. The thought of this made me happy. So I boogied up the hill as fast as I could to learn what was going on. I could hear shouting and arguing before I got to the door and saw people visibly upset and crying when I entered the house. Something told me this was not going to be good.

Ugh.

"We're moving to Indiana, Stevie," I was told.

What in the world? That was far! I certainly did not expect this. I did my best to advocate for us staying in Georgia, but it all fell on deaf ears. I remember walking away from my mother and relatives in the kitchen, and out to the garage to talk to my dad, when I noticed that the U-Haul was already quite full. We didn't have a whole lot of stuff, so I only assumed that the packing was pretty much done.

"Are Lucas, Josh, and I gonna have to share a room when we get there, Dad?"

"Well, no son, you're not. Josh is staying here in Georgia with Grandma and Grandpa."

The world stopped spinning. My mouth ran dry. I felt dizzy and overwhelmed with absolute rage. Heartbreak overcame my body and mind. I lost it. I absolutely exploded with sadness. Right back into the space shuttle I went. And what made matters much, much worse, was that the packing was indeed done. We were going to be leaving within a matter of a few minutes. I would only have about a half an hour with my older brother to say good bye. and zero idea of when I would see him again. This was earth shattering for me. I was beside myself. I cried and pled with every adult in the house not to let this happen. But it was indeed happening and happening fast. Everything was a blur. I felt so helpless and unheard. True powerlessness had overcome me and I was sad.

Why was life like this?

It wasn't long after we hugged and cried together and said our goodbyes, that we pulled out of the driveway in the U-Haul. Without another vehicle, my little brother and I sat in the back of the U-Haul, talking to our parents through the little connecting area for the first few legs of the journey and napping off and on the whole way. Lucas and I were going to be staying with another aunt and uncle while mom and dad got on their feet. They would be staying in a homeless shelter in Valparaiso called the Spring Valley Center. Lucas and I would be attending South Central in Union Mills. My aunt and uncle fostered a lot of kids I guess, so at least I would have friends to play with when we got there. And I would get to see my grandma. I was very excited about!

Where, oh where would this next season in life take us all? I had to say goodbye to Georgia and all that I had known, and hello to Indiana and all sorts of unknowns.

* * *

Once we were settled in with our aunt and uncle in LaPorte county, things seemed to level out quite a bit. We would talk to mom and dad on the phone often, and visit them on the weekends. Sometimes, we opted not to visit them in the homeless shelter though. They fought a a lot. Mom would blame dad for us being in such a place and back and forth they would go. So sometimes, we would choose not to go there, and sometimes we would go to gramma's. Gramma was the best. And she still is. She is such a sweet lady. She lived in this place in downtown Valparaiso, called the Valparaiso Women's Club. I guess she was kind of the caretaker there by cleaning and maintaining the place in exchange for reduced rent costs. When I would go and spend the weekend with her, I would "help" her clean the common areas and take the trash out and stuff.

Part of gramma's responsibilities was to check in on the other residents from time to time, so as we went about our business this day, she would knock on their doors and say hello. There were about three floors inside this place and many, many doors to knock on. So this was taking forever. We would dust the wood and wipe it with Pledge, clean the mirrors in the bathroom, and she then would knock on another door. Empty a trash can, replace paper towels in the common area kitchen, and knock on another door. And on we went. We finally got to the top floor and were just about finished up with the day's tasks, when we came to yet another door to knock on.

We could both hear that the TV is on inside the room, but no one answered her knocks. She knocked again and again, nothing.

Finally, frustrated or "flustered" as gramma put it, she set her cleaning supplies down and used her master key to open the door. She announced that she was coming in, and as she pushed the door open, we could see pretty much the entirety of the room.

It was basically a studio apartment with a closet. There was a dresser inside the closet, a TV on top of a large desk, a tall floor lamp, and a queen size bed. And laying there, slumped over on her face, was a woman who had clearly fallen off the bed onto the hardwood floor. It was the first dead body I had ever witnessed. I immediately knew she was dead, and so did gramma. She tried to give her attention briefly anyway, but it was obvious that she was long gone.

I have learned in the years since that she had died of an overdose. How very sad. I was in absolute shock. I immediately disassociated and stuffed this one down. But the effects were there. This was terrifying. I don't think I slept for a month. I swear man, it seemed like terror and chaos awaited me around every corner for most of my life. I almost didn't have a choice later on in my adulthood but to laugh about all of my life's misfortunes and adventures. This was no laughing matter though. I had no other tools or people to process it with. I just didn't know what else to do. It was like life was just one big sick joke most of the time. And it all shaped me, honed me, and refined me into a very jaded, cynical, pessimistic, and maladapted young man. That poor lady. I wonder what her story was to get her to the point she had died. That was someone's daughter. It is so very sad.

If we all only knew other people's stories, maybe we wouldn't be so quick to judge. I hope her family was able to find closure and heal from all of that.

* * *

Acute Trauma.

It's so interesting to me how this is the year 2023, and it feels like we are in some kind of revolution so to speak. People talk about quantum leaps throughout history, like the steam engine, the combustion engine, the microwave, the Space Shuttle, the cell phone, and microprocessors. Those are quantum leaps. I believe that we are in the midst of a quantum leap, which will bring about a new age as we speak.

The revolution, the quantum leap, and the new age that is upon us though is not necessarily that of technology like before, but it is one of self-awareness and mental health and wellness. We are learning more about ourselves and from each other than we ever have before in the history of mankind—and it is really exciting. Soon we will all be so well educated on the topic of self-awareness and mental wellness, that we will actually be dealing with well-rounded, developed, and healed human beings on the regular. And it begins with, again, exposure.

Many have to be brave enough to expose their own traumas, and their own struggles, to allow others to see and feel what they went through to gain the courage to confront their own struggles and demons, which will then ease the stigma of mental health issues. Going to a therapist or treatment for mental health and substance abuse issues should be just as widely accepted as going to a doctor for a broken leg—and we are fast approaching that.

I really hope that someone can read my experiences and feel inspired enough to take that courageous step toward conquering their own past traumas and finally find the clarity and peace that they deserve.

You are NOT what happened to you. Things happen to us, not because of us.

Time Capsule

"I try not to think of hard times
I try hard to let the past go
I thank God that I'm a changed man
but some days I'm that same asshole"
Jelly Rol l- "Same Asshole"

Time Capsule, Noun: A container storing a selection of objects chosen as being typical of the present time, buried for discovery in the future.

Buried for discovery in the future

Ain't that the truth. That is exactly what I have recently been learning, That I myself have been a time capsule: only not for objects, but for memories, hurts, and feelings.

I have been a time capsule of my childhood traumas, things buried deeply inside of me, only to be dug up in the year thirty six, dusted off, examined, filed, processed, and let go of.

As I stated in my entry before this one, I have been back in therapy. I don't know what the particular reasoning is, but this time around it has really been effective. I have finally been able and willing to honestly look at my past and openly admit to another human being the things that I have been through and have witnessed. But what's equally, if not more important, is the way that I have been able to connect some dots in my mind, and in my heart, as to who I am, and why I am the way I am.

You see, this entry is called Time Capsule, because I believe if you are anything like me, then that is what we can become at a very early age, as a result of protecting ourselves from harm. Someone once told me that, "Not everyone who experiences trauma goes on to become addicted, but everyone who has addiction, has experienced trauma."

I believe that 100%! You see, from the time I was young, as I outlined right before this, I had a really hard life. I had been through, witnessed, and experienced things that no child, hell, no adult ever should. I suppose, that is when I entered my own "Space Shuttle" as a way to just disconnect, and avoid certain feelings and experiences. But that set the precedent for the rest of my life, which is in fact, the core of addiction.

Using drugs is all about escape, and I suppose I was the Harry Houdini of drug addiction. I was a real life escape artist. I didn't even really know at the time of my first cigarette, or my first beer, that that's what I was even doing. It was just instinct. It was something I guess I had learned at what, nine years old? Seven? Who knows, but enduring what I had at such an early age, robbed me of my innocence and forced me into "the wolves' den" of survival and self-preservation, at an age when most kids like playing with toys and sidewalk chalk. But I had no survival skills, other than closing my eyes, thinking of something different, disassociating, and wait for it all to be over. As I got older, I would find new or different things to lose myself into: baseball, TV, acceptance from others, attention from a girl, being a class clown. Anything to keep my surface-self visible, while concurrently hiding my internal self. What also came along with that, which I find interesting, is that I would compare other people's "outsides" to my very own damaged and hurting "insides." I couldn't, or wouldn't, express or expose the things that were hurting so badly inside of me. I just put on a brave and happy face to try to fit into this screwed up world. At the same time, I would judge other "happy and enthusiastic" people up against the very things that I was hiding from myself.

I have been quoted a few times, saying, "You just don't get it, deep down inside I'm just a lost and broken hearted little boy." That was my self-image and identity for a very long time, up until recently.

What's also interesting to me is that with all of this going on, while I'm growing into adolescence, and adulthood, I'm still disassociating, and detaching—but the things that I have buried down deep are still there. Never fully processed, never fully acknowledged, never exposed. Hidden from myself. Yes, that is possible, believe me it is.

The dusty old time capsule is buried deep in the secret places of my mind, like a physical malignant tumor, actually wedged inside my brain. And like any invasive material lodged inside our body, if it isn't treated, if it isn't removed, if it isn't exposed and handled with care, infection looms. The infections that come along with this particular ailment are: anger, sadness, self-pity, resentment, damaged future relationships, drug addiction, depression, poor interpersonal relationships, fear, inabilities to cope, and all of the etceteras.

By shutting down to protect myself, by compartmentalizing everything, by stuffing it down deep inside of me in the time capsule, I might as well have wrapped a bundle of dynamite around it with a thirty-six year long wick. But how was I to know? I was just a child when all of this shit started forming my young and vulnerable mind. I still had so much awe and wonder. I still rooted for the good guys in the movies. I still played with and used my imagination. I was adapting to and surviving life as best as I could.

How in the world could I have known that this was unhealthy? How could I know that this was not normal?

I had never done life before, as far as I knew, so how was I supposed to know that certain things were okay, and others were not? I was literally just kind of drifting along, with very little protection, zero modeling, and zero refuge.

I thought all kids were forced to watch two adults engage in oral sex at the age of nine. I thought all kids were forced into a room to beat the shit out of each other. I thought all kids went to six schools in six years and were dumped off from relative to relative while their dads chased their moms all over the country, not returning for months, or even years. I thought all of this shit was normal in my twenties, hell, even into my thirties. I was just a kid.

I knew right from wrong, but I didn't quite grasp normal from abnormal. After all, normal is just the sum total of what we are exposed to most, right? I had nothing to compare it to. This is what I knew. I knew it didn't *feel* okay, and my internal moral compass told me that this was not okay, but I had nowhere to go with it—I had no refuge. I had no safe place. Everything and everyone around me was a complete fucking shit show.

I don't think I ever actually felt any kind of inner peace until I got fucked up for the first time. Every experience and every person I had ever encountered before that first numbing from substances was accompanied by this "Long Black Shadow." Everything was tainted and blurry. Getting fucked up, I suppose, was a way to just numb it all away. What's interesting to me about that last thought, is that I remember the first time I got fucked up.

I remember my first cigarette buzz. I didn't take it thinking, "Oh this will make all of my pain and traumas go away." It was an after the fact realization. During the onset of the cigarette buzz, and during my first drunk, I noticed that I had no internal pain, I had no horrible memories. I could no longer feel the pressing of the tumor on my mind. It had temporarily numbed it. As I know now, it was like putting a band aid on a broken leg.

But how was I supposed to know? I had been flying solo and flying blind for sixteen years, hell, for thirty six years. Learning and trying to unlearn as I went. Survival Mode since the 1980s.

One of things that I learned recently, as we unearthed the dirty old capsule from its deep and dark hiding place inside my mind, is that everything I experienced, everything I witnessed, everything that was modeled to me, went into this thing—to the point to where it was busting at the seams, and spilling into my present and active mind. Everything that I thought was "normal," everything that I thought we all went through, all of it became "who I am" and molded me into the adult human that I am today.

Trauma Repetition.

I come from harm, I come from trauma. I come from broken and damaged, fucked up relationships. I come from loneliness. I come from uncertainty, and though I suppose it was an instinctual defense mechanism—shutting down and stuffing it all away—it never actually went away. It was silently and insidiously dictating everything I did, and everyone I went around.

I had such an incredible fear of abandonment, and as a result, when people would bully me, or try to exit my life, when a woman would cheat on me, when I felt like a relationship might end—I would run *TO* that person, instead of realizing that I actually deserved better.

I did my best to do and be the opposite of everything I went through, but instead became an exact replica. I suppose that stuffing things down, and hiding from them, actually kept them even more so present and active in my mind and spirit. I was allowing them to fester, grow, and adapt to my present circumstances, events, and relationships. like the tail was wagging the dog, or like a ventriloquist's dummy.

I suppose that is why in my addiction and downward spiral, it was like watching myself do things in the third person. Because it was in fact, not my present and current self running the show, it was all of my past survival mechanisms kicking the can down the street in an effort to continue the numbing that I started at around elementary school.

Interesting.

* * *

Initially, the time capsule was inside of me, as I was in the space shuttle, but eventually, I entered the time capsule myself. It consumed me. They say that when we get clean, we are the age at which we started using.

Arrested Development.

Until around age twenty-six, the prefrontal cortex is not fully developed which makes a lot of embarrassing sense to me. I suppose that makes me about being twenty-two-years old for all intents and purposes right now. It is our present and current relationships that bear the brunt of that, unless we do something about it. As I have re-engaged into therapy, I have slowly been connecting the dots of my entire life. Things happened *TO ME,* not *BECAUSE OF ME*—and that provides me a great deal of refuge. So long as I am recognizing that harmful patterns from my past will and do crop up from time to time, I can take the pause to change that thought to something positive and beneficial. I can avoid staying in that rut of perpetual shitty thinking and behaviors. It is on us to fully examine our whole life from the "helicopter view," like watching the Macy's Thanksgiving Day Parade, not just one float at a time, but with some help, by taking an objective and outside look at how we became who we are.

Connect our dots, open the time capsule, examine the moments and events, process them, and then toss them into the sea.

We are not responsible for our addiction. We are not responsible for what happened to us. We are not responsible for our traumas, but we are responsible for processing them, addressing them, healing from them, and making the necessary changes to avoid the perpetual lineage of passing them down over and over.

We cannot change what we refuse to confront.

Solitary

T hink about and ponder this for a moment: What is the absolute worst punishment a person can be given? I mean realistically, and legally, what is the worst type of punishment that can be handed down to a person? I understand that I am asking a question whose answer is a matter of opinion here, but humor me a bit. Is it the electric chair? The firing squad? The gas chamber? Is it the movie style torture interrogations that we sometimes see in scenes of spy films, done by the counter terrorist groups? I don't think so. You see with all of these previously mentioned terrible situations a person can find themselves in as punishment, they're all typically quite brief in length. They're all very short lived and temporary, no matter how awful they may be. I would think that life in a really shitty and dangerous prison is about as harsh of a punishment as possible, but there is still one rung to go down from there. After all, they still have a way to punish you while you are serving life in that shitty prison. And that way is to place you in solitary confinement for very long periods of time.

Solitary confinement, the hole, Seg. (Segregation).

They strip you of all of your privileges, all of your commissary, and put you in a cinder block room all by yourself. There is zero human interaction, often for many months at a time, and if the sanction is to be harsh enough, years at a time. This just goes to show you, that no matter how hardened the criminal, or "bad-ass" a person is, the basic need for human connection is something that we all need in our daily lives. Without it, we can go clinically insane.

I came to Indiana with my family, only to once again be living with another aunt and uncle who were very much warped. I had experienced my first twelve or so years feeling very invisible and very unimportant. I had experienced many things by my thirteenth birthday that some combat vets never do. I certainly was not lacking in crazy stories to tell, or in the wide breadth of experiences that I had had up to this point. I was lacking so very much in the areas of human connection, bonding, emotional regulation, communication skills, anger management, overall maturity, relationship skills, and processing and coping abilities. I didn't know what I had actually experienced intermittently to be trauma, or what I was feeling at any given moment. I certainly didn't know how to communicate the feelings I was having, or who was safe to do so with. This was a really bad state to be in, and I was very much at a disadvantage here.

So here I was, living with an aunt and uncle who I had never met before and all of their biological kids, plus a bunch of foster kids, in a state I had never been to, fully traumatized and violated. I remember having the "left for dead" feeling often, although I couldn't really identify it at the moment. I just knew it didn't feel good, and I often felt like an alien in my own skin, even in a room full of people.

I always carried this shame with me everywhere I went, like somehow everything that had happened up until this point was my fault. I know how ridiculous that may sound, but as I understand it now, it is actually quite common to bear the shame and guilt of past events, as if they had happened because of me, not to me. What's interesting is that even the adults around me at any given time didn't seem to pick up on it. We would be at family functions, or family would come over to my aunt and uncles', and I would recoil and isolate from my own cousins and other family. The over all consensus was that, "Oh, he's just shy." Nah, man, I wasn't shy. I didn't actually know these people, and I couldn't trust the humans I did know, so I definitely wasn't gonna get close enough to them to hurt me, so I would just hang back away from most people. This is the whole loop of it, because I had become so isolated and emotionally withdrawn from people as a result of everything that had happened up until now. I had a hard time making friends or connecting with people because of my hypervigilance, thus reinforcing the feelings that I had of, *I am not likable, no one wants to love me.*

As a result of all the constant movement, relocating, and being passed from relative to relative, I never established a sense of belonging. The only place I ever really felt like I belonged up to this point was on a baseball field.

Playing baseball was where I felt seen. It was where I felt valued. It was where I felt like I actually had something to contribute. Baseball was a way for me to lose myself. It was a way to escape all of my thoughts and feelings. The only thing I had to think about was playing the game that I loved. There was no pain here. There was no trailer trash, violence, molesting, fear, abandonment, worry, none of that was on the diamond. It was just my teammates and me playing a game for the pure fun of it, and I was pretty good at it too. In another life, and under many different circumstances, perhaps I would have been able to go pro. Not in this life though, and that's okay.

Particularly damaging to me personally was that a vast majority of the trauma and pain that I had inside of me came at the hands of my own blood family.

(Again, I am NOT placing blame here. As of right now, January 24, 2023, I have better relationships with my family than I have had in a very long time. I loved them all then, and I love them all now. I am not trying to sit here and paint my parents, or extended family in any kind of negative light. I am simply trying to convey how things throughout my life made me feel, and ultimately impacted me in the long run).

Feeling safe at home, or wherever I was living at the time, was very difficult for me. I believe this is why the second I caught a whiff of independence, I took it and ran. I also believe that this is why I always found myself people pleasing and trying to fit in. Fitting in is the opposite of belonging. I know that now. When someone doesn't have a sense of belonging within a certain system or community, they will reach for validation by fitting in where they don't belong. That was me to a T, and that is also a very interesting concept. I don't feel like I belong anywhere, so I try and fit in where I certainly don't belong. This left me again and again still feeling very isolated and very much alone, even once my parents finally got on their feet, as promised.

* * *

We finished up the year at South Central and moved into an apartment in Valparaiso. I was going to be attending Thomas Jefferson Middle

School. I remember being nervous about this, because I had heard the adults around me talking about how snobby Valparaiso was (Their words, not mine. Although I don't all the way disagree). However, I was very much accustomed to the starting a new school thing. I had done it like eight times now, including this one, so what the hell, it couldn't be all that bad. And it wasn't. I had become very chameleon like in my ways of survival. I could "get in where I fit in" pretty well, because I carried with me a sense of not belonging. It was the only real means I possessed at getting along.

I remember the first day of school at Thomas Jefferson. I was standing in line for lunch, and I felt a tap on my shoulder. I turned to find a girl standing just behind me.

"Hey, my friend thinks you're really cute. I think she likes you." Then she points over to a group of chicks sitting at a lunch table.

"Yeah, her name is Lauren Laurenson," she said and started laughing in my face, as all of her little friends joined in. She had learned my name/nickname was Steve, Steve Stepherson (Pronounced Steverson) and decided she was going to deal a major blow to my already frail and damaged sense of self, self-esteem, and self-image with a damn name joke.

Bullying. Rejection Trauma.

I don't even know why I included that last little bit, but it came out, so it's staying. It's not like in the grand scheme of things it's really all that important. The timing of it all really did suck though. I was already eaten up with all kinds of negative shit, and now I was essentially getting bullied by a little four-foot-nothing-female.

It was just about the status quo though. Move, make a fresh start, get settled in, get some hope, and then BAM—kick to the nuts. I was used to it by now.

(And yes, this entry that I am writing here sounds really "victim-y" I know, but I am trying to convey to you what kind of head space I was in at the time. Don't worry, it changes. Trust me. If it hadn't, I wouldn't be able to write about it like this.)

I ended up pretty hurt by the lunch line thing, and kind of resigned myself to just trying to make friends a little closer to home. I started with the kids who lived in my apartment complex, then the kids who rode my bus, and then outward from there. The overall theme here was that I was always seemingly searching for a place a fit in. This was because I always felt so isolated. I felt like an alien in my own skin. I carried so much shame and guilt over things that were not my fault that they became my identity. I constantly felt like I had nowhere to go.

I remember throughout my life thinking, "I want to go home, the only problem is, I don't know where that is."

I wanted to experience some kind of real human connection. Some actual bonding, a real lasting friendship. As I would find out over the course of my life, I was not well adapted enough to maintain and nurture friendships and relationships once I had finally obtained some. Because of how my perspective had been shaped, and how essentially deformed my mind was, I ended up running people off, or walking away from them once I had experienced any kind of vulnerability with them. I was totally screwed up. It was not a good stretch of life, emotionally, mentally, or spiritually. It seemed as though I had been born into and raised in my very own solitary confinement.

"Spent my lifetime in this cage
I've built around me
Bangin' on the doors"
—Cody Jinks

The Porcupine

Recently the image of the porcupine has been stuck in my mind following a therapy session. The porcupine is not to be screwed with. It is fierce and damaging to anyone who threatens it. With an artillery of sharp points, one swipe of its tail sends its adversary running and howling in pain, ending up like a bloody pin cushion. Just think about it: if you ever saw one, would you want to approach it? Take zoomed-in pictures of it from afar maybe, but get close enough to it to wind up on the receiving end of those brutal quills? Absolutely not. Porcupines are sketchy looking little buggers that deal damage to anyone who threatens them, large or small, whether we mean well or intend to do harm.

The reasoning that this animal's image has stuck with me recently is that I found myself pondering, "Are porcupines born with those sharp quills? Wouldn't those sharp spear-like weapons be damaging to the mother at birth?"

It turns out porcupines are not born with sharp quills. They are born with soft quills that harden over time, as they mature and venture out into the world. How metaphorical.

Likewise, we humans are not born with "hard quills" either. We are born into this world, for the most part, perfect and innocent, shameless and soft hearted. As we experience life and venture out into the world, we develop hardened quills—or don't. Even if they do develop, and we become this prickly ball of angry defense, at the end of the day, the quills only serve as one thing: a Defense Mechanism.

I feel like this analogy of the porcupine is relevant in my life, for I too have slung my quills at people as a form of defense whether they deserved it or not. I believe we all have. But I wasn't born with the ability to sling quills. It was learned and adaptive. I know that now.

The more I talk about and ponder on my life in reverse, and the traumas and experiences that I have had, the more I understand "the sharp points" or at least try to. You see, I used to always share my story in a very condensed version for Keynote Speeches, or Breakout Sessions at various conferences. I used to talk about traumas and negative experiences from my using days, as a way to spread awareness about what addiction *REALLY* looks like.

It came up recently that most, if not all of my negative experiences from using, were essentially "self-inflicted," or at least somewhat within my control. I got to pick and choose the risks I would take in pursuit of my drug-seeking lifestyle, so that was an interesting point.

Self-Inflicted Trauma.

Is that an actual thing? I certainly understand the thinking behind it but wouldn't that be more of a "play stupid games, win stupid prizes" type thing? Anyway, I digress there. But looking back on a couple talks I gave in particular, I remember being "double minded" while delivering them.

During a presentation in Fort Wayne, Indiana, and another in French Lick, Indiana, I was talking about the lifestyle of using, and the traumas that occurred as a result, which led me to those impossible situations. The space shuttle launch that took me outside of myself and allowed me to hide in the world of drugs, that in turn, conjured up all of the experiences I was sharing about. What I should have been talking about to begin with was the space shuttle launch. Interesting.

I am not a victim. You can save your sympathy for the infomercials on TV. I made choices, and some of those choices led me to some really ugly and life threatening places. But how much responsibility can we really put on an eight year old little boy? A ten year old little boy? We are all born into this world dependent. Dependent upon the humans who created us, or the humans who adopt us, or the system if no one does.

Many of us end up experiencing the world relatively defenseless and naive. Sitting here this morning, I feel like I have much better understanding of why and how things turned out the way they did. I'm getting to a point in life, at the age of almost forty, where it's just about time to close the old story, and only focus on the new. As much as I absolutely love what I do, and who I am today, I don't just want to be this former heroin addict, drug addict guy anymore. I mean, that will always be a part of my story, and a big one, but it's time to fully explore and release. Explore the past, investigate it, know it, learn from it, and let it all go. It's really important for me, and anyone reading this to know that we can. It doesn't matter where we come from, or who our parents are, or where we live, what color we are, our traumas, pains, an old story can end and a new one begin We can, and it is our responsibility, to investigate and reflect back on our harmful patterns and how we became who we are today—both good and bad. Then we can in turn, use our discoveries and new found wisdom to enrich our relationships and break harmful cycles in our lineage and legacy. We don't have to sling quills even when we feel threatened or harmed in some way. We must learn to restrain, and let be what is.

I suppose I started developing my quills around the age of ten. Maybe a little sooner. Up until this time, I suppose I still had the luxury of my childhood innocence. I had the God given ability to still see the world with wonder and joy. Although terrible things had already long since been happening to me, I think maybe I was able to chalk it up to whatever the fuck my little mind was able to.

I mean, hey, it is totally normal to be forced to do horrible and disgusting things or get the shit beat out of you right? All kids experience that, that's just part of life right?

By the way that's sarcasm. It's *not* normal. It's horrible and evil and damaging and leads to a lifetime of trauma. People who commit sex offenses against children should be given life in prison without the possibility of parole, in my opinion. But it wasn't just that. The beatings, the moving, the uncertainties, the instability, Being counseled on how to talk to Child Protective Services when they come and ask about a number of things, having to borrow money from my teachers in elementary school for lunch. My teachers bringing me lunch to school because they were sick of paying for my lunch. Being dumped on relative after relative. And not seeing Mom or Dad, or either for up to a year at a time. Getting my head split open with a golf club, or being beaten bloody with a broom stick. Repeatedly molested, run over, and being wedged in the middle of an ongoing family war between Maternal and Paternal sides of the family. Witnessing a suicide attempt, and finding a dead body!

I mean fuck man, none of these things are even in the universe of normal, and all of these things happened before my 18th birthday. All while riding this invisible wave of life, trying to navigate and find myself, and be a little boy. All while just wanting to go to the same damn school system for consecutive years. I remember somewhere along the line, just checking out. Getting into my space shuttle and detaching from it all. I became a real life Harry Houdini, by the age of twelve

The thing about it is, I don't think I ever actually detached. I mean, is that even possible? No matter what, no matter how hard we try, don't we still witness it to some degree? Every time something would happen, or a crisis would occur, or my so called stability was threatened, I would detach in my space shuttle, to protect myself and a new quill would develop. This became My M.O., "detach and grow a quill." Where once was a soft and delicate little fuzz patch—resembling the dwindling innocence I still had remaining—a hardened and dangerous quill would form. Just waiting on someone to threaten that vulnerable place of mine, so I could hurl my manifested defense mechanisms right at their face, keeping everything that threatened me at a safe distance.

I was sick of getting hurt man. I was sick of having to constantly adapt to this version of life that I was getting. I know that we all play the hand we're dealt to the best of our ability. But someone has to teach us how to play the game, whether its Texas Hold'em or Go-Fish. Someone has to teach us about healing and processing and understanding where our quills come from, otherwise we are stuck in the balloon factory, and everything that gets close to us is in danger. It is important for us to truly understand where each of our "Sharp points" come from, and then lean in to them, study them, investigate them and know that we didn't just decide to develop them. They are a result of our past hurts and pains. We are products of our environments for the most part. I mean, shit, I'll be forty years old in three and a half years, and I am just now truly understanding this shit and at a point where I am ready to lose the quills. That's important work, losing our quills. Shedding that old self that no longer serves us.

It dawned on me recently, how important this is, losing the quills—those sharp points of maladaptive behavior from my past, because I was actively burning my life to the ground, slowly over the course of about two years. It didn't matter that I hadn't shot dope or smoked crack in a long time. I was still relying on my space shuttle, time capsule and sharp quills as ways of defending my still wounded heart and spirit. I was still acting, reacting, and behaving in many ways, like I always had.

"Oh you hurt me five years ago, well let me continue to sling these quills at you, to keep you far enough away from me to never do it again. Oh you fucked me over. you fired me, you made fun of me in high school, you broke up with me, you didn't invite me, you _____. Well let me just make sure you get a face full of quills—resentment, bitterness, anger, gossip, etc. to keep you from ever getting close enough to harm me again."

It's what I learned to do a very long time ago to protect myself. I was just a child when I started developing my "sharp points," but I was alone a lot in this world early on, with no protectors, almost to the point of Hyperbole—like my karma was so bad in a previous life, that I was reborn into this one to know only suffering for a very long time. Then came the world of drug addiction; crack and heroin addicts and dope dealers, and more quills formed. By the time I actually got clean, the dust settled from the giant bomb that just finished exploding after twenty nine years of nuclear fallout—My head was spinning, My heart was destroyed, and I was this ugly, angry, ball of prickly defense mechanisms that served no one, and harmed everyone.

It has taken some really dark places and horrible-yet-again-self-inflicted-traumas to get to this place of understanding this. There really is something to that whole, "I'll show you, I'll Kill me," cliche that we hear so often in the various fellowships, because that's literally where I was not so long ago. "Oh you fucked me over? I'll stick this needle in my arm then." I'll slowly slip into a horrible depression, consider suicide, write suicide letters, burn them and then just climb into a bottle of booze and flip out on everyone I know, because I just can't shake this pain and fear that I'm living with every day. Covered in sharp points on the inside and out, beaten and broken, pissed off at the world, expecting so very much of myself; so many others expecting so much from me.

All I really longed for was to just be able to fucking breathe and feel some actual peace and joy in my life for the very first time.

So much has happened so fast. It seems like I was just sixteen years old hitting my first home run in the All-Stars Tourney, and now I'm almost forty.

I'd been in the space shuttle for a long time. But I finally feel like I have reached my stopping point, a point of inflection. A rude awakening. A point in my life where I realized that the past ain't changin', and there is nothing I can do about it except heal. There is so much power in healing. Shit, there's power in *trying* to heal. Learning and unlearning all of the things that formed the quills. I do *NOT* have to be who the world made me into being. I have the power to unlearn, un-do, and un-be. In my God Given form, just as I am right this moment, I am okay.

I believe that is how we break these generational curses that plague us as a society. By learning about ourselves, by understanding our quills and how they got there, by leaning into our sharp points, unlearning our maladaptive behaviors, and "un-being" who we once thought we needed to be.

Like the baby porcupine, the porcupette as it is known—we humans are not born with "sharp" or "hardened" anything. I think about my Grandmother when I write this; She used to talk about how innocent and perfect new born babies are when they first enter the world.

"The world out there took a naive kid, scarred his heart and beat him down, and this song is me, coming back around, from out of town."

Learn.

Unlearn.

Undo.

Un be.

Understand.

Let be.

Let go.

No one wants to hug a Porcupine.

Compromises

"If you don't stand for something, you will fall for anything."

Fitting in is the opposite of belonging. If we don't have a sense of belonging, then we will attempt to fit in where we definitely do not belong. Water seeks its own level; low self-esteem and low self-worth create low standards.

Ain't that the truth?

I actually settled into Valparaiso quite well, once the awkward newness fell away. I knew that I would have an *in* to make some friends no matter what, and that *in* was baseball. But this world that was Valpo, as we called Valparaiso for short, was a little different than the other towns I had experienced. Here, the kids who played sports were the cool kids. I certainly did not consider myself cool at all. Hell, I didn't even know what cool was.

I actually had no idea who I was. I had like zero identity, zero direction, and zero sense of self. I basically felt like I had just emerged from over a decade of absolute chaos—like that of an Atom Bomb explosion. Giant mushroom cloud erupts, death all around me, screams, cries for help, chaos and panic everywhere, and then I emerge a complete total stranger to myself. Like I had just appeared, with only the painful memories from the explosion left inside of me. I didn't know who I was, what I wanted, or where I belonged. Totally banged up from it all.

I had only what I could carry: remaining trauma, shame, guilt, insecurities, fear, loneliness, self-pity. An inner child that never felt good enough, worthy, valued, or noticed, A desire to feel like I mattered, and a love for baseball. (Not a victim stance, not

Hyperbole. This is where I was in life). I was so inside my own little world so often, that, I know it's hard to explain, but looking back, I was never fully present. I escaped with everything. Music, riding my bike, baseball, movies, TV.

I was just kind of floating along all accidental, like on a breeze. I would think about my life up until then often. I would remember back to all of the ugliness and pain that I endured. I remember many times actually pondering on my life, and actively probing myself, "So, Stevie, this is what you have experienced up until now. What are you going to do about it?" That type of stuff.

Thank God I did have people intermittently throughout my life who believed in planting seeds. For without them, it would have been incredibly easy to just become what the world had tried to make me into. A cold hearted, scorned, spiteful, hateful, resentful, mean-spirited person. But I wasn't going to allow that to happen. I had seen some really kind-hearted things in spite of the chaos and trauma that ensued. I just knew that when I was given the chance, I was going to make a difference one day. I knew that deep down inside I was a good person. I was just dealt a really shitty hand, and one day soon, I would be able to step out on my own. If I could just hold it together, one day I would get my chance.

So, I just kind of went through the motions as best as I could I suppose. I played baseball, and I had a couple friends that I rode bikes with all over town. Immediately after school, if I didn't have practice, and all weekend long if I didn't have games, I was gone. I was out of the house with my buds riding bikes all over Valparaiso. Sometimes we would go fishing, and sometimes we just hung out at a friend's and played video games. I never said no to a friend asking me to hang out. It made me feel good. It made me feel like I fit in somewhere. That ended up blessing me with friends from all over the "grid" so to speak. The jocks who played sports, because I played sports, the kids who once rode my bus, but now rode bikes to school, so now I rode my bike to school too. A couple buddies of mine loved WWF wresting like I did. A couple buddies who loved fishing, and a couple buddies who loved video games. I was constantly trying my hardest to always be on the go and to always be "in" somewhere. I had no actual consistent group of friends, with but a couple of exceptions. However even those friendships drifted apart eventually, and this is why I feel like my first "drug of choice" was Acceptance.

Acceptance from friends. Feeling seen. Feeling like I fit in somewhere. This was a very dangerous thing for me, looking back, because couple that with low self-worth, which equals low standards, and couple that with little to no moral compass, or direction in life, I now stood for basically nothing, so I would fall for anything. Does that make sense? Like, throughout everything that had happened so far, I still somehow managed to come out very naive. Lack of mentorship and guidance will do that to you. Plus couple that with growing up in chaos, which left me with this innate need for adventure, which is actually the comfort in chaos response to it all, and I was fucked. It was only a matter of time until just the right "carrot on a stick" was dangled out in front of me.

I have heard a lot of people throughout my life say this exact phrase over and over again: "I believe I was an addict before I ever even used a drug." I myself have said this countless times, and every time I shared it amongst other addicts, it was received with head nods of agreement. But what does that mean, and how can that be? I think what that phrase really means is probably something like this: "I suffered through extensive trauma throughout my life, and the very first time I used a chemical it worked. It numbed me and took away the pains. It was a remedy I found that I hadn't known I was looking for, and I was hooked on mind and mood altering chemicals ever since. Anything that gave me a head change is what I wanted. I had previously used other outlets to escape and self-medicate, but once I found drugs and alcohol, self-medication just became so much easier."

So as you can see, I hope; *I hope* I have painted a pretty accurate picture of who and what and where I was. I was on a collision course with addiction and didn't even know it.

A traumatized and violated kid, naive as shit, with a need for acceptance, ongoing need for escape, and no sense of belonging. Just wanting to fit in. Always on the go. Hardly ever home, unless it was to sleep. No sense of self or identity. No direction. Hardly any kind of moral compass, although I did know right from wrong. No boundaries or understanding of boundaries. A people pleaser. A tagalong. I was prime for the pickin' when the time would come. And it would.

* * *

Time marched on. I stayed on the go. Different friends seemingly every weekend, to the point where my parents couldn't even keep up. Baseball friend, bike buddy, video gamer, this part of town, that part of town. Rich friend, poor friend, etc. I was constantly chasing and moving, always trying to be in the mix as best as I could.

What I know now, that I so clearly did not know then, is that I was trying to fill a void. I was trying to fix my insides with external validation and influence. I also know now, that then, I certainly would have benefited from extensive amounts of therapy. But, as it goes, hindsight is 20/20. Life can only be lived forwards and understood backwards. That's just the way it goes.

I hated cigarettes as a child. I hated cigarettes as an adolescent. Everything about them disgusted me. The way they smelled, the way the butts accumulated in ash trays, the ash. The way they made smokers' voices sound, everything. They grossed me out. I hated that my parents smoked cigarettes. When I was riding in the car with my folks, and they would smoke, I would always ask them to roll the windows all the way down, because I didn't want to smell like the smoke. It was nasty, and I could never understand why someone would want to indulge in such a gross and self-destructive habit. I was actually embarrassed at times that they smoked.

I had grown up around smokers all my life, and the idea of it was just nasty. I remember vowing to myself as a child that I would never smoke a cigarette as long as I lived. I hated them that much.

Ya know, it's crazy how people have so many different "isms," needs, morals, and values. Sometimes we are willing to compromise one for another.

The point that I am getting to here is that I absolutely hated cigarettes, but I absolutely needed and loved feeling like I fit in somewhere.

Eventually the time came when I was with my bike-riding friends—I think maybe I was in eigth grade, going into ninth— when I was offered my very first cigarette. Something was gonna have to give here. And because I had such low self-esteem and self-worth, I was essentially defenseless. I found myself in a situation that was low standard, but I had low self-worth, so I lost. It was too easy for me to give in. I had no reason not to. I didn't love myself enough to say no. Something was about to be compromised.

Do I stand on my morals? Do I stand on my vow to myself that I will never smoke a cigarette as long as I live and risk losing a friend? Or do I take the cigarette and gain some much needed style points from this group of friends?

Decisions, decisions. Well, I took the cigarette immediately, because I certainly wasn't going to lose my friends and end up stuck back at home. That was the very place I was trying to avoid. Light me up!

I fucking hated it. The smell, the taste, it made me feel physically sick. I remember having to sit down, because it made me so damn dizzy. I remember my friends laughing at me because of it. Not in a making fun of me way, but in a, "I remember my first beer" kind of friendly ribbing. It was gross.

"Don't worry dude, you'll get used to it," I was told.

But why the fuck would anyone want to get used to this? I got about halfway through my first cigarette. A Camel Menthol Light, and the buzz of the toxic smoke had really begun to set in. I was in love. Unknowingly to me, this was exactly what I had been searching for. A chemical escape. It was so easy! It was damn near effortless. All I had to do was light a smoke, inhale, and it gave me a head change— all of my cares, worries, fears, doubts, insecurities, and pains all just melted away. It was like 1,000 pounds of weight had just been lifted off of my shoulders.

I had no idea in this moment, that six years later I would be a fucking heroin addict.

I just wanted to fit in. I just wanted to feel seen. I just wanted to escape. And so I compromised my code. I compromised my values. I sacrificed my promise to myself. And this is when my journey into becoming the *Junk-box* began. This is when my obsession with getting fucked up kicked in. This was the very first of many compromises to come.

Of course I am going to make compromising decisions. My core beliefs were that I didn't matter, no one wanted me. I was a mistake and a burden. At least by using chemicals with my friends, I felt like I was visible and that I mattered somewhat. This was my time to finally be noticed and celebrated.

So compromise, I would.

We get to our rock bottom, one compromise at a time.

I had to fill the void and fill the void I would.

DOPAMINE

Dopamine is a chemical released in the brain that makes you feel good.

A Drug of Choice. Not exactly the correct way to put it. At least not for me. It's not even about drugs. I mean, maybe to an extent. But the chemical itself wasn't as much of a factor as some may believe. This idea is really just kind of like a preferred flavor. I preferred opiates. I preferred heroin. But did I really?

No, I preferred "oblivion," "blotto," "just shut it off." My drug of choice evolved, and I made my way to the deepest of bottoms. One compromise at a time. Small compromises at first, increasing in size over time. Sacrificing my future for the moments. Sacrificing more and more along the way. But all of this, in and of itself, was a compromise to my truest self.

I preferred a bond. I preferred belonging. I preferred to feel loved. I preferred to feel.

My first drug of choice? Not the traditional chemical. But a chemical reaction that occurred in my brain. A dopamine hit. The chemical reaction that occurred in my brain when I felt this was, *ACCEPTANCE*. The feeling that I was okay, that I was loved in spite of all my flaws and insecurities, just as I was day in and day out. That I was good. That I was loved. That I mattered to someone. I loved my family, they did their best. I loved all of them, but I only really felt bonded with few of them and that was ripped away. Then I was shuffled around like a kid in the system.

I looked for something to bond with. I looked for someone to bond with. I am not sure why I never bonded deeply with them like

I should have. Maybe it was me? I searched for outside validation. I searched for a place that I fit in. I sought for ways to fill this void inside. The more I fed the void, the deeper it became.

At first it was baseball, video games, acting out. Then being the class clown, getting a girl's attention. Finding the wrong friends. Finding the right friends. Anything for that dopamine hit. Instant gratification. I had to chase it.

My first cigarette wasn't enough. My first drink wasn't enough. Weed, no. Sex, no. Video games, no. I had to chase it. The more I fed it, the larger it grew. Maybe just one more will satisfy. Nope. If I hit a home run on the ball field, I needed another one.

I just wanted to feel special. I just wanted to feel celebrated. I still do. I just wanted to feel relevant. I just wanted to feel noble. I just wanted to feel something, but also, nothing at all. I had to chase. I had to be on the move.

Looking back on things, I wasn't chasing towards anything. I was running from everything. Pot became pills, pills became powder. My friends became my adversaries. I became someone else.

Just chase it. Just get another one. Shut it off. Shut it down. Get high, stay high, nothing matters when I can't feel.

Oblivion, blotto, blackness. Out of sight and out of mind. Anything for a dopamine hit. Anything to make me feel something other than what I am.

Why work hard? Why sacrifice? Why study? Why practice? Why go home? Why tell the truth? Why be me? When this one ten dollar bag of weed makes it so much easier. To do nothing, to be nothing, to lie, to be someone else. To just fucking escape. Increase pleasure, decrease pain. Both please. Just stay numb, chase towards and run away from the exact same things. The generational loop in perpetuity. Run from my broken home. Run from my lack of bonds. Run from my childhood. Run from the beatings and the embarrassments The trailer park run from watching dad hitchhike on Highway 74 and out of my life. Run from the welts and the heart aches. Run from the domestic violence. Run from the insecurities. Run from the pain.

Chase towards the numbing of pain. Chase towards the insecurities. Chase towards domestic violence, towards the heartaches, the welts Chase towards that highway, and the trailer park embarrassments. Chase the beatings, chase the childhoods, chase the fractured relationships. Run to what broke you, create a broken home . . .

I'll be damned. I ended up becoming everything that I was running from.

* * *

This is the result of a phone call that I took from a gentleman yesterday. He is an Atheist, I am a Believer. But we share something in common. He didn't push his beliefs, and I didn't push mine. This is the beauty of recovery. It's the clear cut difference between religion and spirituality. Religion is for those afraid of hell. Spirituality is for us who have been there. We share that common pain. That survivors' bond. Recovery is where the priest learns from the plumber. Zero judgement. Wounded warriors all.

> "We're just two lost souls,. swimming in a fish bowl."
> —Pink Floyd

* * *

This is the beauty of it all. There is no drug of choice. It is all the same. We're all just wanting to feel optimal, or nothing at all. We addicts. We get clean and get super into working out, or shoes, or clothes, or the opposite sex. Or work, . or art, or Music. Maybe it's dogs, or reading, writing, and helping others. It can be meetings, purpose, or church, or God. Food, family, or Netflix. It could be cars, or money, or nothing. Or, we fall back into it once again to shut it off.

Everyone is addicted to something. Everyone just wants to feel loved, to feel special, be respected, feel celebrated, and feel a purpose.

Addiction is emotional. We are driven by chemical reactions in our brains. Some of us more than others. Increase pleasure, decrease pain.

Dopamine.

* * *

Addiction Interlude

The next few chapters are some insight into where using drugs took me. I went from smoking that first cigarette at around fifteen years old, to trying every drug that was made available to me. It all started with that first compromise. Once I began compromising my values, it got easier and easier to say "yes" to chemicals. I ultimately ended up strung out on opioids—heroin specifically, and crack cocaine. I was in and out of jail and prison for most of my adult life.

My first book, *Junkbox Diaries*, details what my life in active addiction was like on a day to day basis. For those of you who haven't read the first book, here are a few previously unreleased entries from my active addiction days to get you up to speed.

Hey Bud

I spent a lot of time homeless while in my active addiction. That's no secret. Everyone who has been following me already knows this. It was miserable. It was very lonely. I cried silently to myself often. I prayed. I hoped in my core that things would some day get better.

In between the twacked out crack highs and the oblivion heroin lows, when I had the mental capacity to do so, I would reflect back on my life. I would kind of just blank out and watch my life story in the forefront of my mind while looking out the window of the CTA bus line, or the Red Line train, or the Blue Line. Or sitting on a bench in Garfield Park, or at a bus stop in Lawndale, while the busy hustle and bustle of local gangs, crime, drugs, and police activity just passed me by.

It was strange. I was present and alert, sometimes, but I could actually watch my life story in a very morbid reflection.

How did I get here? How did I actually end up in this place and in this time, this very moment?

During my comings and goings, I met a lot of sad, lonely, and broken people. I encountered some of the forgotten ones. I saw what the bottom rung of our broken society looks like, and for a brief moment in time, we shared each other's pain.

You know what's interesting? Today, there is absolutely no way that I would ever go back to those spots in the city. I would never in a million years go back to those benches, bus stops, or gang ways. No way. It's far too dangerous, for me today. But, back in the day when I was in it, it was weird. I was a regular in some of the most depraved and deadly parts of the most dangerous city in the United States, and very few times did I ever actually feel in danger, save for being robbed at gun point, or afraid of the cops.

I hope this makes sense. Yes I was scared, but I was scared *FOR MYSELF*. I was more afraid of facing another day than I was of walking into an unknown alley way, to buy an unknown powder, from an unknown gang member who was visibly brandishing a very large hand gun. I don't know, it's strange. It's almost like this survivor's bond that we all shared. All of our lives were shit. I can't even begin to understand what would drive a nine-year-old boy to sell heroin on a bicycle, but I bought it from him every day. I wonder if he's even alive today? Anyway, that was a rabbit hole of thought, and not where I intended this entry to be going. I aimed at the beginning to share with you some of the sadder souls I have met, and one of the more insane and depraved. So here we go.

* * *

While living my life on the bottom, I would frequent the area just off of Ohio Street and Homan Avenue on the Chicago's West Side. Incredibly high crime area.

God I can still see it right now with my mind's eye.

Open air drug market, addicts everywhere, dealers everywhere. Screams, gun shot,. blue lights flashing on local Chicago Police Department cameras, which seemed to be on damn near every corner but did nothing to stop anything. Then there was me, stinking, unbathed, strung out, 125 pounds soaking wet, right in the thick of it all. I was hollow, I was alone, I was scared. But it didn't matter because I was not even steering the ship because it was like watching myself walk through life. Like an outer body experience, just kinda drifting. Watching this nightmare unfold day after day. Sometimes, maybe for a few minutes, maybe for an hour, I would encounter a fellow dope fiend just as lost as I was. Just as hopeless, just as broken. For those brief moments in time, I would have a friend, but sometimes it was just a chance encounter like, "Bud."

"Bud" was clearly not his real name, so I'll use it here. Bud lived in an abandoned building on Homan between Ohio Street and Chicago Avenue, I think. Now I had always seen this guy coming and going. Scurrying around like a crackhead, making dope fiend moves, ripping off white kids from the suburbs. Kids from Indiana, Illinois, and Wisconsin who came to the West Side for the promise of the best shit around and a few extra bags that they could then skim from their friends back home for making the trip and taking the risk. They were too scared to actually go to the source, so they entrusted guys like Bud to make the run for them and bring it back to them.

I obviously wasn't one of those kids.

One day, while waiting on the plug to get to the spot, Bud and I struck up a conversation, the topic of which I have no fucking clue. But there we were, among a throng of other awaiting dope fiends, two of which were a pregnant couple. I think things took a turn for the scary when I had mentioned that I was a lone wolf who only got to smoke my rock and shoot my dope comfortably when I found an entry to an abandoned building—or a tucked away corner somewhere. Bud invited me to come and get high with him in his "house." I didn't think anything of it. I wouldn't be there long anyway. Being a panhandler, and a petty thief without a car and on foot never really netted me much, maybe one rock and one blow per trip, so I'd be there, what, maybe twenty minutes? So I took him up on his offer. The plug got there, served us, and we were on our way. Bags in our cheeks, pipes and needles in our pockets, we scampered over Homan Avenue, through the gangway, around the back, and into Bud's dwelling. I'm getting nauseous and sickly feeling recalling this memory, but I promised to never hold back, so I'm not.

We entered the "house," which was basically a one room apartment located inside a completely abandoned building. To be honest, I was actually kind of impressed. He had somehow acquired power. He had lights and even an antenna TV rigged up inside this little crack shack. He had a bed, a couch, and even posters on the wall. I guess necessity is the mother of all invention, huh? So we sat down and started smoking.

Neither one of us spoke for about twenty minutes. Those of you in recovery who have smoked crack before know why. It is not a very social drug or high. As we started to come down and stop shaking, we both prepared our heroin to "get right," and now we were able to actually speak to one another. I don't recall about what, but we spoke, and it was casual. Sometime later, Bud said that he was about to make another run. He told me that I was welcome to stay but not to steal anything, and he would be right back.

Well, shit, that sounded good.

"Go right ahead, it's cold outside. I'll be right here man, thanks for letting me chill for a bit."

In no time flat he was out the door. After quite some time, he still hadn't returned, and I could feel inside me that something wasn't right. I got up to walk out to the gangway to smoke a cigarette, but when I got to the only door to the outside, I noticed something very strange. I had to do a double take. I looked at the big heavy fortified door and noticed that there was a massive chain on it. At first my strung-out brain couldn't quite compute what I was seeing. I grabbed the knob and pulled the door inward to open it, but it would barely budge.

What. The. Fuck! This dude left the apartment and had this whole chain set up long before I arrived. He had fashioned it to lock from the outside in! He had actually chained me inside!

Oh no, this was not good. I ran back up to the landing and into the room where we had been chilling. I stuffed all of my paraphernalia and checked the windows. Barred and locked. Of course they were! I ran back down the landing to the door and yanked it as hard as I possibly could. Nothing. It was becoming very clear to me that he had done a very good job at keeping me contained inside this little room with no way out.

PANIC! SHAKING! FEAR! What was about to happen to me? I have got to get out of here, and fast. My survival instincts kicked in. Search the apartment and find something to break out of this place as quickly as possible. Drawers, under the bed, behind the couch. Nothing. Holy shit. Will I be beaten? My God, will I be raped? Or worse, murdered? I gotta get out of here! My hands are shaking as I type this.

I felt like I was gonna vomit, and I absolutely TOSSED this apartment, searching high and low for anything I could find to get out of there. I can't even recall where it was, but I found something I thought I could use. A claw hammer. I got to work. There were about fifteen nails pounded flat into the back of this VERY HEAVY, probably oak door, holding the massive chain in place. With nowhere to grab the nail heads and simply pull them out, I violently pounded against the section of nails where they bent over and made contact with the chain. Violently pounded. Loud as hell. If Bud were within earshot, certainly he would hear it. If he came rushing in to stop me, I remember having the image of bashing his brains in with the now tool, as well as weapon, that I clutched in my right hand. I did not care. This was life or death.

One nail broke, then two, then five. I was slowly breaking these nails free and pulling each chain link free as I went. It was working, but I wasn't quite there yet. More nails broke, more links freed. Finally I got to the last one and was able to pry the door completely open. I stuffed the hammer into my waistband, bolted out the door, and around the corner toward Chicago Avenue, where I would wait and jump on a bus in plain, public view just in case something happened. As I turned the corner from the gangway and out onto the side walk of Homan Avenue, here came Bud with about six very sketchy looking men with him. I have never run so fast in my life!

"Motha fucka," I heard Bud kind of say to himself and the others. "Steve! What the fuck white boy!"

I heard the stampede of footsteps racing behind me. The closer I got to Chicago Avenue, the safer I felt. And I got there, right next to the Family Dollar store, and turned the corner. As I did, I looked behind me to check the distance, and it was clear to me that Bud was obviously frustrated. He kind of did the "Ah Damn/Oh Shucks" shoulder lift and downward fist punch in annoyance as he realized I had gotten away. The group of men gave up their pursuit, turned around, and headed into the gangway. My heart rate finally slowed as I got onto the CTA bus, headed for God knows where, but far, far away from here.

Holy shit, what could have just happened to me?

Phew, I survived another day. Thank God I'm outta there.

Relief—but then dread. Because I knew that if I wanted to get my fix again, I would have to go right back into that Lion's Den in just a few short hours . . .

Incomprehensible Demoralization

Incomprehensible means difficult or impossible to comprehend or understand.

Demoralization is the process of **demoralizing** someone.

Demoralizing means causing the loss of hope or morale.

I have encountered some very ugly, very scary, and very lonely individuals throughout my life. It is no secret that I too, have been one of those people. Addiction is one of those things that so many people claim to understand, but unless you have lived it, you have no idea what you're really talking about. I could write for a million lifetimes and still not cover everything that I have thought and felt throughout my journey. It's literally like living multiple lives in multiple dimensions. I try my best, as I felt led to write about my experiences. For some reason this one has been surfacing and resurfacing in my mind.

* * *

I have always been what is known today as an empath. I have always felt people. I have always had a heart for others. I rooted for the underdogs in sports and in movies. I grew up a child in Georgia, and as all kids in Georgia do, I loved the Atlanta Braves. I remember watching the 90s Braves team in the playoffs one year with my dad when they played against the Pittsburgh Pirates. Now, I don't really remember the circumstances, but I'm sure it was in our favor. The manager went out to the mound to pull the pitcher for the Pirates, John Smiley I think was his name—I could be wrong, but that sounds right. Although I was cheering and rooting for the Braves, I remember looking at John's face on the television screen and seeing how sad and disappointed he was. I felt his pain. I felt his sadness. I immediately switched allegiances and started rooting for the Pirates. I have no idea why, maybe because I was like six-years old, and when we're kids, we're naive. I also have no idea why I chose to share this with you, but I am. Anyway, the point that I am trying to get to, is that I have had this inexplicable empathy . . . for everyone It's very strange, and it's also a priceless gift in my life today. I also cried during the movie, *Rudy*. Every single time I watch it. *Rudy* is the single biggest reason I am a Notre Dame fan to this day. But I digress.

* * *

Anyway, the reason I include this little preface to the next portion of my psychobabble is that I think all of us addicts—no matter how judged, no matter how condemned, no matter how misunderstood we all are—are all very soft hearted, vulnerable, fragile individuals. Because of this, we all get hurt easily. We take longer to heal emotionally, and we tend to endure more trauma then most. We also relate to people on deeper levels then we let on, and if you're anything like me, our gears turn *WAY* longer than the average normie.

It's weird to explain this, but if you're an addict, you certainly understand. It's like this great riddle of sorts to solve, this whole, "Well you're out here stealing from your gramma and family and manipulating people to get heroin, but yet you have this ultra-soft heart. Is that what you're telling me?"

Well yeah, it is. Once we're in the grip of active addiction, the lifestyle isn't intentional. I didn't wake up every day and DECIDE that I was going to rip gramma off or steal a lawnmower. It's instinctual, like breathing. I needed my dope, I needed my fix like we all need air. It's so very hard to explain, but even though I was living like a scumbag daily, my heart was still very much open to others. Once again, if you're not an addict, you probably won't understand.

Even throughout my active addiction, when I was at my lowest, and sleeping on the Red Line or the Blue Line, wandering the streets of Chicago all alone, I always tried my best to save at least a dollar or two to hand to other hopeless, lost, hurting souls. I thought deep inside of me, that even though I'm out here living the way that I am, doing the things that I'm doing, maybe, just maybe, this one single dollar bill will shine some light into this poor hurting soul's life. Show him or her that someone sees them, that someone acknowledges that they're there. Once again, I'm not sure why I share these things, or if they even make sense, but I have been thinking a lot about this lately so I'm going write it. These open hearted empathetic feelings led me to some of the most heart-breaking scenes one could ever imagine. Very closely together I might add.

* * *

I had made my way over to Chicago and Homan yet again—even after Bud tried to lock me in that little crack shack of his. I had no choice, I was living on instinct. I had to sustain my habit, no matter what the cost. So I did.

It was almost like the movie *Groundhog Day* where once again, it was always the same. Hustle, get money, get dope, shit happens, repeat. That much is no secret to anyone who knows what drugs are, and this was just like any other day.

Maybe I had come up with fifty dollars somehow, which was my "try to get to" amount with each run. Then I could get a piece of crack as well as some dope to come down and not be sick. My routine stayed right in line. I went to the spot, got my drugs, cheeked it, and went on my way. Next came the challenge of finding a place to smoke and get high where one, no cops will see me; and two, no fellow dope fiends will bother me for a hit. I always said yes unless it was my absolute last hit.

So where to go?

You would think that I would have these places down pat, and I did, but so did every other junkie on the West Side. It was all on a first come, first serve basis, and they were almost always occupied. This time it was no different. I ended up settling for a dumpster that was enclosed in a brick horseshoe shaped alcove, behind the Family Dollar store, right there on Chicago Avenue.

The squeeze was tight, but I went ahead and tried, barely able to slink between the green iron of the dumpster and the brick wall beside it. Just behind the dumpster was a very small but manageable spot where I could do my thing, and no one could see me. I prepared my stuff and did my thing. Barely through my crack, I heard someone coming, so I had to do my best crackhead-weird-ass-mannequin-stance, so no one in Chicago could hear me breathe.

Hopefully they're just taking the trash out, and they'll go away.

No such luck. They're coming back here. How am I going to explain this one, some white kid standing back behind this dumpster all weirded out? I think I'm going to jail . . . ugh. Going to jail all cracked out is the worst. Didn't even get to do my dope yet. But it wasn't the cops.

As soon as this older black gentleman, in rags similar to mine, appeared around the side of the dumpster, I knew I wasn't going to Cook County Jail. But what was about to happen? He didn't even say a word. He saw me, and I saw him. He didn't ask me for a hit, he didn't say anything. He gave me a head nod to let me know that we saw each other and that we're both cool.

I recall very vividly seeing this pain, fear, and loneliness in his eyes. We were the same. We were both broken people. Then he took his shoes and his socks off, pulled his pants down just a little, and leaned against the brick wall!

I've gotta get outta here! I finished my hit and pocketed my kit to leave. As this man finished up shitting all over the ground inches from where I stood, he bent over and picked up his own socks, to wipe himself with, then pulled his pants back up, put his socks *BACK ON*, and then put on his shoes!

As he was squeezing back through the dumpster and bricks, he actually spoke back to me and said something like,"I know white boy, but it's all I have."

I was absolutely dumbfounded. No way did I just witness that. As grossed out and disgusted as I was, it's weird, although I would never do what he just did, I felt his pain. I felt what he said. I had literally just witnessed someone's lowest, most vulnerable, secret pain, and felt that. But it smelled horribly bad, and I had to get out of there. I wasn't sticking around the West Side for this shit.

I used my "one day fun pass" to hop on the Kimbal-Homan bus back north toward the Dunkin Donuts where I picked my food out of the dumpster each night and found a place to shoot my dope and come down. That was way too weird for me for one day.

* * *

I swear to God I can't make this stuff up. Just when I thought my day and life couldn't have gotten any more bizarre or flat out screwed up, it did.

I remember getting on the bus and heading back toward Diversey and Milwaukee. Once I found a seat and was able to somewhat chill, I found myself in some kind of stunned disbelief. What in the hell did I just witness? Holy cow what kind of life is this? Although I had a million and one thoughts swirling through my head as anyone on uppers does, I kept coming back to that man behind the dumpster. His eyes. The emptiness, the pitiful sadness. He literally had no other choice than to do what he just did . . . What kind of life had led him to that very point? I cannot even imagine.

I stared out the window of the CTA bus and listened to the voice on the speaker name off the stops until mine came. I got off the bus and made my way toward an alleyway next to an old Polish bar that I used to frequent. I knew it wouldn't be occupied, and it wasn't.

As I rolled up my sleeve and did my thing, I couldn't help but think about that poor man. I finished up, collected my items, and made my way back toward Six Corners, which is where Milwaukee, Irving Park, and Cicero all intersect. Night was approaching fast, and my mind was completely exhausted. My spirit drained, my body sickly and tired. This was all too much.

I can't continue to do this shit was probably my most common thought throughout my days—and today was no different. I was tired, hungry, and depleted. I couldn't even make it to Six Corners, and even if I did, what then? Who gives a crap. I'm just gonna find a bench to sit down on. I was completely broken. day in and day out. This was just another shitty day during my shitty ass life. I found myself a cold, hard, wooden and bolts bench to sit down on. Before long, I was nodded out asleep.

I came to—I don't know how long later—with someone sitting next to me. It was cold as shit and dark. Late October, or early November, I think. There was a nearby street light, and traffic was still on the move, so it couldn't have been that late. This person sitting next to me is someone I weirdly still think about, someone who I pray for some times, like the man behind the dumpster. I hope they both made it out of their own hells and found life again.

This person sitting next to me was a woman. A very old looking, very worn out, smelly, but also, a very kind woman. She was a prostitute. No, I did not engage with this woman, if that's what you're thinking. The reason I know she was is because, weirdly, over the next couple days, this woman became my friend. Almost nightly we would end up sitting on this same bench in the same smelly clothes, worn out from the same lifestyles, and weirdly enough, I actually looked forward to it. I was not threatened by her, and she was not threatened by me. I don't remember her name, but I do remember her. This woman was very sad. She had ZERO teeth, I mean zero. She had these little black almost hole looking stubs in her mouth, and she may have weighed about ninety pounds.

The thing physically that stood out to me most about her was her right index finger. It was black, she was white. I don't know what could have caused this—some kind of horrible infection like gangrene I'm sure, but it actually looked like a beef jerky candy cane. As gross as that sounds, that's the only way to describe it. It was all shriveled up and had the curl on the end like a candy cane. I have always thought that this woman had injected that krocodyl drug and had contracted some kind of flesh-eating bacteria. The thought of this poor woman still makes my heart so sad. We actually would talk. We would find ways back to this bench, and there we would sit. I don't remember what we talked about, junkie stuff I'm sure, but I do remember that she had kids. She did mention that, and I have always wondered about her poor children. Did they even know where she was? Did they even care? This poor soul would sit there, as would I.

Then she would just hop up and say,"Ope, I got a date."

I don't know what's nastier, her selling herself, or the fact that someone was willing to pay for it. I remember one time in particular that she got dropped off after one of her "dates," and she came walking back up to the bench and said something like, "Hell yeah, Mother Fucker, I just got me 12 dollars."

Twelve Dollars.

Holy shit. I don't even know what I was feeling or why this memory disturbs me so badly, but it does. This woman with no teeth, who smelled worse than me, whose finger was rotting, who spoke so normally and never really seemed dangerous at all, had kids, and just sold her body for twelve dollars. I remember feeling so much pity for her. I remember feeling so sad. I always seemed to take on the peoples' pain that I met, along with mine, but for whatever reason,

I always felt like there was hope for me. In this moment, I felt so hopeless for this woman here.

It's a very rare and scary feeling to look at a person, or a time, and realize that there was no hope there. This was one of those times. There are so many people out there like this. Just existing. The man with the socks, the prostitute with the finger, the pregnant girl in the apartment, Bud.

This is what addiction does to people, this is what it did to me. This is where it took me. I saw things and people and places that I never thought I would. It's so much more than an egg in a hot skillet, and "this is your brain on drugs." I still think about those poor, sick, sad, and suffering souls. They're all a part of me. They're all a part of my story and life, and I hope they all made it out. Or at least got to experience love, laughter, and joy once more, before they finally nodded out behind a dumpster somewhere for the last time.

* * *

People talk about statistics, numbers. They talk about us like they're tallying up an RSVP for a wedding or something. I know that it's so truly sad that we addicts die. I will never discount it. But it's not just that we die. It's how we die. I think about living a day like that poor woman, or having to wipe my ass with my socks and then put them back on so my feet don't freeze off, and then passing away all alone on a park bench, or in an alley.

It breaks my heart as I write this. Those people once mattered. They still do. I feel them. I feel their pain. That was someone's little girl, or dad, and now they're probably gone. Now they're probably one of those statistics we read about.

God I hope not. I pray that they made it. I know what that hopelessness feels like.

Incomprehensible Demoralization.

That's what addiction is. Summed up in two words. It is the stealer of children and hope.

I don't know which is worse.

Feeling my own. Or witnessing someone else's.

Dr. Pimple Popper

Being an addict in the grip of active addiction is something else. I have spoken about this numerous times, how when we were kids, we would see Scruff McGruff on TV and the guy who fries an egg and says, "This is your brain on drugs, any questions?" Not to discount those efforts to thwart drug use in the then current generation, but that never did anything to make me think twice about using.

In fact, when I was in high school, and they did the Red Ribbon Campaign, we were all asked to sign the "Red Ribbon Pledge" that we would, "Just say no to drugs!" Well, my wild ass made about three hundred copies of my signed pledge, because when we turned them in to the local McDonalds, they would give us a free cheeseburger for signing the pledge and doing our civic duty. Well, I would go out and get super high, drunk, and really loaded. I would then take my gigantic stack of signed pledges to multiple McDonalds and get straight stupid on free cheeseburgers. I was crafty like that.

I do try to incorporate some humor into my entries, but there is absolutely NOTHING funny, fun, or good about drug addiction. It is the absolute most godless, loveless, friendless, joyless, and most disgusting miserable life that I could ever imagine. I had to figure that out on my own I suppose. I guess I'm a hands-on learner.

* * *

I already told you about my nasty MRSA/staph infection that I had in my foot and leg. It almost cost me my foot from the ankle down, my hearing, and my life, as my fever got up to 104.9 degrees.

This is the result of being a nasty, unwashed street junkie. This was something that went on for years, off and on.

* * *

I see a lot of shared photos, and memes of people who are using meth. I see how their faces become sunken in, covered in sores from picking at the imaginary bugs or critters they think are crawling on them. I don't know, I never really got into meth. I have tried it a few times, but all it did was make me super geeked up and I ended up driving around on my buddy's golfcart in Peachtree City. I drank an entire thirty pack of Milwaukee's best light beer, trying to come down from the high. It didn't help, and I ended up driving the golf cart for so long that it died. I had to leave it on the side of the cart path and walk five miles home while I was high. Yeah, sounds like a great time, doesn't it? I never really got into the whole speed thing, but I did smoke a lot of crack when I had heroin with me to immediately come down. I don't know, different strokes for different folks, I guess.

Anyway, I always had the misconception that facial and body sores were meth exclusive. I always thought that the picking at myself and getting all scabby and nasty was only for those who used meth, because it made them tweak and pick at themselves. Turns out I was wrong. I never really put two and two together until after I got clean. I can say that about a lot of things.

I'm not sure when it started happening, but I imagine that it was sometime well into my eighth year of using heroin, when things really started to get sketchy, nasty, and almost took my life on many occasions. I noticed that every once in a while, I would get just the tiniest pimple looking thing on my arm, shoulder, or neck. I would do what most of us would do—pop it and go about my day. No big deal.

Then I would notice another, and another. Pop, move on, no big deal. On occasion I would take a shower at a two-dollar flea bag motel, and I would feel a little better and somewhat relieved that I got a chance to clean myself. Another little pimple, another pop, on we go. No big deal.

One day I was going about my daily rituals of most likely, either panhandling, ripping someone off somehow, conning people, etc. . . Whatever the hell I was up to at this particular phase of my life, when I noticed that there was a very large spot of discomfort on my back that felt really hot. No big deal, a nice amber colored thick shot of dope would take the pain away. And it did for a couple days.

Eventually this spot on my back became so damn unbearable that I had no choice but to walk into a local emergency room and have it looked at. It was so embarrassing, having to walk my unwashed, stinking, strung out, junkie looking self into an emergency room, to have something on my body that was CLEARLY a result of my chosen lifestyle, looked at. I swear that I looked and felt . . . *GREEN*, just completely nasty and utterly filthy. I felt so unhealthy and sick, but the physical pain in my back outweighed the emotional pain and the sting to my pride. I knew that this had to be addressed.

In seemingly a of a couple days, I had developed a giant boil-like sore on the center of my spine. The doctors already knew what was going on and what I was. They offered *ZERO* pain medication to alleviate what was about to happen. You know what I got? A bag of ice. They laid a bag of ice on my spine for about ten minutes to numb what was about to happen.

It didn't work.

The doctor removed the bag of ice, and on the count of three, lanced the giant, hot, smelly boil on my spine wide open! I could feel the metal tearing the flesh on my back, followed by the relief of the pressure releasing, and then the smell! It literally smelled like rotting corpse was leaking out of my back. Then they stuffed it full with some kind of absorbent gauze, told me to have a nice day, and sent me home.

If only hospitals had people on standby to catch those struggling at their bottom when they came in. Trust me I'm working on that as we speak, I have authored three bill proposals that have been accepted into legislature in Indianapolis as of 2021. Protocols in this state are going to change if it's the last thing I do.

Imagine this: imagine being so mentally, emotionally, spiritually, and psychologically drained and exhausted with life. Imagine being so traumatized, at your own hand, that you hated who you saw in the mirror so much, that you spit at your own reflection every time you saw it. Imagine feeling like God and the world actually hated you.

Couple that with feeling so god-awful and horribly dope sick, in constant physical pain and trying to go about your day sick with withdrawal, fear, anxiety, panic, and paranoia. All of these feelings compounded by the very thing that you crave more than anything. It's the only thing that will take the pain that it causes away; that or finally jumping off an overpass above the Dan Ryan hoping the fall itself would kill you. If not, maybe you could time it well enough to land in front of a Brink's Truck, but you're too chicken to ever actually kill yourself, so again you feel like a failure because you're too much of a wimp to take your own life Welcome to heroin addiction.

Now, imagine all of this unfolding *CONSTANTLY* between your ears, inside your poisoned mind, while you grime your way through life and have to steal, panhandle and beg, just to get a bag of the thing that's killing you. It's causing your body to have physical reactions and symptoms, and now I crossed a point where these little "pimples" are happening more and more.

More trips to the ER, more ice bags, more lancing of the boils. They were on my arms, legs, back, and neck.

Once, I had one just under my eyebrow, and at the time, I was somewhat thankful. It was just the tiniest little one, smaller than the average pimple. I squeezed it, and it popped, and everything was fine. Until I woke up the next day and my eye was completely swollen shut, and it stayed swollen shut for almost two weeks.

These were not pimples. This was cellulitis from living like a dirtball. My skin and body were actually starting to break down and rot. All of this no doubt, is what finally gave way to my MRSA/staph infection that had me in Saint Mary's Hospital in Hobart for eleven days.

I didn't care anymore. I was on a suicide run. I just wanted more dope and more crack. I was determined to get as much as I could and hope one of these shots would be enough to finally do the trick and kill me. I could finally nod off into the big sleep, overdose, and my pain would finally end for good. I was done living this miserable life. I was done going into the hospitals to get the boils lanced and removed. They were just reappearing elsewhere anyway, so what was the point? All of these visits damn near put me in bankruptcy. Once I got clean, if I ever did get clean, I was going to be on the hook for all that money, so screw it. I just wasn't going to the hospital anymore. (I am STILL paying off old medical bills from my using days, almost six years later, to the tune of almost $20,000.) These are the unspoken, unknown prices that we pay to play the game.

Addiction took me further than I wanted to go, kept me longer than I wanted to stay, and cost me a helluva lot more than I wanted to pay.

* * *

I was done going in and out of these hospitals to be looked at, judged, and humiliated. The pimples, abscesses, and boils continued to become more severe. It came to the point where I started noticing they were actually developing little green, grey, and yellow phlegmy looking cores in them and wouldn't pop. I would squeeze and squeeze, and they would just ooze and bleed. Gushing, foul smelling ooze, pus, and infection would run out of my arms, legs, shoulders, and eventually, right in the middle of my forehead. A giant knob had formed smack dab in the middle of my forehead. This one scared me to death, because of its proximity to my brain and eyes, so I didn't mess with it too much. I would shoot some heroin to numb the throb of the infection, mash down on it, and try to catch the ooze before it got into my eyes. I would wipe the blood and pus away from my face, put a bandanna on to somewhat disguise the giant sore, and go about my day.

But finally, it got to the point where it was just too much to bear. No shot of dope would kill the pain. No bandanna would hide the giant sore, and I didn't want to go back to the hospital.

So, I did what I had to do.

I shot a massive amount of brown liquid into my left arm. Then I found needle nose pliers, and walked into the Speedway Gas Station on Swanson and Highway 6 in Portage Indiana. I went into the restroom and locked the door behind me. I took a big blast of crack, shot some more dope, and squeezed all of the liquid out of the wound as I possibly could. I forced the pliers down into the stinking, infected flesh on my forehead, and dug that dime-sized, green, black, and yellow mucous plug out of my face.

I thought I was going to bleed to death right there in the restroom but thank God I was able to get the crimson gush of blood under control. I'm sure the entire restroom smelled like a corpse, but I actually did it, I got it out. There was so much morbid and disgusting relief that came along with this little victory of mine. I instantly felt physically better. I stuffed some paper towels under my bandanna to absorb any blood leaking, cleaned up the "operating room," stuck the pliers in my pocket, and went about my day.

As luck would have it, I found a fifty dollar bill on the floor of the gas station on my way out. Talk about impeccable timing. Not bad pay, for an excruciating time spent operating on my own face in a gas station restroom. I'm kind of a jack of all trades.

(Egg cracks, and hits hot skillet) This is your brain, this is your life. This is your FACE on drugs. Any questions?

Pizza Pizza

I have met a lot of interesting humans throughout my life. I have met a lot of interesting characters throughout my using days, and while incarcerated in particular. I have told you about many of them thus far. I'm not exactly sure what always prompts my writing, though I choose to believe that it is somewhat inspired writing. I never want to just jump in here and start writing just to fill the space, not that my inspired stuff is particularly much better. I just want it to actually have some meat and substance to it.

Imagine being subjected to a life where going to jail—beginning at the ripe old age of eighteen and on through your late twenties—was actually an improvement in your life circumstances. Yes, you read that correctly. Imagine going to jail, and actually feeling safe and provided for. Isn't that sick? And no, jail and prison are not nice places. I have witnessed some of the most disgusting and horrific things I could ever imagine inside the walls of incarceration—but that just supports my previous point. Imagine that your life is so messed up, and you're so desperate, lonely, strung out, and lost, that once the initial shock of being cuffed, going to jail, getting booked, and getting over the dope sickness, you actually feel a great deal of relief. It is such a sad and awful truth for so many of us out there who are struggling and still sick. I don't know, maybe I'm the only one who has ever experienced this, but I doubt it. Every single time I got arrested, I was scared because I didn't know what was in store for me, and I was about to be dope sick for about a month, but I also concurrently felt relief. Relief, knowing that I wouldn't have to sleep outside anymore, or eat out of garbage cans, or shoot dope again for a while. It is really a sick, sad world for so many of us out there.

Once I got over the dope sickness, and acclimated to whatever pod or dorm I was assigned to, I actually felt somewhat comfortable. Yes, I missed my family, I missed my son, but this is the duality of being an addict. We're survivors. We can adjust and adapt instinctually to almost any environment. I guess it comes from the years of trauma, grief, loss, PTSD, and undiagnosed mental health issues that go into making a low bottom addict such as myself, but I speculate.

Though the sadness would come, and I would get into my feelings and miss my people on the outside, I was so accustomed to this carousel of jail, drugs, homelessness, I could actually compartmentalize most of it. I think this is why they say, "You really only do two days when you're locked up: The day you come in, and the day you get out." The rest is just kind of like being in some type of purgatory, or a dreamworld of sorts, but it is very much real. Although we do tend to get acclimated and comfortable with the humans we're locked up with and our surroundings, we have to remember to stay alert and proceed with caution and respect, because there are some very dangerous people inside those walls.

* * *

During the daytime hours, as many of you who have been to jail know, we're allowed to come out into the day room, watch a TV with no sound, play cards, make phone calls, etc. . . and this is when most of the dumb shit goes down.

Dudes talking shit constantly. It's annoying. Everybody's somebody special when they're in jail. It's weird, and there should be some psychological studies done on this topic in particular, but I think as a lay person, maybe it's ego? A defense mechanism to shield them from the fact that they're just another broken hearted, lost, forgotten, lonely person inside a jail with people just like them. They never shut up, and pretty much everything they say is bullshit. That's why I jokingly say that J.A.I.L. stands for: Just Another Inmate Lyin'.

The daytime hours are when we play cards and go to programs, and the mail comes, etc. That's when we tend to find our little cliques of in jail. The daytime is, for the most part, pretty easy going I suppose, but it's also when the most chaos happens. Fights, arguments, etc. . . It can be so annoying. Fighting over dominoes, cards, eighty-five cent Ramen Noodles. My all time *favorite* argument, fighting over which rapper makes the most money! My God, I have actually seen dudes come to blows over which rapper has more money, Drake or Eminem. Holy shit, the ignorance inside these places. It's also incredibly sad. The fact that two, three, or seven grown men would actually beat each other up over such a petty disagreement shows me the level of maturity and lack of nurturing that these once little boys with dreams had.

I mean, think about it. As we speak, there are thousands of grown men sitting in prison or jail, with a known or unknown amount of time staring at the floor watching their shitty lives unfold over and over in their heads. Wondering why their fathers didn't want them, or why their mothers sold their bodies for crack, or _____(fill in the blank); and why they got turned onto drugs in the first place, only to escape from the trauma in their lives so that they could feel better, even for just one second.

Then they got so strung out that the only choice they had was to rob a liquor store and now they're stuck in prison for twenty years. I mean really think about that. Think about what a shitty hand that is to be dealt. Especially when you only have one life to live, and that's the one you get. It breaks my heart.

Now you're forced to again compartmentalize and create a persona to be inside the walls so that you can "get your respect" and feel visible, probably for the first time in your entire life. The only outlet you have is to finally explode on someone and smash their head with a food tray, and thus earn yourself a month in the hole and a year added on to your sentence. So much for the "correction" in Department of Corrections, huh? Yeah, it's a twisted world man. Tens of thousands of good human capital are just thrown away into the system of privatized prisons and jails. Talk about "Heads in beds." It's sick. So much potential just flushed down the tubes because, they're "drug addict losers". UGH. But anyway.

As you can probably tell, I'm a bit of an empath. I can pick up on, and feel energies, and I tend to have a bleeding heart for the lost ones. I always have actually. I have always had an affinity for the underdog. I love watching people "come back." It is literally my favorite thing in the whole world—Hence my career path. "For the Lord does not despise humble beginnings, but rejoices to see the work commence." The Big Book, from the Alcoholics Anonymous program, says that watching "The Light come on," is the bright spot of our lives, and it's true. I love seeing the lost souls turn their lives around. It makes my heart skip a beat when I get the texts from those that we have worked with thanking us, and celebrating sixty, ninety, one hundred-twenty days; one, two, or three years of sobriety. It's truly awesome the potential that we addicts have—when we realize it.

So yeah, we have established what the daytime hours are like; and the nighttime hours, at least from my experience, were very much different. But again, I'm an empath, so I think I just naturally feel and interpret things differently.

To me, the nighttime, considering the circumstances that I was presently in, and the ones I was recently in—were strangely very peaceful. There was almost like this weird, eerie serenity to it. It's hard to explain. I could actually FEEL safe. Locked inside this little box, nothing could get me. No monsters, no dealers, no drugs, and no needles could find me here, and I could just pray and dream. I swear I could pick up on all of the others throughout the jail feeling the same things. Slowly drifting off to sleep to the sounds of humming and dimmed luminescent lights, sometimes flushing toilets, and maybe the sound of someone sharpening a shank, but the doors were locked and no one could get us. I could let my guard down and just fall asleep. Lamenting, dreaming, reflecting. Not having to act or lie anymore for the day. Almost like, "Phew, I survived another day, praise God." Then I would drift off, thinking about what possibilities the future may or may not have . . . Only to wake up to more of the same old bullshit tomorrow. UGH, it's like Groundhog's Day in there.

* * *

Let's kind of compound all of those previous ramblings above into one moving forward. I think most of you get the picture, and those who have been to jail get it, so this is nothing new. We get to know people and all of their bullshit lies. We clique up, play spades. We tell jokes, and we bullshit. And we compartmentalize.

But not every single person that we meet in there actually fits all of this. At least not in full. Sometimes we meet people in there who are brutally honest, to a flaw. One gentleman, who I will not name, because I do not name names, is the one I want to tell you about.

Remember when I said that we do get comfortable? Jail is actually an improvement upon our drugged out lives, but we must also proceed with caution because there are some truly dangerous people in there. We never really know what guys are in for, because they all lie. This young man is exactly why I say that, and you wouldn't know it if you saw him on the street walking past you. He looked totally normal. Literally normal. He didn't use drugs, he didn't get angry, and he shared his commissary. He was a genuinely— SEEMINGLY—regular dude. We actually had to ask him to have his newspaper article mailed in because we didn't, and couldn't, believe what he was in for—*MURDER!*

He sure as shit murdered someone! I had been sharing coffee, and playing cards with, and making slams with a stone cold killer— and I mean stone cold! This dude would laugh and joke with us, and play Monopoly with us like he wasn't facing seventy five years and like he didn't take someone's life in cold blood.

He would tell you all about it too. No remorse whatsoever. It was one of the strangest interactions I have ever had to this day. If you asked him, he would straight up tell you, "I fucking hate drugs and don't understand why someone would do drugs. My Step Dad got my mom addicted to heroin, so I fucking smoked his ass. Put like eight rounds right in his back, then walked to 7/11, got a burrito, and a Mountain Dew and waited for the cops."

Whoa. I'm guessing that this young man had some type of psychopathy or some type of mental derangement, but he seemed super normal. I can't even explain it. He is definitely still sitting in prison right now listening to punk rock music and drinking coffee. This dude loved coffee. He would order like five bags a week, and just walk laps and tell jokes.

Very scary to think that there are so many people like this walking the free world and we would never know it. I guess this is why they say we walk past a murderer more than fifty times in our life and never even know it. Gives me chills, but I'm also thankful that I know how to handle myself and I do my best to treat everyone with respect. This young man also had a dark side, as if you needed me to tell you that after what I just told you.

Now, I've seen a lot, I have lived through some crazy things, but this absolutely takes the cake. The title of this chapter is "Pizza Pizza," and here's why.

* * *

In jail, guys get really creative with their commissary. We can make just about anything out of seemingly nothing. We can make twenty-pound burritos out of Ramen Noodles, crackers, Cheetos, salami, pickles, whatever. We can also make homemade microwave pizza out of commissary items. You break up the crackers, noodles, and Cheetos, get them moist with water from the sink, and mold them into a crust on the microwave plate. Then microwave it until it hardens into a crust. Then pour on the sauce, meat, and cheese items from the commissary as toppings and VOILA! Jail Pizza.

One night, maybe about an hour and half, before lock down, we were all just kind of unwinding, watching a show, chilling and talking. My punk rock friend sits down across from me. Normal night. No red flags, no chaos. Pretty chill day and night. I think it was a Tuesday. That's when commissary came, and we all ate like fat rats that day. So, my friend sits down across from me. He has a clean rag in his hand, some bleach and cleaner. He has his commissary items out. Looks like he is about to eat again. Not sure where he put it all, as he was a little guy, but he loved to eat. Whatever, do your thing man. He grabs the microwave plate to disinfect it before he starts cooking his nighttime meal. No big deal. Very methodically, very causally cleaning the microwave plate. Then he prepared his crackers and noodles. Chillin' like Bob Dylan.

"Damn man, eatin' again, huh bub?" I casually say.

"Yeah, Herb. Makin a Pizza," he says.

"Man, you really can eat dude. Think you wanna let me get a piece of that?" I ask.

"Yeah, I'll share it with you, but I don't think you're gonna wanna eat this one dude" he replies.

"Why, what are you making it out of man?" I ask.

Then he looks me dead ass in the eyes, and says, "FLESH!"

He runs up to the front of the Pod, smashes the glass microwave plate against the one-way bulletproof glass, shattering it into jagged shards, and he starts cutting, *DIGGING* into his arm, and *DEEP!*

Instantly the whole pod freezes and is stunned at what we were seeing. Thick, dark purple spurts of blood geyser out of his arm and soak his jump suit. Myself and another man run and tackle him to get the glass out of his hands.

"Grab some towels! Grab some shirts," we scream as we have him pinned down. We're covered in blood and smell like metal. It's loud and chaotic.

"Hit the Button! Hit the Button," we all scream, and guys are jumping up and down trying to flag the guards down. It must have taken almost five whole minutes for the guards to see us, react, and get inside the Pod. By now, the three of us are soaked in thick red and purple blood, and our punk rock friend is as white as a ghost. We are ordered to lockdown. But my friend who helped, and me, are ordered to strip down and shower immediately and brought fresh clothes. We shower as the medics arrive and take our friend out on a stretcher. Never to be seen again . . .

None of us slept or felt at ease that night. Not even close. There was no lamenting or peace or quiet that night. Just the smell of old stale blood, and the sounds of racing and processing minds as to what in the hell had just happened.

Another trauma piece of wreckage from the lifestyle that I had been living. So, when they crack an egg and say, "This is your brain on drugs," what they really mean is, "This is your life because of drugs."

I still think about that guy once in a while. He really was a decent enough guy, but he had a demon. I hope he got the help that he needed.

Trigger Warning

I think it was around 9 p.m. and I was standing all alone on Chicago's South Side. Halstead and something. There was a Walgreens there, that's about all I know for sure. I had just come out of a black hole of street level heroin and crack. I can't really recall what I did to come up with the money I had, but I had some and stayed super high with it as a result.

Now I was coming to, which meant it was time to go back into one. I didn't even have a cell phone. I had been out wandering the streets of the "wild hundreds" (a section of the city which refers to high crime, drug, and murder rates in streets which are numbered 100 and up) for many days now. I was dazed and confused. My jeans which now sagged off of me were covered in black soot marks from setting my hot spoons on them after I cooked, and before I injected. My feet hurt. My Soul hurt, but I just couldn't stop the chase. I was incapable of thinking about anything other than the next bag.

I looked around, assessed my surroundings. It was nighttime, and I was white. Clearly, I was up to no good, but I only had one needle and maybe two bags of heroin on me, so I was fairly confident that I wouldn't get arrested if I got bothered by the cops. My bag was in between my ass cheeks, and the cops never looked in there. They weren't going to take me in for a needle. They would just destroy it and send me on my way back to the nearest drug store to buy another ten pack over the counter for three dollars. Crazy system we have, huh? Anyway, it was time to make a move. I had to find some cover for the night, or at the very least get loaded enough to pass out on a bench somewhere. It wasn't cold out, I remember that much. I had several hundred dollars, so I would be able to get a hotel room if I absolutely had to, but that would be dope money lost.

A pay phone! Okay, so what am I gonna do with it? I'm gonna call my guys, duh.

I enter the Walgreens and get change for a few single dollar bills. I hit the pay phone, and scribbled on the inside wall of the phone booth were words reading something like, "Got money? Call the crack express." I thought it was a joke—pointing fun at dope fiends like me. But I figured, "ah what the hell?" So I called the number . . .

"Good evening, _____'s Livery Service, this is _____."

And I hung up. I checked the Yellow Pages of the hanging phone book for the name they just told me and it matched, I picked up the phone, inserted two quarters and dialed the same number again. Same greeting, same person.

"Um, yeah, my name is Steve. I'm calling the, uh, express number."

"Where you at, Steve?" I looked at the streets and told them I was near the Walgreens on Halstead.

"Okay Steve, go sit on the bench in front of the store. What' chu wearing?"

I told them, sat down, and waited. Not exactly sure what I was thinking here, but when you're this far gone, this far in the grip, I didn't really care if I lived or died. I mean honestly, what's the worst that could happen? LOL, my God I was sick.

About fifteen minutes later, a newer dark colored almost cop car like tinted out Ford or Mercury something pulls up, and there's an old black man driving it. He had on one of those really nice looking Kangol Hats, but facing forward, not flipped around. This man actually looked like an actual chauffeur.

"You Steve?"

"Yeah."

"Hop in the back man, let's go."

"Okay . . ." *Maybe this isn't such a good idea.* But I got in the car anyway.

"My name's Edward, Steve. Nice to meet you, young man. What kind of music you like to listen to man?"

"Oh I listen to everything sir. You can put it on whatever you want."

So, where you from, Steve?"

"Uh, Valpo . . ."

Edward was clearly watching me, more than he was the road. He was very familiar with the streets and this process. He was clearly a local and had to be almost seventy. He was making small talk to feel me out and see if I was cool or not.

OOF, this is making me sickly feeling just thinking about this memory.

We exchanged small talk for about five minutes. There was no meter, and he never asked me where I was going. Finally he interjected, "So how much you try'na spend?"

"Um, I don't know, like a hundred dollars. Sixty for rock and forty for some boy (Heroin)."

"A'ight man, I'll let them know."

He makes a phone call from his cell in a low muffled voice. About three minutes later, we pull into a driveway, and he asks for my money. I ain't falling for this shit. He insisted that since this was the first time, he had to go in, and he had to watch me get high and check out how I carried myself while doing it. This was clearly a sophisticated ring I had stumbled into. So I gave him my hundred dollars, and he was back in the car in less than two minutes.

We drove around for literally hours while I smoked and shot dope. He would even offer the back dome light to assist me. I had just found a new friend and this dude was super cool, not weird at all. We would talk, and he would laugh when I got all stuck and weirded out. I have no idea where I ended up that night, but I made sure to get his number before he dropped me off. He even took appointments to pick me back up the next day, or even, "When you get your check."

All his card said was, "Taxi Cab Edward." I use the name here, because he actually once told me that that was *NOT* his real name.

"It's just what everyone calls me."

I'll be damned. A real-life crack and heroin chauffeur. He was ALWAYS prompt. I never had to wait around, and it was always him, which looking back, was weird. You would think that this type of service would be in high demand. It was very low key, and the dope was always, always good. Never once did I get ripped off or shorted. Hmmm . . .

So Taxi Cab Edward and I became friends. We would talk about all kinds of things. It was kinda like a fucked up modern day cracked out version of "Curtis Lowe" (a song by Lynyrd Skynyrd).

That old man would pick me up all over the city and drive me to the best spots and let me do all kinds of drugs in the back of his car.

One time I got some crack that absolutely rang my bell and almost cost me a finger. I had never had shit like this before, and I used to smoke crack by the wheelbarrow. One blast, that's all it took. I mean I smoked it all, but it took me about three days to do so.

It was nighttime, and we were driving around somewhere, Edward and I. He handed it to me and warned me to "be careful with this shit. Tell me what you think."

I would have, if I could talk. Sparks of sizzling debris, the taste of nail polish remover, a dash of egg, and the loudest high pitch sound I have ever heard in my life were running through my ears and brain. I was stuck like Chuck, completely locked up. Damn near rigor mortis in the back of this car while Edward laughed his ass off.

"You ain't gonna throw up is ya Steve?"

I started to slump over at the same time I absolutely spun out of my gourd. As the numb wore off and the locomotive left my brain, I started to notice a pain in my left ring finger. I had slumped over, locked up super hard, and melted the tip of my finger on the hot end of my Pyrex crack pipe. The nail had burned down in a crescent shape and was painfully throbbing. *UGH*. I quickly shot some dope to numb it away and put this crack up. There was no way I was driving around smoking this shit. It was way too good. I would freak out if I had to look out windows on this shit. Once the heroin did its job and I was coherent again and talking, I had to ask Edward for a big favor. I had to ask him to give me a ride all the way back to Portage, Indiana, from the south side of Chicago.

"Oof man, Edward. I'm fucking burned-out man. I been going hard in the paint for weeks with ya man. That one put me in the dirt dude. I need to go home to finish this and rest for a couple days man."

"I hear ya Steve, Tell me how to get there."

No questions asked. He drove me back to Portage, dropped me off, shook my hand, and I never saw Edward again. I was back in town now and would have access to rides and stuff. I would end up going another direction and using with "friends" from now on. To be honest, and I know it's sick, but I wonder what ever happened to that old man.

The next morning, I awoke in my parents' motel room where they had been living. A massive, horrible hot white pain burned in my finger. It had swollen to about three to five times its normal size and width. I could see my heartbeat in the fingernail. With every lub-dub of my heart; my fingernail would concurrently beat, "black-white." More of an ill looking grey than black, and my whole finger was dark blood red. I had to go to the hospital. But first, let's shoot some dope. The heroin coursing through my blood was still not enough to stave off the pain in my finger. I knew this was bad, and it was about to get gnarly.

I checked in and waited. And waited and waited. Finally, they called me back to a room, and I waited some more. The on-call doctor appeared, sat down next to me, and picked up my left hand as I winced in pain.

"Ohhhh, yeahhhh," he says in a very shrill and pity filled voice. "I'll be right back sir." Moments later he returns with a pre-filled syringe of numbing agents, shoots my hand and finger up and disappears again. About five minutes later he comes back and pokes my finger with a prick-tool thingy to check if I'm numb enough for him to do whatever he's about to do.

Ugh, this shit makes me cringe.

He pulls out some weird looking hand tool from his coat pocket. This thing had some kind of like snail antennae/wishbone looking prongs on the end of it, and he was going to use it to burn my nail open to release all the pressure from it.

Oof.

And that's exactly what happened. The little tool thing came to life and sparked as it met my nail and instantly a giant gush of hot red blood shot out all over the doctor, myself, and some even ended up on the ceiling tiles above our heads! You could tell that we both weren't expecting such an explosion, as we both let out our breaths at the same time in a "phew" type fashion.

"How in the hell did you say this happened, Mr. Stepherson?"

"I burned the shit out of it on the end of a hot crack pipe, in the back of a taxicab, on the South Side of Chicago sir." (Like it wasn't no thang.)

"Oh. Well that's pretty hard core, and I appreciate the honesty, sir. Now, you wanna see something really cool?"

"I mean, yeah, sure Doc."

Then he pulled some weird looking pliers out of his coat pocket and very casually placed one pincer end underneath the tip of the deformed and melted nail. I heard a very noticeable *CLICK* sound, and the nail bed disconnected from the nail and the cuticle gave way. *Ugh.* Then the doctor held it up in the light to inspect the nail and picked up my hand to inspect the bed. He rinsed both with some type of cleaner and then got out a little dentist air tool. He blew my nail bed back open with the little tool, eased the nail back into the bed, and washed them both with cleaner.

"You're lucky you came in when you did. I don't know how you pulled that off, but if you had waited much longer, you probably would have lost at least half of that finger dude. Maybe you should stop smoking crack sir." Then he wrapped my finger up in some gauze and taped it up.

Yeah, maybe it is time to stop smoking crack, I thought to myself.

Hard maybe.

I knew deep down inside it was way beyond time to stop. I was so sick and stuck in the grip man. I couldn't even truly think about getting some help.

Anyway, I still had some of that shit left back at the house and a couple bags of heroin. So I was gonna go back and get all weird yet again . . .

So yeah, that's my, "How smoking crack in the back of a taxicab almost cost me my finger," story.

Yeah, I don't miss that shit.

Stalactite

Stalactite: (Noun) a tapering structure hanging like an icicle from the roof of a cave, formed of calcium salts deposited by dripping water.

Recently there have been a lot of headlines in the wake of COVID-19. I saw an article locally about a parade of people rallying and driving around Westville Prison because they were concerned about the wellbeing of the inmates inside and the quality of care they would receive. Westville prison had a pretty bad outbreak of COVID-19 which left a lot of people pretty ill. Although many were concerned about the virus and i's potential impact on those who may be exposed, that's only the beginning of the absolutely horrific things that these men and women are exposed to everyday. This idea just gave me the inspiration to bring it to light.

I know, believe me, I know—there's going to be a lot of people clamoring, "do the crime do the time," and "put them under the jail," and all that. To those people I say, "judge someone else when you're perfect," and "don't judge others because they sin differently than you do." Also, yes, crime should be punished, but the time away from the free world, and their families and society, *IS* the punishment. This goes far and beyond that. But I digress.

* * *

July 12, 2007. I believe it was a Thursday. It was also my birthday. Go figure. I stood in an orange jumpsuit, shackled around my waist and wrists, with leg shackles. The now retired judge, who ironically would be the one to marry my wife and me, really laid into me. My grandmother sat crying in the on-looking crowd. My head down in shame.

"Mr. Stepherson, you are incredibly fortunate that you were able to receive *ANY* kind of plea deal with the state and that I am feeling gracious this afternoon. I am going to accept the terms of this deal and sentence you to the Department of Corrections (Corrections—what a joke), and if I ever see you again sir, I am going to max you out.

(She wasn't lying, the next time I saw her, she did in fact sentence me to life—life of marriage with my beautiful wife Tiffany. LOL).

Once I was sentenced, all I could do was, "wait for the bus," as they say in jail. I had absolutely no idea when it would come either. They keep it very quiet when it came to that, for security reasons of course.

I didn't have to wait long, it was about two weeks. My door popped at around 4:00 a.m., and the guard said to me in a chipper voice, "You get to go today!"

Oh, goodie. It was about a three-hour drive to Reception Diagnostic Center Prison, (RDC), in Plainfield, Indiana, where I would spending the next two weeks getting blood drawn, my head shaved, my balls felt up, teeth examined, and questioned by all kinds of strangers for placement into the prison system.

It was *HOT* in Central Indiana, in late July. On the fourth floor of "The Range" with no air conditioning, the windows seemed to face the blazing hot summer sun all day, every day. The place smelled like sweaty ball sacks, onions, and shit. Believe it or not, this wasn't even why I wrote this entry. God it makes me sick to think about what I saw next.

* * *

General Service Complex, Dorm #9, Westville Prison, Westville, Indiana.

August, hot as shit. This place was underneath Ten Dorm I believe and had two great big, long wings that extended in opposite directions. In the middle of the long hallways, which housed about sixty guys total I think, was the "Cage," where the Guard would stay inside and hand mail out, answer phones, etc. Also in between the long corridors were the bathrooms—roughly eight toilets; four facing one way and four facing—you guessed it—right back at the other four. This had to be by some sick design. Waking up and having to shit, no dividers whatsoever, damn near elbow to elbow with three other guys, while four other guys stared back at you, was uncomfortable to say the least. God the smell.

Then there was the shower, which was supposed to be set up like you see in the movies, or in a gym locker room—shower heads all the way around to accommodate multiple men at the same time. There were about ten shower heads, but only one worked and the water was *ICE COLD!* One would be lucky to get a shower once a day, but most of the time it was every other day. Sometimes I was too grossed out to shower, so I would "bird bath it" in the sink and just hope I didn't smell. I was grossed out because there were just way too men screwing, each other in there.

(Not that I believe being gay is wrong, but there was just something about loud gay prison sex late at night while I was trying to sleep, that made me sick. Although I never actually saw it (thank God), it was not a well-hidden secret. Now I knew why all the other men slept with head phones on. *Ugh.*"

Even still, I don't think that was the worst of it. In between the two long hallways, next to the cage, and next to the shower and bathroom area—was the Day Room. The day room is where the guys spent most of their time. There were two TVs, one of which was exclusively for sports. The other TV was for movies and regular programs, although for some reason they really seemed to like to watch soap operas on this one. *General Hospital* and that kind of bullshit. So, one might be lucky to catch a glimpse of something that actually interested them, maybe twice a week. Maybe. This was also where we would play cards—spades and poker mostly. Guys would study their Bibles and for their GED, and the artists would draw and watercolor. So hopefully you can kind of see this wonderful world that is GSC 9 Dorm—and yes that was sarcasm, it just came out, so try to keep up.

* * *

I remember vividly sitting in the day room, still somewhat new to my new world, and just kind of scoping the scene out, getting my bearings about me. One day I was sitting there watching the soap operas kinda. I didn't have headphones so I couldn't hear the sound, but I was really just kind of staring off into the wild blue and daydreaming.

All of a sudden I heard a very loud crunch and a bunch of people yelling "OOOOOOOOOOHHHHHHHH!!!!!!!"

My head snapped toward the sound of the chaos when I saw a young guy absolutely stomping another guy's guts out against the roll bars, after he had just knocked all of his front teeth out with a lock. That was the crunch I heard, his teeth breaking and coming out of his mouth. The guard didn't even move with any sense of urgency, this was clearly a run of the mill normal for him.

"Back to your rooms guys," he said as he casually called for medics to come to our section of the world and get this battered young man into to the infirmary.

Whoa, that was intense. I would just continue on throughout my stay, with my head down, and not borrow anything from anyone. Which was a very good idea from what I'm told.

"If you see it, you're a part of it." So, I did my best to see as little as possible. But I did in fact, see something that still makes my stomach turn and my heart hurt to this day.

One morning, I was sitting in my same, "please don't bother me, or talk to me seat" that I always did. I was a couple seats away from an older man who had clearly been locked up a while. He had very long hair. They shave your head at RDC, and this guy's hair was to the middle of his back at least. I was scanning around quietly, and I noticed that the ceiling was crudely cut open. About twenty-five feet long, and about ten feet wide, in a jagged long rectangle. Pipes and all the innards of the building were exposed, and the pipes had rags and towels crudely wrapped around them. I asked the man with the long hair why they had towels and rags wrapped around the pipes. He leaned over and told me it was to stop the drips. He told me that maintenance wound come in once in a while and replace the towels and clean the area, but that must mean like once or twice a year. Over the next month or so, I watched that place in the ceiling like a time lapse photographer. The fluid behind the towels began to saturate, and the dripping began. I made sure to stay away but would watch as the drips fell down and would hit one man in the head, another on the shoulder, and another. Then men seemed to be so accustomed and used to this, that they would casually just swat the area and wipe the drip away, like a gnat at a barbecue or something. A couple days later, more drips, then more. After about a week I started to notice a little tip starting to form where the heaviest of the saturation was forming. Then it became a little cone. The more it dripped, the heavier it got, and the larger the formation grew and sagged down. Eventually it became a cluster of about one foot long grayish-brown-amber colored nasty looking rods hanging down, and again, I asked the man with the long hair what in the world that was. He casually leaned over and said, "Piss, shit, cum, and hair from upstairs in 10 Dorm." I think I turned green when I learned this. All of these formations conveniently dripped right over the tables where we would eat our commissary and sit and write letters to our families. Every once in a while, they would yell something that I cannot remember, but it would summon the "Dorm Bitch," and he would come with a mop on a long stick. Everyone would clear the area, and he would push the stick up into the gaping hole in the ceiling and knock the formations down to the floor, then collect them in a bucket, and mop the area where they fell. Then life would return to "normal."

So, if you think that COVID-19 is something to be alarmed about in our prison system, maybe you need to think about what life before COVID-19 was like on the inside.

We need prison reform.

Why?

I didn't always want to keep using. In fact, most of the time I was using against my will. It had stopped being fun a long time ago. It was more like a job now. Wake up in instant pain and agony the second my eyes opened and I became conscious. Covered in sweat and goosebumps. Bones hurting, skin crawling. I remember vividly that when I was dope sick, everything smelled funny. I don't know why, but when I was sick, no matter where I was, I always smelled this old mattress smell, like some rank old rubbery smell. And the panic, my God, the panic that came along with being dope sick.

Imagine waking up and your first thought upon awakening is sheer and utter dread. Every damn day. Chills, then hot. Sweats, then freezing. The only thing that was going to take the pain and misery away was the very thing that continued to cause it. Perpetual insanity . . . I truly believe, in my off the cuff opinion here, that 90% of all heroin addicts are truly miserable. The only reason we keep going is because we get so horribly dependent on the drug physically, that we wake up every day and literally have no choice in the matter but to keep doing more.

If I wake up in horrible agony every day, and know in my mind that this drug is destroying me, I only have two choices: go through the pain, delusions, insomnia, and psychosis of withdrawl for God only knows how long—the last time I detoxed was cold turkey in a jail cell, and I was sick as a dog for two weeks and didn't sleep at all for twenty eight days—OR, do whatever it takes, steal, lie, beg, manipulate, rob, or con someone to get the very drug that's killing me, just to stave off the hell for one more day. Why, to me it's a no brainer. I am going to do whatever it takes to get that bag, and *MAYBE* I'll try and get clean *TOMORROW.*

This is why crime is so common with heroin addicts. The crime is a symptom of a MUCH deeper issue here. I have never committed a crime clean and sober, ever. Anyway, tomorrow had come for me a few times during my career as a dope fiend. Those moments of clarity, and desperation that we hear about and see in movies, but they're always few and far between for addicts like me. I used for what, almost fourteen years, and actually reached out for help, honestly, without jail or prison hanging over my head, what, maybe eight times?

I couldn't take it anymore. I wasn't dope sick, but I knew that I was going to be very soon. My day of crime had netted me about six or seven bags, which were definitely already gone, and about one hundred dollars in currency. I wasn't sick, but my cycle was about twelve hours, and I had just injected my last three bags. The time was now. I had to make a move or God only knew how long it was going to be until I had this window of willingness again.

I picked up the phone. I am not going to mention any names, or institutions here, as I never do and never will, because this is my story and no one else's. I called a local hospital here in the region, which has a long running reputation for helping addicts and alcoholics get clean and sober. This would be my second try contacting said hospital. The first time they flat out told me that they couldn't take me. Which was cool, I guess. At least they didn't give me the run around that time, and I appreciated that in some sick way. I think the run around, and being passed from help line, to help line is insulting, discouraging, and makes an addict feel just as hopeless as the needle itself. So, I called the place this time and explained my situation in almost embarrassing detail. Embarrassing because I did this to myself. I take ownership of that. Also, because I was so pitiful, scared, vulnerable, and poor. I just didn't want to hurt anymore. I told the voice on the other end of the line that I needed and wanted help. I would come there and walk willingly into the world of recovery, if they could just show me some love, tolerance, give me a bed, and help me not wake up so sick tomorrow.

"I just can't go on like this anymore. Please help me."

The voice on the other end of the line was very kind. They were patient with me and sounded like he or she really wanted to be that beacon of light for me. They instructed me to pack a bag with clothes and hygiene for seven days and said that they did in fact have a bed for me and would hold it until about 10 p.m. that night. I told the person that, yes I had a ride and would be there immediately. But I also wasn't stupid. I mean, I may have lived in abandoned buildings, eaten out of garbage cans, shot heroin with toilet water from the nastiest places known to man, and smoked crack out of a plastic pen tube, (which tastes amazing and I'm sure the thick black smoke coming off of the melting plastic is super good for you and all), *BUT I AM NOT STUPID*—So I took my cash with me, just in case something happened and they turned me away. I know that hospitals, treatment centers, detoxes, etc. may not always be able to take me. But believe me, my dope dealer always will . . . that's a sad fact of life right there.

Anyway, I walk into the hospital lobby, with my little roller suitcase stuffed to the gills with anything I thought I might need. The second I walked in, this wave of relief and a glimmer of hope washed over me.

I was finally going to get free of this on my own. I know it's going to work this time because I really want it. I had finally reached a point where I knew that this doesn't work, and I'm desperate enough to try anything that might work. This is it. I'm so close I can taste it. I got butterflies and shook with anticipation. It was finally happening. I walked my 125-pound ass up to the desk and explained to the lady behind the registration counter who I was and why I was there. The time was about 6:00 p.m. She had me fill out some basic paperwork, and I complied. I handed her the paperwork and sat down with my suitcase and waited. And waited, and waited . . . They're probably just moving someone or getting my bed ready. I'm just thankful they finally said they would take me this time. I shouldn't be getting sick for several hours now. I had some time. I'd go outside to smoke and grab a pop from the machine to pass the time. I'd stare at my phone. I'd stare at people.

Finally, after about two hours, I went back up to the counter just to check in and see what was going on. The lady informed me that she was waiting on a superior to let her know what to do. Okay.

Another hour, another check in. Nothing. More waiting. As time hammered on like a locomotive at a snail's pace, powerful, noisy, determined, and slow as hell, I began to grow increasingly anxious and impatient.

I'm actually writing this without effort. I'm just banging away on this keyboard as I watch this next episode of, "My life Fucking Sucks," playing out in my head.

More time, more check ins, no news. The time is now well after 10:00 p.m., and now I am being informed that I *MUST* wait until the morning, when this so called superior, or department head, or whoever the hell this person was, actually comes to the hospital physically. Well that's not what I wanted to hear, but oh well, what choice do I have? I can make another ten hours or so, I have some cash so I won't be hungry or without smokes, I should be good. 8:00 a.m. comes quickly, I'll just close my eyes here and hope to sleep through the night and when I wake up, it will be time to get better.

I did sleep through most of the night, up here and there to go out and smoke, but for the most part I did sleep. The problem with sleeping on opiates, at least for me, is that I tend to sleep it off. I always wake up dope sick, and this time was no different. I was now once again, a sweaty, anxious, goose-bump covered mess. But hey, it was 8:00 a.m. and time to check in so that's good.

I walked up to the counter and talked to a different lady this time and explained my situation and what I had been directed to do. She took my name, grabbed my form, and walked back into the back. She came back about ten minutes later, and it was very clear that either she had no idea why I was there, or that they had zero intention of admitting me for detox.

Holy shit, this is not good. So, I asked for her supervisor, because my name is "Karen" and I want to talk to the manager. This gentleman came out and explained to me very matter-of-factly, that he did not care what anyone told me to do, it was looking like I would not be admitted for detox. Then very casually, he walked to the back to attend to all the important people . . . I was shocked, I was crushed, I was on the brink of tears, I felt like this was some kind of very cruel joke. I fought back the tears and very calmly looked at the lady and told her what I had been instructed to do.

Then I proceeded to look her dead ass in the eyes and said, "Listen, lady, I need help. I was told to come here almost twelve hours ago. I'm dying, I'm desperate. And if you guys don't take me like you said you would, I'm going to walk outta here, and I'm going to fucking kill myself."

That got her attention.

She said she would be right back "Just wait right here, Mr. Stepherson. Someone will be here for you," and she was right. She went into the back and called the cops on me. Two uniformed officers came walking into the lobby, told me to grab my things, and then escorted me off the hospital grounds. They walked me to a nearby pavilion and issued me a no trespass warning. They told me if I ever came back to that hospital that I would be arrested. I had never felt so defeated in my entire life.

* * *

After I had finally gotten clean and had been at the Respite House for a while, I joined a baseball team with some of my recovery buddies. We always joked and said it was an "old man" league, but it sure was fun. It felt good to be back out there on the ball field again. I felt young, I felt alive, I was having fun. It was so nice to get out there and chatter and mess around with the guys on a Sunday afternoon, even though I quickly realized that my best baseball days were long behind me. But it was still fun and that's what mattered. We played every Sunday all summer long. We traveled all over to play too, Chesterton, Portage, Valparaiso, Hobart, and other towns. I played all over the field as well. I was the "utility guy." I was not afraid to play any position, except second base, I don't know why but playing the two bag was always weird for me. Maybe it was the positioning on the field? I have no idea. Other than that, it didn't matter where I played, as long as I was in the game. One game I was assigned to play short stop, which I love playing because it gets a lot of action. It gave me a chance to show off my arm, shooting guys out at first base across the diamond, and hearing that loud *POP* of the leather. Seeing the dust fly out of the squeezed mitt and hearing the "bang bang" of the close play always excited me.

Then there's turning double plays, which I have only done a few times, but man is it fun. Just the whole culture of being out there, the chatter and the shit talking is so fun to me. I miss my old playing days. But on this day, I got a lot of action. I was dusty and dirty by like the fourth inning. On a particular play, I had to dive out toward the short-left field grass and behind the third base bag to try and keep the ball in the infield. I did in fact make the grab, but I was too deep in the infield and the guy was too fast, so I just had to "eat it." No play.

I noticed that I may have tweaked something in my lower back, but no big deal at the time, just kind of sore. I finished the game, and as the day progressed, I noticed that my back pain too, was progressing and that I was going to be super sore in the morning— and boy was I. The second day after was even worse.

Thank God for Tiffany, bless her heart. She would be having to help me with my socks and shoes for the next couple days. Getting old is fun. Ibuprofen, Ben Gay, Icy Hot, ice packs, heat pack, nothing seemed to ease the pain. Finally, around night at four or five, I made a decision that the next morning I was going to go to a local urgent care and see what they had to say. I was not being dramatic either. This was bad. I couldn't bend, I couldn't tie my own shoes, I couldn't drive. Maybe I had torn or broken something. I needed an X-ray at least.

The place I had selected to go, was here in Valpo, and they opened at 9:00 a.m. Tiffany helped me with my socks and shoes, and I hobbled my old man ass out to the Explorer. I was at the urgent care place at 9:01 a.m. I wobbled in like Quasimodo and explained to the lady behind the desk why I was there. She asked me for my information and had me fill out some forms.

I love filling out forms, said no one ever. But I did as they asked, and once it was time, they asked me to come on back. A lady came back to visit with me and asked me some basic questions. What brings you in, etc. . . I told her what happened on the ball field and explained to her how it hurt and what not. I then proceeded to «Red Flag» myself, like I always do. To "red flag myself" means to out myself as a recovering drug addict. I told the lady right off the bat that I cannot have narcotics and will not be accepting any opiates for pain. Motrin 800 and *MAYBE* a muscle relaxer if needed would be fine. She acknowledged my request and took me for some X-rays. She then accompanied me back to the room where I waited for the doctor to come and explain everything to me. It took a little while for them to read the films, but eventually the doctor came back in. He was cordial and kind for the most part. He explained to me that I had a lower lumbar strain, and although not really all that serious, it could be quite painful and uncomfortable for a while. I once again red flagged myself to him and explained to him that I cannot have any narcotics, no opiates, nothing that gets me high. He nodded in acknowledgement and left the room for a few minutes. A short time later he came back in with some basic information on what my injury was, some home remedies for easing the pain, and some prescriptions to help me along in feeling better.

"Ok, Herb, I'm sending you home with two scripts today. Motrin 800 and Flexeril, to help ease the muscles and the strain." He handed me all of the information and thanked me for coming in. He instructed me to stop at the desk and sign out and to take it easy for a couple days and I should be fine in no time. I complied. I stuck the information packet in my back pocket and headed out the door. I hobbled out to the Explorer and gingerly eased myself into the driver's seat. I leaned up on my right butt cheek and pulled the information out of my back pocket. It was as he said. I was skimming over the information he had provided and then returned back to the front page to examine to scripts he had written me.

Hmmmm . . . he told me that he had written me two prescriptions. I thumbed through them and there it was. A little blue piece of paper, prescription number three, stapled so nice and neatly, sandwiched between the other two scripts and the information on my injury, Hydrocodone 10s. I stared down at the scribbly writing of the doctor and simply could not believe my eyes. I had very clearly told not one, but two different trusted people in the medical field that *I DO NOT* and *CANNOT* have any narcotics. I don't even know how to articulate all of my thoughts on this, but there is very little chance that this was some kind of honest mistake. This man had clearly slipped this prescription for opioids into this packet, and then failed to tell me about. Unbelievable.

So, I can't get the help getting clean when I do want it, but I *CAN* get the pills when I don't want them . . .?

My question for you, reader, is **WHY?**

Interlude

So, as you can see, my life had gone from a horror story to a nightmare once I began using chemicals to cope with my life and its circumstances. We may not always possess the ability or know how to make our lives better instantly, but we can always go and make it a whole lot worse really quick.

My life was absolute hell for about thirty years, either because I was born into chaos, or brought it upon myself as a result of being addicted to powerful drugs. I

used to often ask and ponder questions to myself, like "Why does God allow suffering, if He loves us so much?" Well, I know that answer now.

For me, God allows suffering for two reasons:

One, so that we can realize our need for Him and dependence on him. That to surrender our will and allow God into our lives is how we win.

Two, so that once we make it through our own suffering, we can use our experiences and empathy to help others who are currently suffering and stuck like we once were.

Experience and Empathy are two of the most powerful principles I have ever come to know, and couple that with my affinity for the underdogs and the soft spot in my heart for them, I would soon be traveling into some pretty amazing places. The following entries are more focused on my thoughts, ideas, and experiences since getting clean and my work in intervention and my life since getting clean from heroin.

Affinity

Once I made the choice to compromise, to roll the dice and pick up a cigarette and it did what I didn't know it could do, I was instantly obsessed with what else there was out there that could do it too. I quickly moved on to alcohol, weed, every other chemical I could get my hands on, and as detailed out in my first book ultimately crack and heroin.

My experiences with trauma were still very much ongoing, and in a sense just getting started. The traumas that lay in wait for me in the world of addiction though, were to be very much self-induced. I came from chaos, so as my life in the addiction world unfolded, I would continue to gravitate to more and more chaos.

This is what one of my therapists referred to as, "Trauma Repetition." The whole idea is "Comfort in Chaos" and down, down, down the spiral we would go . . .

As I believe I mentioned before, I always seemed to have this inherent affinity for the "underdogs" of the world. I think it is because from a very early age, and as a result of everything I had been through, I knew suffering. I knew what it felt like to be invisible, unheard, insignificant, brushed aside, neglected, abandoned, and essentially thrown away. So I always felt this kind of like survivor's bond with similar types in movies, TV, sports, and in real life.

I remember the first time I watched *Forrest Gump*. I was absolutely blown away. This man had had the most incredible and interesting life, even though he had been born with so many disadvantages and had so many obstacles thrown at him. He was born with a learning disability, a back as "crooked as a politician," and he didn't have a father. He was named after the founder of the Ku Klux Klan. He was bullied, beat up, invisible to most, and ignored. He was taken for granted and taken advantage of. He was shot in the ass, the woman he loved always left him, and no one liked him. He was very much an outcast of society. But the things that really made him special to me, were his innocence, integrity, humility, and his giving nature. His loyalty to friends, and his moral compass. Someone must have planted the right seeds in his heart because they went on to become very fruitful later in life. The thing that really stood out to me about him was that he never really did anything over-the-top spectacular. He just always did the right thing, and that was all he ever really needed to do.

It's funny how this world works. They say when the student is ready, the teacher appears. When I was desperate and lost as an adolescent, with no real mentorship or examples on how to live and do life, I was able to find messages. I was able to learn and able to feel meaningful life lessons in the most unusual of places. It's kind of like I knew deep down inside that if I was going to somehow make it out of all of this, then I better take on a heart that was hungry for wisdom and be able to recognize it when I heard it.

Forrest Gump, and stories like his, provided me with great inspiration. I knew that I too was at a disadvantage in life. The cards were truly stacked against me. School and college weren't much of an option to me. I just knew that deep down inside, if given the opportunity, I could go on and be somebody someday. All I had to do, was do my best to be a good person. I knew I was gonna fail at that at times. But, if I just truly followed my moral compass, and held on long enough, one day I would get my chance. That, and lots and lots of prayer and faith were seeds that were planted in me, in second grade in Tennessee and gave me unwavering hope. Even in the most hopeless of times.

It's crazy, the dichotomy or duality of the mind. I would go on to become a homeless, strung-out street person for many years. But through it all, I always held on to hope. I just knew if I never gave up, one day I would be able to finally turn it all around. And I was right. It just didn't happen quite like I thought it would and had.

When God calls us to our purpose, remember that He has already factored in our foolishness.

Brother's Keeper

The **Big Book of AA**, page 67: "We asked God to help us show the same tolerance, pity, and patience that we would cheerfully grant a sick friend. When a person offended us, we said to ourselves, 'This is a sick man/woman. How can I help him/her? God save me from being angry. Thy will be done."

February 7th, 2020. 1:48 a.m., Friday morning.

The name on the call log written in red, because I had missed the call while I was sleeping.

I hate getting those calls. Not because they sometimes disturb my sleep—I rarely sleep through the night anyways. But because they are *NEVER* good calls. No one has ever called me at that time with good news, or to tell me how well they're doing. I awoke at roughly 6:30 a.m. and saw the missed call. Instant concern and worry. I returned the call and heard the voice of an old friend. Someone who I love and respect immensely. Someone who I still as I write this, admire very much. This is all still very fresh in my mind, and I am still processing, so please bear with me. (I figured this was as good a way as any to flesh this out.)

"I need help Herb."

"Oh, buddy, I know."

I could hear the grief, the brokenness in his voice. He was lost, he was hurting badly. I could hear the shake, I could feel his tremors, his voice cracking. The utter humiliation. And his self-pity. He proceeded to walk me back through his now two-years long relapse. I asked questions, and he answered. He would take breaks too, take that breath—that deep from the soul desperate and ugly breath—

and then return to his story. We talked for about forty five minutes and really re kindled our old friendship.

He needed help, and I wanted to help him. I needed to. We came together with a plan of action and made all of the necessary arrangements. Work was notified, and family and friends made aware. He was in bad shape, but he had a willing heart. He was ready to finally pick up that 1,000-pound phone and ask for help. He was ready to let someone else in.

When the pain of change is less than the pain of being the same, we take action. We make adjustments, we ask for help, and we follow through. But he, my friend, is what you would refer to as the "low bottom addict." Like me. I could tell by the way he sounded, and the things that he told me—like the way he had been using—that he was going to need some assistance to get moving and get to a hospital for some help. That did not go well. I sent over an escort to pick him up. A man who'd been sober fourteen years. A man ready to help him.

But my old friend was so fucked up and out of his mind, that this was clearly not the time to try and get him to make a move. Eventually, after several hours of hanging out with him and working on him, and his inability to stop using and come down—we had to reconvene. My escort and I made a decision to take a step back for a while and allow him to come down a bit. He was not at the time a danger to himself or anyone else. In fact, he had some company there with him, who seemed lucid, rational, and sober. This person had agreed to keep an eye on him for the next several hours and to stay in communication with us. He was safe and would be taken care of. We agreed to let him come down, sleep it off. We would re-visit things in the morning.

February 8th, 2020, 9:18 a.m,

This morning we decided that I would take a shot at him. I would go over to his home and see if I could get him moving. After all, were long-time friends, so this should be easy enough, right? No problems at all . . .

I knocked on his apartment door. Nothing. Waited. Nothing. Again, and again, and again. I know he's here, his car is in the parking lot, and there's no footprints in the snow near the entrance to his place. I call his phone, and I can hear it ringing on the other side of the door. He is definitely here. I knock harder and harder still. I walk around the side of his apartment and rap on his window, again, and again. Nothing. No motion, no stirring. Now I am consulting with my team on the phone. Roughly twenty minutes of knocking on his door and window, and about seventeen calls to his phone. I am now fearing for his life. Had he passed away inside? Was I only a matter of minutes too late? Should I call for help? One more knock on the door, and if I don't hear anything I will have to call emergency services . . .

Finally, a noise from inside. Some shuffling of feet. Hands meet the door on the other side. The dead bolt disengages, and the door pulls inward toward the guts of the house enough to reveal my friend, and a very large handgun . . .

Instantly, and I mean *fucking instantly*, my blood ran ice cold. I instinctively show him my hands. I am not 100% sure how the next moments went, as I was on extreme alert, and fearing for my life. I believe I blacked out from fear and was running on 100% survival here.

"Whoa, buddy, it's me. It's Herb . . . «

"Herb, you're not Herb, who are you!?"

"Buddy, it's me. It's Herb, it is Herb, man. Please. I can leave if you need me to, but if you let me in, you gotta put the gun down."

I remember having this "run-like hell" thought, and I could not take my eyes off of the pistol. At first, I thought to myself that maybe it's a BB gun and this is just a scare tactic. But the more I fixed my eyes on the weapon and looked it over, the more I feared that I may die right here. I had to get my eyes off of the gun and make eye contact with him. It's crazy how it takes so long to explain something that happened in a matter of maybe ten seconds, but it seemed like an hour. I was finally able to peel my eyes away from the pistol, my guess is that it was a 9 mm, or a 45—I don't know guns, but it was absolutely large enough to bore a massive hole through whatever it was pointed at. Right now it was fixed dead center in my chest. Sternum shot. I'm gone if he pulls that trigger. I worked my eyes up to his, and the moment we made eye contact I knew that I was safe.

"It's me man, remember_____? (removed to protect his identity.)

It's so funny, strange, and interesting to me—but maybe I myself am more fucked up than most, delusional at times. As my buddy was pointing that gun at me, he identified me in his mind. I could see all of his hurts. I could see his pain, and maybe that's what he was actually pointing the gun at all along. I just happened to be standing in the bullet's path. As soon as this little interaction finally caught up in his brain and he processed it, he immediately lifted the gun away, pulled the clip out, and took the bullet out of the chamber. He then set all three parts of the weapon on the counter and threw his arms around my neck, and sobbed. I mean, sobbed. That "gnashing of teeth" from the gut and soul brokenness sob that only the most desperate of men or women can make. The sound of a soul in pain.

We hugged it out for several moments. Then to the double shoulder pat and squeeze as we looked at each other. This man was once a mighty, mighty man. Very much in shape, a seasoned veteran of life, a hard-working father, and a mighty man of God.

Today, as I looked him over and evaluated his condition, I would venture to say that he was MAYBE 120 pounds, soaking wet. He had little frail flamingo legs. Gaunt, cheekbones blaring through his face. He appeared to be about eight-five years old. Frail and decrepit so sad and heart breaking to see. I felt as if I could actually hug him and squeeze him to death. His clothes barely stayed on. I threw his arm over my shoulder and walked him to his couch, like trainers help an injured football player to the sidelines.

He sat back on the reclining portion of his couch, and I knelt on one knee next to him with a hand on his shoulder. He lit a smoke. I took in the scene. Burn marks littered his arm of the couch. "His Spot," no doubt. Today was one of the most powerful days in recent memories for me. Today was fucking brutal, personal, and sad. I stood and made my way to the foot of the reclining portion which held his feet up and stared down into the eyes of my friend. He nodded out for just one quick second, then he took a drag of his cig. This man was in total spiral, physically withering, and spiritually dead. A shell of his former self. He was once a life speaker, a service giver, a leader and mentor. Today he was at rock bottom from a relapse after two-years run of sobriety. Couch covered in burn marks, house shuttered in. No blinds allowing so much as a thin line of sunshine in. Complete and utter despair. Delusion, paranoia, all of the tell-tale side effects that we drug addicts know all too well.

But my friend was not using cocaine, crack, meth, heroin, pills, or powder of any kind. He was not using any of those My friend was using the legal shit. The stuff they tax. The stuff they sell over the counter. They push it down our throats on TV, they glamorize it with celebrities. My friend was using alcohol . . .

"Sorry, buddy. I just woke up. I'm ready to go Herb. I'm beat."

"I know brother. Can I make you a pot of coffee? You got a coffee pot?"

"No, but do you mind if I take a shot?"

I could smell the burning amber liquid as he painfully gulped one down. Then another, and a third. He grimaced as he choked the last one down and finished his smoke.

We chatted for a while. He mostly listened, but when he did speak it was, "I'm sorry, Herb." "I'm Scared," and, "Fuck." A lot of "fuck." And just that, nothing more. There was nothing more to say.

It took some time, and constant nudging and moving him along, but I was actually able to get him to firmly commit to going. I gave him a deadline of about an hour to be dressed and ready to go. During that hour I witnessed someone's rock bottom. I had to help him shower, not like that—but I had to get his towel for him. I had to turn the water on for him, while the poor, frail, suffering, and naked man stood on the other side of the shower curtain. I packed his clothes and toiletries. I helped him with his socks and tied his shoes for him. I put his shirt on for him and gathered his pocket stuff—wallet, phone, smokes, and etc . . . Once again, I was going to have to basically carry this man. This time to my car, but I promised my friend that I was going to help him, and that I was not going to leave without him—and I meant it.

Today was one of the most powerful days in recent memory. Today, I saw someone in their most vulnerable and desperate place. Today, I saw someone's secret place. I saw their pain, and I latched my strength to his lack of strength. I carried my former mentor out of his apartment and to my waiting car. I loaded his things, and we pulled away. He silently cried in the back seat while I tried to keep things light and positive. I played music and offered him something to drink. He declined. He cried silently. He grimaced in spiritual pain. But even still, through all of that, I saw something in him. I saw relief. I saw hope, and I saw that he wanted to do this. I have chills as I write this. God bumps.

Today was one of those days where something just comes through, ya know? Today was one of those days where you can just feel something special. Something cosmic. God was with us today. On the doorstep, in his apartment, and in that car.

Tomorrow, my friend will wake up with one day sober.

Symbols

I went to see an old friend of mine recently. He was in the Porter County Jail, again. He had been on Methadone for a while now and just could not seem to get off of it or stay on just methadone. I have come to find out that most, who end up on methadone, stay on it for the rest of their lives, or for a very long time.

It is very difficult to come off of methadone, because the providers tend to move you up so fast and to such a high dose, that people become horribly dependent upon it. Add that to it being so addictive—most would agree that the withdrawals are worse than heroin itself. I wouldn't know. I was never afraid of heroin, but methadone scared the shit out of me. The detox from methadone is from what I've witnessed, absolute hell, and this young man was in the full throes of it. He wasn't shaking in the typical sense of the word. The only way I can describe the way he was moving is that he was quaking. Like there was an epicenter of pain sending seismic vibrations from deep inside his core. His skin was ashy grey and splotchy. His pupils like that of a giant squid; huge saucers with zero colored bands around them. I could see the way his hair, matted to his skull from countless hours of non-stop sticky detox sweats. He couldn't stop sniffling. He was so sick. God, I don't miss that.

I could tell that he was not so pleasantly surprised to see me. Surprised, probably, but not in a happy way. Usually when they see me, they know what's coming. I am rarely in front of drug addicts with happy news. But this was truly different. He was an old friend of mine, and I wasn't there to intervene, scare him or give him some kind of come to Jesus moment. I was just there to talk to my buddy, a person who I have always been quite fond of. At first he was quite resistant, which is so interesting to me by the way. Here is a man, almost forty years old, sitting in jail, strung out on dope, no job, no car, no apartment—not two nickels to rub together, and yet still so full of bravado, and ego.

Why is that? Why are we addicts *ALWAYS* the last to know that we're licked? It's like that meme where the house is on fire and the little character is in the middle of the picture is saying, "This is fine, no big deal, I got this . . ."

We do not got this.

It took about thirty minutes to really get him to let his guard down and start openly talking with me. At which time I asked him a very simple question, but to the addict who still suffers is a very hard one to answer, and I ask it all the time: "What do you want?"

One of my favorite quotes that I use all the time is, "If you don't know what you want, you'll damn sure never get it."

That was the case for my friend here. He didn't have a clue, as with many addicts that I talk with. The only thing that we have ever known, is the getting, using and finding ways and means to get more drugs, so what's the use? Dreams? Goals? HA! Not a chance, I just wanna get high and fuck shit up. That's what I am, and that's what I do right?

That is the IDENTITY that we CREATED for ourselves. It is what and who we associate with. I never, until I got clean, had anyone challenge me about priorities, goals, or success. I just had a bunch of using buddies that I got high with. I had no clue what I wanted, or who I was, or who I wanted to be. This is common for we addicts, especially during our first five years, which I lovingly refer to as the "wooden nickel."

My friend here didn't even fully understand the question. He repeated it back into the air, not really back to me, multiple times. At first, he repeated it back at me, with kind of an agitation. Kind of like he was pissed off that I would even dare to ask him such a thing. Like he knew that I knew, he didn't know, because I did. I didn't either for a long time, and he was kind of insulted at first, but I maintained the flow, and kept emotions to a minimum. I kept control, stayed calm, and led with love and respect. "It's just a question, buddy. It's just us here."

"I don't fucking know, Herb. What do I want?"

"Only you can answer that man."

He kind of zoned out then. That dissociative thousand-mile stare of a truly broken man. I could see him traveling his rabbit hole of secret places, the way only a truly lost soul can. We can time warp and introspectively transcend all of our past, our present, our desires, our longings, and our fears concurrently, while thinking about a present question or situation—merely trying to avoid it. It's like watching a movie in our hearts and heads, behind open, dead eyes, while asking ourselves a thousand questions that we simply cannot answer. We snap back to reality typically with an, "I'm fine," or "I don't know," dismissive response. God, I *hate* that I know that. It's such an empty and awful feeling.

I was able to kind of nudge my head down into his field of vision and regain his focus. I asked the question again, after his journey of introspection, and this time, he locked in on me and spoke some truth.

"I still don't know . . . a house, or apartment? A Girlfriend? A Job? What do I want, Herb?"

Then he found some confidence in his answers. "Yeah, an apartment, a girlfriend, and a job. That's what I want."

Now we are scratching the surface. You see, I thought those were the types of things that I wanted when I first got clean, too. But just like anger is a surface/secondary emotion—those things and ideas were secondary things too.

I thought that once I got back on my feet and stopped shooting dope, that all I had to do was play the country song backward—the dog would come back, the girl would return, or I would find another one. I'd get the truck and the house and etc.—that that's what recovery, life, and success would look like. But those are all SECONDARY or surface ideas. Those are all symbols, that I connected with what I *REALLY WANTED.*

When I heard him say that he wanted a job; I heard, "I want to feel like I matter, and I can depend on myself. I want stability, and to be able to provide for, and be proud of myself."

A job is just a status that my mind equates to being self-sufficient and trusting myself to be secure enough in my place in life that I can lean on myself and be what I see as a real man. I want to feel like I am enough to myself, and to others. I want to prove to my family that I can make it on my own, and a job would be a great way of showing them that.

When I heard him say that he wanted an apartment, or a house, I heard, "I want a *HOME*, a safe place of my own. A sanctuary where I can truly be myself, free from judgement. A place where I can feel secure, stable, protected, and still. I want my own refuge where I can return to from my job and feel *PROUD* of for being able to provide this safe place for myself. I am going to enjoy it and take comfort in knowing that I no longer have to borrow or beg for a warm place to sleep. I want a place, a location, a spot, where I feel like I truly belong. Where I deserve and long to be. Just for me, and maybe a family one day.

When I heard him say, "I want a girlfriend"—I heard, "I want a wife. I want to feel truly *LOVED* by someone who doesn't judge me and loves me for who I am, not in spite of who I am. I want a real friend, a partner and a teammate. Someone who I can *TRULY* depend on. Someone who isn't going to leave me, like so many others have throughout my life, whether I pushed them away by using or not. I want someone who I can do life with and share life with. I want to feel seen, appreciated, and celebrated. I want someone to *CHOOSE ME*, not just be obligated to take care of me because we share the same blood as family. I want someone who loves me with a fire, and who can't live without me, or me without them. I want a dog and pictures on the wall. Christmases and a life we can enjoy. That's what I heard". Everything else was just symbols . . .

That's exactly what he meant too, because when I told him this, the flood gates opened. We had touched a part of him that had been suppressed for so long. He was still that scared, lonely, broken-hearted little boy. We both were and we connected, and he knew it. He cried, I listened. We continued talking for about an hour. Eventually we laughed, and we reminisced about some of the old times. His light was slowly starting to come on, and for a moment, I could see that he wasn't in jail. He was starting to envision his life with a purpose. He was starting to taste that his future and his life could be better than he had ever imagined, and it felt so reassuring to see.

I think that that's a pretty common theme for most of us addicts out there. That's what we want, we just cannot grasp the actual fruit of the idea below the surface. We long for deep, meaningful relationships and purpose, but we have seldom truly experienced them, due to our using. Sometimes all we need is someone to talk to, a fresh perspective. Someone who can help us wade through the murky waters of our secret places. Someone who can reiterate what we just said, right back to us. Someone who can translate things into a language we didn't know that we understood. Someone who can show us what our symbols and ideas may actually mean below the surface.

Money, cars, clothes, status. House, fences, pools. Jewelry, toys, vacations, power, etc. . .

These are all just things. Symbols.

What do the symbols of your life say about your true self below the surface? What priorities of yours do they reveal?

Midas

An older gentleman said to me on our way home from a meeting many years ago, "Herb, let me tell you something young man. I want you to listen to me when I tell you this; everything that your recovery blesses you with, your addiction will try and use against you,". He was right.

You know it's funny, you write one book, and everyone thinks you know what you're talking about, and I do. It's just that being a published author, especially when it pertains to the subject matter of addiction and mental health, puts one in a precarious position. It's like all of a sudden that, and the field I work in, somehow gave many people this idea that I was somehow cured and had some kind of answers. All I ever did was share my experiences and do my best to be a good person and a helper.

Life absolutely took off for me once the book dropped, and I began my work in intervention. It all happened so fast; it was like a blur. Offers were coming in from all over the place. Come speak in Idaho, Come to Southern Indiana, be on this radio show, this podcast, etc. I was contacted by celebrities, newspapers, politicians, families in need of help, churches, radio stations, TV, you name it.

It was like a dream come true, with some exceptions, of course. I wouldn't change it, but let me tell something right now:

Every gift has a cost.

* * *

Tiffany and I moved in together once I left the halfway house. I was working at the first intervention company, and we were just riding the wave. You wanna talk about starting from the bottom, and now we're here, that was us.

We took over a home on Kinsey Street in Valparaiso. We had no furniture, no beds, very few of our own clothes; and the house was absolutely trashed. The last five or six weekends while I was at the halfway house, we spent getting the house ready and livable. The yards were horribly overgrown, and the inside of the house looked like a trap house. We worked tirelessly getting the place ready, and when we moved in, all we had were a few bags of clothes, some blankets, pillows, and a couple donated wicker chairs and table. We made a pallet on the floor and slept there the first several weeks.

Over time, we accumulated the stuff we needed. A donated TV, small sectional, kitchen table, dishes, etc. I worked at the intervention company, and she worked for a nursing agency. We were grinding. Things were an absolute blur. Kids, school, an hour commute to and from work for me every day. Book signings, birthdays, speaking engagements, TEDx talks, travel. We were cooking! Meetings, sponsorships, probation meetings, family trips, new piece of furniture.

We got a dog, Reba. She is the sweetest. She's an all-white with blue spots and one floppy ear pit bull and she's my second-best friend. My wife is my first.

* * *

Life simply could not have been going any better. We were two determined love birds. We were ascending. Tiffany had been an underdog story herself in her own right. A single mother of three, doing the best she could, working, cooking, being a mom, and all that comes with that.

I was just a disaster when we met, but we have somehow continued to make it work, through thick and thin. When we first got together, I didn't even have a bank account. I opened my first checking account with fifty bucks, when I was working at the insurance agency. From there it was baby steps in the right direction. Little by little we climbed. Sometimes we had to overdraft an account to pay a bill, sometimes we didn't. We were determined to succeed, and we loved each other very much.

I had so much going on. I didn't know if I was coming or going half the time. I had all of my, what I now know to be, "Professional

Life." Interventions, book signings, speaking engagements, writing, appearances, meetings, etc. I had all of the personal life stuff, wife, kids, step-kids. We weren't married yet, but we all lived together. It was pretty obvious that this is where it was headed, or at least I hoped so.

"Baby Momma Drama," and all the crap that came along with that. Court hearings, etc. I did my best to squeeze in some "Me Life"—meetings, sponsorships, journaling, etc. It all seemed so surreal. Days passed by sometimes quickly, sometimes slowly, but where oh where, did the months and years go?

We were laser focused. One day I decided to get myself a secured credit card. The type you have to pay a deposit for, and the credit card company gives you a card with limit on it. A beginners' credit card, to start building credit with. That was my very first piece of the American dream right there.

We were determined. Our conversations were ambitious and driven. They were very goal oriented. Our first year at the house on Kinsey was amazing. We hung out in the back yard when we could, we went for drives, and took the kids to do fun stuff.

We traveled all over. Tiffany and I flew to Arizona, then Washington, and drove into Idaho; I had been paid to come and give a keynote speech for the Idaho Juvenile Justice Association. It was one of the coolest experiences of my life. Driving down through Eastern Washington, all the hills, mountains, and geography were just breathtaking. Massive combines glided through rolling hay fields, kicking up giant clouds of dust that were cut through by setting sun rays, and back dropped in bright pinks and purples. It was one of the greatest moments of my life. We ventured into the local towns exploring. I remember this lake; it was as smooth as glass and as clear as a diamond. The only thing that came cutting through it was the Washington State Row Team, practicing out on the water. This was all just too good to be true.

* * *

We got our first Christmas tree as a family, financed our first car, celebrated birthdays and continued to climb. I thanked God every single night for delivering me from such a horrible previous life to such an amazing one. I was so proud.

It was really easy to keep busy during these times, because there was always so much going on. There was always a task to handle, there was always something to be done, and we did them well. A secured card credit card turned into multiple credit card offers, which turned into multiple credit cards, which turned into a rising credit score. I utilized the marketing skills I'd learned at the insurance company at the intervention company. I was learning as much as I could, as fast as I could. After all, I was at a disadvantage already and had a lot of time to make up for. I had to pin my ears back, put my head down, and go. And that is exactly what I did. I was a workaholic, I was locked in. I was Dad, Step-Dad, interventionist, author, boyfriend/fiancé. I was a dog dad, speaker, brother, friend. I was living the dream. We were living the dream.

I was always working. It was annoying to some I am sure, but how could I waste such a beautiful and wonderful opportunity? The position I found myself in allowed me to do what I had always wanted to do, help others. It was a double blessing that I was able to support my family while doing so. We were on top of the world. Phone calls, emails, conference calls, hikes, cookouts, bills, life was chugging along. I continued to say yes to everything. Keynote speech—yes. Interview for newspaper—yes. Give a talk at a church—yes. Book signing at Barnes and Noble—yes. It seemed like the more I said yes to, the more the opportunities came. We couldn't miss.

* * *

We went from a pallet on the floor with no other furniture, to a fully furnished house, and a new-to-us car in the driveway. We were making it. Task, task, task, goal, goal, goal. Work, work, work. God was really smiling on us. I had attended the Indiana Dunes Great Banquet, and so had Tiffany. We were really growing at a rapid pace. Before we knew it, we were in our second year at the Kinsey house. What a blur. We were knocking off the old collection accounts on our credits from the previous years, when we both struggled independently. Together we thrived. We had her three children, and we had Lucas as often as possible. We would enjoy home cooked meals together and family game nights. We did s'mores in the back yard, and we went to Indiana Beach. We were all so happy.

* * *

One Friday evening, I had to make a run over to the local gas station for some smokes and fuel in the Buick Envoy. Tiffany asked me to grab her a few Scratch-off lottery tickets, which I always thought were a waste of money. Begrudgingly, I said I would.

I had my feet up on the ottoman while watching the news while she scratched at the tickets with a coin. I sipped my coffee and gazed off at the talking heads on the screen, when she interjected the silence with a loud "BABE!"

"What, thirty dollars down the drain, babe?"

"Bullshit, I just won $5,000.00," she screamed.

I couldn't believe it. I had never seen anyone win anything on those damn things. But there it was, right in front of my eyes. She sure as shit did. Like I said, we just couldn't miss. It was a winning streak like nothing I had ever experienced. We used most of it to pay bills, and credit cards off.

We used a piece of it to purchase Chicago Bears playoff tickets. It was the very first time both of us saw the Bears play. It was one of the best days of my life. We didn't get the win. As I am sure you know, this was the infamous "Double Doink" game. But it was an experience unlike any other. We even met Travis Kelce. He was there watching his brother who plays for the Philadelphia Eagles.

* * *

It's crazy how everything was happening. I mean, I had never experienced anything like this in my life. What a plot twist. I had gone from lost soul, heroin addict to all this. It didn't seem real, but it was. Life had become such a wonderful adventure of tasks to be handled and goals to accomplish. I sent a copy of my book to the White House, and Donald Trump sent me back a hand signed thank you card that I still have to this day. This was right around the time he had donated his quarterly salary to combat the opioid epidemic, and I had sent him a book as a thank you. It was awesome to get a handwritten thank you back from the President. I mean, how many people can say that in their lifetime? I was offered a new and better position at another intervention firm, and then another. Progress after progress, success after success, step up after step up.

One beautiful evening on a pier in Hilton Head, South Carolina, I found myself down on one knee proposing to Tiffany in front of her whole family and a bunch of strangers. It was amazing, and she said yes. We were both so happy and on top of the world. It was the best day of my life to that point. I hope it was to her as well.

We were killing the game. It seemed as though everything we touched turned to gold.

I also had the amazing and incredibly stressful privilege of giving a TEDx talk at Valparaiso University. "The Myth of Rock Bottom," was what it was called. The overall idea of it is how we can always bottom out again, even after what we think is our rock bottom. We can always dig another one.

A'int that the truth?

My, oh my, how foreshadowing that was indeed.

Rise and Fall

We had really been on a miraculous turn-around of our lives, and on an incredible trajectory. Everything we set out to accomplish, we crushed. It's really interesting too, because prior to all of this newfound success, we were both really struggling independently in our own rights. But together we seemed to really kick some ass.

I would say that now we are right around our third year in the Kinsey House. I had previously been with two different intervention companies and was now working for a third. Each time I made the decision to move on, it worked out and proved to be the best decision for our family. Tiffany and I had been talking about me leaving the agency I was with at the time and starting our own company. We believed that this would just be all around the smartest and most logical move to make at that point. I had hours totaling close to 7,000 by this point and had long since become well established, educated, and experienced in the field. We had done countless interventions in all fifty states, several times over.

We would talk about it, and the "put a pin in it," talk about it again, and "put a pin in it" again. I knew that deep down inside it was what I really wanted to do, but I was scared. Like terrified.

I said, "put a pin in it," but looking back, what I really did was procrastinate. Kick the can down the street. I think that in retrospect, this is when the fear began creeping back in. It was paralyzing at times. Eventually, the time came when I just knew that I had to do what I had to do— and that was take the leap of faith, take a risk, and trust that this is what I was supposed to be doing.

My wife and I set a deadline to tell my current company that I was going to be leaving. It came and went. *Ugh!* I just couldn't seem to pull the trigger. I was completely gripped the fear. So, I did all of the behind-the-scenes stuff first. I began building the company unofficially, so that it would be a smooth transition once I finally did part ways with my current employer.

We started by filing with the Secretary of State Office and all of the paperwork that came along with that. We hired an attorney to be with us throughout the development of the company who is still with us today. We built a website. We created logos, cards and fliers and readied ourselves to launch, the second the severance was official. All of the groundwork had been done, and there was nothing else to grasp at in the way of excuses. Now to just finally take the leap. I was so stressed out.

What if it all failed? What if it all fell apart? What would we do if this was the wrong move? This is definitely when the fear returned to my mind. I couldn't sleep most nights. When I did sleep, I had awful dreams. I dreamt about all of the worst-case scenarios that were undoubtedly heading our way once we did this. I ruminated on this decision for weeks.

Finally, I just couldn't take the stress of it any longer. I knew it was past time to get on with it, so I made the phone call and let the company know that I was resigning. To my surprise, it went a lot better than I thought it would. I suppose the fear of a situation is often times worse than the situation itself. I was quite relieved indeed. But the fear was still there, it had just morphed into other ruminations.

It wasn't that I doubted my own abilities. It was that I had never been fully and totally self-sufficient before. It was time to man up. We were now small business owners, and the success or failure of this company was going to be 100% on our shoulders. It was liberating and terrifying at the same time. My wife was so supportive and encouraging through the whole process. She would always remind me that God didn't bring us this far, to only bring us this far. It always sounded good, and briefly made me feel better, but it didn't seem to take the pressure off. The amount of pressure that I now felt on a daily basis was unlike anything I had ever experienced before.

* * *

I can imagine that everyone wants to work from home, myself included, but working from home brought about a whole new day to day, and list of difficulties for me. I could tell right off the bat that this new way of life was going to require a tremendous amount of discipline and self-made structure. I went from working more than forty hours a week in an office with several other humans, to working from home completely alone and isolated from human interaction for forty hours a week. This was a major shock to my system, especially since I am such an outgoing and sociable person. My little joke, when talking to people about the new venture was, "Everyone wants to work from home, until they work from home," and I believe that. I have now been working from home for about five years, and it is not as easy as one might think.

Anyway, back to then. At first, I seemed to adjust alright, or so I thought at the time. I spent many hours each week, marketing and "banging the drum," so to speak. The first few months were not easy. It wasn't long into this that I began to doubt that this was the right decision to make. No matter what I seemed to do, the phone didn't ring. It had become eerily quiet. The fear began to build.

I think it was about three solid months that we didn't generate any business. Nothing. I spent the days sending emails, following up, dropping into various places throughout the region, doing my best to stay visible and available if someone needed us to help. Nothing seemed to make a difference. I was becoming more and more stressed out by the day. The pressure was building and building. Fear followed me around like a long black shadow. It had really started to take over my mind. I was so hyper focused on growing the company, I was obsessed. Obsessed, full of fear, overwhelmed with pressure, and stressed out nearly all the time. I felt like I was chasing my tail. Perhaps I needed to just swallow my pride and ask my former employer for my job back. Maybe this was all a mistake.

It's very strange though, the duality of the mind, I knew and could feel that this was what I was supposed to be doing, but nothing was working. The only thing that was happening was, we were falling further and further into debt, and I may have been developing an ulcer. The fear grew, and the pressure built up. The rumination continued. I found myself pacing the floor of the house to the tune of miles a day I would guess.

I talked to Reba as if she were a person. Think *Ace Ventura, Pet Detective*, telling Spike the monkey that he couldn't feed him until he found Snowflake the dolphin. When we got Luna, our little Boston terrier, I talked to her too. I don't think those dogs know or understand how much they have done for me. My mental health was declining.

Recently, I learned that for those of us with PTSD and Borderline Personality Disorder, immense amounts of stress are absolute destroyers. Plus, keep in mind, I was at that point in time 100% untreated. Yes, I was clean, I was sober. I had been so for quite some time. I had done the CD&A (Chemical Dependency & Addictions) program in the Porter County Jail a couple years prior. I spent a year at the halfway house, and I had been to thousands of meetings and worked the steps. I had been through the Great Banquet, so my faith had recently been reignited and I had a working knowledge of recovery and staying the course. But I was still very much untreated. I had never been to an actual treatment program.

For those of you who have read my first book, you know that. I couldn't get into one. I didn't have insurance, and I was poor. I didn't matter to treatment centers. I was a have-not. It was always, "We will put you on the list and call you." They never called. So, I utilized what I had, whatever the State of Indiana mandated that I do.

Looking back on things, this is when the "Kerplunk Sticks" began to be pulled, one by one. Fear and stress became my way of life. I was able to finally get the company going, and we were getting busy. But here is a very interesting point about me at this time: I was unhealed from an entire lifetime of trauma and drug addiction. My mind had not ever been able to fully process everything that had transpired, and I certainly hadn't had any kind of real professional help. When the fear, stress, rumination, etc. returned to my brain's pathways they stuck. It was like I had reverted right back into that old chaos and trauma repetition. Even though the company had begun to take off, and my family life had been going really well, it didn't matter.

The fear, paranoia, stress, and rumination had already gotten in on a deep level and were not leaving. My entire mindset had changed and was changing still, going in the opposite direction that it was supposed to be going. What's crazy about all of this, is I couldn't see it. I thought that stress, and all that I was experiencing was a normal part of owning a small business, and it is. But I had yet to be fully diagnosed, and I had no idea what was going on inside my mind. Looking back, I have a couple ideas about this: 1)—I was still disassociated from childhood the whole time, to some degree. And 2)—this is when I began splitting. I am not entirely sure on this, but either, or both, would make sense. I just held on, white knuckles and all.

I know how this may sound to some, "First world problems," and "Must be a tough life," are a couple phrases that come to mind. I am not complaining. I never was. I am just trying to express what was going on at the time. What's more though, what's even more important and more impactful than all of the pressure, and stress, is that I had stopped taking care of myself.

* * *

Life is a shifty and intricate dance of balance and circumstances. It's really easy to lose sight of certain things sometimes. You see, the devil, the negative forces of this world, they come disguised as everything you ever wanted. As my friend said to me in the car that night, "Everything my recovery was blessing me with, indeed my addiction was using against me."

My therapist and I went over this in treatment. She called it "Dealing with Immediates." It is also known as being, "task oriented."

I became enamored with the grind of life. I became preoccupied with rebuilding my life, which is a good thing, but balance is so very important, and I had no concept of balance at the time. Part of the trauma brain is all, or nothing thinking, black and white thinking, handle tasks, stay busy.

"Our addictions always resurfaced or continued to progress, taking on many different forms, until, in desperation we sought help."

It's true. I had essentially relapsed on work, on chasing the American Dream, on building credit. I know that may sound crazy, but think about this, isn't addiction all about escape? It is, and I was losing myself in my work, I was losing myself in the "task, task, task," and didn't even know it. I was not losing myself to escape my current life at the time, my life was going awesome! I was immersing myself in work, I was escaping into the tasks. I was dealing with the immediates to escape the unhealed parts of my past, unknowingly to me. Subconsciously, I was right back into the patterns of "losing self." Even though we were succeeding, doing all kinds of good things, and helping a lot of people, all of those "right now tasks," or "immediates" took my focus off of what I should have been doing all along, which was healing.

There I was: a workaholic, under immense amounts of pressure, mostly self-inflicted. My fear driven and unhealed mind was escaping from my untreated traumas the way it always had—by losing myself in something. Only this time not chemicals, but work and dealing with the immediate tasks that life brought about, AND receiving all kinds of accolades, acknowledgements, and adulation for my efforts, which reinforced that I was on the right track. And here came the ego. The mind is truly the most fascinating place in the entire known universe to me.

The ego can be a defense mechanism for so many of us, especially those of us with troubled pasts, and low self-esteem. It certainly is for me. It seems like the lower my self-esteem, the bigger my ego. It also seems like the tougher the circumstances, the more difficult things become around me, and inside my head. My ego tries to shield me from harm. My mental health was declining. I was stressed out all the time. I was fear based in my thoughts, I ruminated often. I was isolated, overwhelmed, and very much "in the weeds," as many of my restaurant people may relate. Life, on the outside of things, was full of accomplished goals and outward successes. My ego continued to inflate with every pat on the back. With every new upcoming obligation, bills that were due, birthdays on the horizon, and all of the stuff that life brought to our door, my sense of self and mental well-being continued to deflate. My mental health was in rapid decline, but the circumstances of my life, of our life, were in rapid incline. How in the hell does that work? It was so confusing and overwhelming for me.

* * *

You see, I didn't go about my days thinking about my past life and all of my past traumas. I had spent decades learning how not to think about that stuff, but it lives inside of us. It is a noun. A thing. My brain, mind, spirit, and heart were wired and tattooed with it. It touched and affected everything I did. What we resist, persists, and it was all still festering inside my mind, because I had never actually and fully confronted it. I was unintentionally and unknowingly still relying on my broken and traumatized mind to handle my new life and all of the shit it was bringing my way. I was still utilizing the same mind, the same tools, and mechanisms I once did—the ones I used that turned me into a heroin addict. Stuff it down, brush it aside, work-work-work, ruminate, white knuckle it, lose myself in dealing with tasks, instant gratification, ego, external validation, etc. I thought I was recovered.

Why was I still feeling like this? Why was I still detaching? Am I back in the space shuttle, or am I still in the space shuttle? I began slipping away.

* * *

As the credit scores went up, my mental health went down. Ego did its best to protect me, but my self-worth and esteem declined. I was falling back into my default mechanisms. My trauma brain, my addict brain was taking the controls again.

People didn't even know, or notice until much later, because I was performing life so well. For all intents and purposes, I was killing the game, but I was dying inside my mind. I was totally blown and overwhelmed now. Totally robotic, autopilot.

I was supposed to be this awesome success story. How is this happening?

So, I stuffed it down, swallowed the pain, and trudged on. I compartmentalized. I disassociated. My ego grew, and my self-esteem shrank.

> *Poor me.*
> *Poor me.*
> *Matter of fact, pour me up one of those.*
> *Everything my life and recovery had blessed me with, had been used against me.*
> *"Recovery gives us a life that takes us away from recovery."*
> *Pour me another one.*

ISM

ISM: noun; **ISMS**: plural noun:
A distinctive practice, system, or philosophy, typically a political ideology or an artistic movement.
"He loathed isms and any form of dogma."
Forming nouns denoting a pathological condition.
"alcoholism"
ISM: **I**. **S**elf. **M**e.

I t was 100% consequence free and seemed to be okay, pouring myself up that first IPA beer. I mean, I had been clean and chemical free for many years. I had never had any kind of real issues with alcohol, other than what I had outlined before in my first book, *Junkbox Diaries,* in that it had always led me to other drugs. For some reason, in that moment, I knew it wasn't going to lead to other stuff this time. In fact, then and now, you couldn't pay me to put crack or heroin into my body. It had been completely taken off the table.

Plus, it was strange. I would do seminars and conferences with social workers, therapists, addiction counselors, etc. and afterward, a vast majority would go out for drinks. So certainly, as long as I could limit it to just beer and not allow it to lead elsewhere, I would be fine, and I was.

Many, if not all of my family, friends, colleagues enjoyed cocktails on the back deck, or drinks on the golf course. All were well to do, professional family-oriented types. This was fine. I mean, after all, we are the company we keep right? So, a few beers with a buddy from church on the golf course, or with my family, or with my wife on the back deck was no big deal, and it wasn't.

Time marched on. The business was growing, the family life

was good. Birthdays, holidays, milestones, credit scores grew. Bank accounts were healthy, relationships were solid. We were on our way to living the American Dream. The pursuit of happiness.

In spite of all of this, the pressure didn't come off. The stress didn't leave. The fear and rumination remained. I had recently reintroduced a liquid solution, alcohol, into my body, which many of you know, raises a person's baseline anxiety. So, the aftereffects of having some beers were horrible and lasting. My fears, worry, and stress were pretty much now full blown anxiety.

As a person with addiction issues in the past, and what I now know to be diagnosed mental health issues of PTSD and Borderline Personality Disorder as a result of the PTSD, this was not good. The slow burn had begun.

Initially, it was still all good, but the formula was there: Previous mental health and addiction issue. High stress professional life and pressure to perform. Declining mental wellness, and increasing social acceptance, notoriety and ego, plus drinking. This was a very dangerous and potentially volatile formula compounding inside my mind and body. Even though I wasn't drinking to excess, or too frequently, it had opened the door to once again using a chemical to cope. "To take the edge off," and that's one of the many things at the core of addiction. Escape. But nothing was or seemed problematic, so it was still all good.

* * *

We had both made a commitment to one another that we were going to be working towards buying our first house. We were both so excited and ready for the next step and so were the kids! This was a big deal! We were living the dream.

We got married in October, and my family from Georgia all came up to attend. My big brother Josh was my best man of course, and it was the happiest day of my life up until that point. Judge Mary Harper, the same judge who had sentenced me to prison many years ago and made sure to include, "Mr. Stepherson, if you are ever in front of me again, I am going to max you out" when she did so married Tiffany and me. How funny, she, the judge, wasn't wrong because the next time I was in front of her, she was "sentencing" me to a wonderful life through sickness and health with my best friend, my now wife Tiffany. My how things can change. I am a very lucky man and felt so very much that way on that day in October. We had so many of our loved ones all together, celebrating our love with us. The sky was the most brilliant of purples and oranges overlooking Lake Louise. We had a band, amazing food, a beautiful wedding cake, and we were the center of the world for one day.

* * *

From there, we just continued on with our goals. We sacrificed in many great ways, pinching pennies and saving money. We prioritized working on our credit scores and monitoring our bank ledgers. We were focused. I was incredibly stressed out through the whole process. I have been incredibly stressed out for about thirty-seven years, looking back. Pretty much the entirety of my life has been spent on edge, according to my therapists. Such is life experiencing trauma and living with its aftermath I am told. At the time all of this was happening, I just thought it to be a normal part of life. So onward we climbed.

I had already "broken the ice" or "broken the barrier" so to speak with drinking beer, IPAs specifically. It hadn't caused any problems and was widely accepted by those around me, so it wasn't made to be any kind of big deal. Plus, I was this author, intervention company owner, policy writer, and expert on the subject matter. So, I gotta guess that everyone around me assumed that I knew what I was doing and what was good for me. Every time I cracked one, or poured one up, and "got away with it," it inflated my ego, and reinforced my behaviors.

As my dad once put it, "They (the world, cops, society, my family, whoever your 'they' is) can afford for you to get away with it 1,000 times, but we cannot afford to get caught or fuck it up once."

From a spiritual aspect of things, the devil, the negative forces of the universe, they want you to get away with it many times at first—that's how we take their bait. We get comfortable in the getting away with it, and then they "set the hook," if that's what you believe.

Anyways my feedback loop was becoming more and more polluted and corrupted. We were doing so well socially and professionally, so no one batted an eye. Social acceptability does not equal recovery, and neither does professional outward success.

ISM, Its Still Me. I am still what I was before all of this. That hadn't changed. Time marched on.

One thing that I can see now, as I look back on the way things all progressed, is that from the time I began to enjoy my first adult beverages again, two things happened: 1)—I reopened those pathways in my brain and mind that are wired toward coping with a chemical. And 2)—I was immediately convicted. I was immediately filled with shame, although quietly.

At first it was as if my conscience was telling me, "You know you can't go around recovery anymore, you fraudulent piece of shit."

So I didn't. How could I, and why should I?

Everything in my life was going so exceptionally well. My life wasn't unmanageable, and I wasn't powerless over anything. If anything, I was more in control of my own life than I had ever been. And just like that, in those exact types of thoughts, I had completely disqualified and compared myself out of the recovery community. My oh my, the power of our thoughts.

In that moment, in that train of thought, I had begun separating myself from my support systems, and now, I had to go back into the isolation and secrecy of my new hobby, drinking.

* * *

Everything was still all good, I had no reason to worry. It's not like shit was blowing up around me. My ego was alive and well. I had this shit totally under control. I was the master of my own destiny.

We were about to buy a house. We had just gotten married, life was good, the kids were good, and we were kicking ass.

My shame grew, as my isolation from my people grew, as a result of trying to stay low key about my lifestyle. My self-esteem and self-worth shrank and shrank. With low self-esteem and low self-worth, come low standards of living. This was about to be really bad, and I had *no* fucking idea.

It wouldn't be too terribly long, and I would be writing suicide letters at the kitchen table and in the basement of our dream home. The very one we had worked so very hard to achieve. I had begun the process of losing my mind. I had begun the process of a full-blown alcoholic relapse, mental breakdown, and was heading toward my total bottom. It was with alcohol, which is a slow and methodical burn. I had no idea what was happening. I had completely separated myself from the world that I needed to be in, by drinking and with the shame and guilt that followed it.

My ego, pride, and status wouldn't allow me to look at it for what it was. I was so self-absorbed and self-centered. It was so easy to trick myself, compartmentalize, and escape. But what I learned recently was that I wasn't trying to escape my current life. I was still trying to escape my previous life, my trauma. Those unhealed parts of me from decades prior. They still lived in me. They don't just go away because I worked some steps, wrote a book, and found God. We can't shake our shadows, and we cannot change what has not been confronted. I was still very much at war with myself; it just looked different this go round. The more I continued to try and keep up with this kind of double standard in my life, the harder it became to hold it all together mentally. It wasn't long until it was no longer a double standard, but a double life. A split was occurring in my life, and in my mind. Each side of the split was battling for control of the show, vying for the stage and ability to call the shots. Shit was about to get real.

Inside all of us exist two wolves. Which one lives? The one you feed the most . . .

Living the dream.

With regularly occurring thoughts of suicide.

ISM.
I. Separate. **M**yself.

Rumination

Sound of alarm breaks through my sleep.

Instantly, and concurrently to my becoming conscious, negative thoughts begin to swirl.

"Fuck."

Turn alarm off.

Feet hit the floor. Deep breath in and out.

"Ugh. Okay let's go. Let's see what this day has in store for us."

Walk downstairs. Take a piss. Start the coffee. Smoke a Cig.

Finish first Cig. Grab a cup of coffee. Return to garage. Smoke another one.

Fear hits. Money worries. Work stress. Check Facebook. Nothing good.

Check bank accounts. Not broke, yet.

Check emails. Back to social media.

Nothing to provide immediate dopamine.

Smoke cig.

Walk inside. Sit down. Turn on the T.V. Watch the news.

It's all bad news. Murder. Rape. Carjackings. Bullshit Politics.

We're all gonna die. We're all fucked. This world is fucked.

Scroll on phone.

Scroll on phone.

Scroll on phone.

Nothing to provide immediate dopamine.

Check Crypto. Still not millionaires.

"Not that it would make me happy anyways."

Smoke a cig. Worry about work.

Worry about Money.

Stress about the hours that lie ahead.

Get the kids off to school.

"Phew. Thank God the kids are off to school."
Refill coffee. Stare at phone. no dopamine.
Negative thoughts invade.
Judge people on T.V.
Scroll on phone.
"I should go do something today."
"Shouldn't I be doing something productive today?"
"Nah there's nothing to do."
"My kids don't love me."
"My Wife doesn't Love me."
"Works gonna dry up."
"This life isn't sustainable."
"These dogs are annoying."
"Fuck those neighbors."
Numb. No thought. Then more thought.
Fuck this. I might as well clean the kitchen.
Fuck this place.
"We're so lucky and blessed."
Try to pray. Try to find gratitude.
Take the dogs out.
Judge what I think I know about my neighbor's lives.
What do they think about us?
They probably hate me, I should go inside.
Shut the drapes.
Stare out the windows.
Pace the floors.
Switch the laundry.
Dryer finishes. Fuck folding it. Restart the Dryer.
Stare at phone.
play a game on my phone.
Think about sending an email.
But no one wants to hear from me anyways.
"Why doesn't anyone call me anymore?"
"They must not want to hear from me. They probably don't love me."
"I should call them. Nah, fuck that."
"I will tomorrow."
"I'm really excited about (This thing coming up)"
The things comes up.
"How can I get out of this?"

God I just wish there was something I could do.
(Finds something to do)
Instantly dreads doing anything.
We need groceries.
Bills need paid.
Car needs gas.
Reba needs her medicine.
Kids need lunch money.
Sports. School clothes. Homework. Football. Vacations.
All things I want.
All things I dread and can't handle.
Smoke a cig in the garage.
Thousand mile stare off into the woods across the street.
Smoke another Cig.
Stare at phone.
Recline on couch.
"I'm Coffeed out."
Switch to water or Peach Tea.
Take Vitamins. Maybe this legal self-medication will help.
Check emails.
Look at phone.
Watch TV.
Intrusive negative thoughts.
Everything is falling apart.
No one wants me anymore.
I'm just a gimmick.
"Why do I feel and think like this."
"God, please remove these thoughts from me."
The thoughts remain.
I take out the trash.
"These kids are fucking lazy."
Take the dogs out. Stare at the grass.
It's getting cold.
This winter is gonna suck.
I hate living here in the cold months.
If only there was somewhere I could go.
Intrusive thoughts.
"Maybe I should kill myself"
Dude. Don't be crazy. This will pass.

"They're better off without me."
"No one needs me"
"Fuck this life shit."
"it's a trap."
Check bank account. '
"I just know I'm failing."
"My wife doesn't want me. My Kids don't love me."
It will all fall apart soon.
I bet our neighbors have better lives.
This is all too much.
I feel invisible.
People only want FROM me.
People are fucked up.
I hate a lot of people.
I have no where to go.
I don't want to go anywhere anyways.
I should probably take something for this.
I don't wanna take any meds.
They wouldn't help anyways.
I should probably delete all this.
No one will read it anyways.
It's all just stupid psychobabble anyways.
I'm not even a real author.
No one cares what I have to say.
It doesn't help anyone.
Yes it does.
Of course it does.
Take a break. Smoke a Cig.
No one is home in my neighborhood.
They're all out living their exciting and productive lives.
And I'm stuck here in my head again.
For the 17th month in a row.
I'm gonna go for a drive, to clear my head.
(Goes for drive) Head does not clear.
I knew it was pointless anyways.
Nothings ever gonna change.
What's the point anyways.
I feel like shit. Not physically, but mentally, which makes it physical.
I have no energy.

I feel so blah.
I should get back into the gym.
I should go for a walk.
I should go play golf.
Why can't I laugh?
Why can't I feel anything?
Why can't I stop thinking?
Tomorrow will be a better day.
I can't wait to go to sleep tonight.
Smoke a cig.
Eat some food.
Smoke a cig.
Scroll on my phone.
Compare my life to everything I see on my screen.
Judge my insides but what I see on TV.
Judge the world.
Feel nothing.
Check my bank accounts.
I know Ill be broke and homeless soon.
Do the dishes, listen to music.
Ahhhhh, the music. The music shuts it off.
Dishes are done. Time to turn the music off.
Take a shower.
Pray in the shower.
Try to cry.
Can't.
Just feel the heat on my skin.
Stare at the white walls of the shower.
Transcend to years ago. Years from now.
Why can't I just be here, now?
Because I'm a fuck up. Because I worry.
Dry off.
Dress.
Smoke a Cig.
No one really loves me. They just wanna use me.
Stare at my phone.
No dopamine.
Just. Stop. Thinking. Please.
I can't.

Stare off into space.
Pet my dogs.
Smoke a cig.
Walk around my house.
judging everyone by what I see in their absence.
All I hear is the TV.
There is no one here.
Think.
Smoke.
Think.
Pace the floor.
Look outside.
Fuck this neighborhood.
Smoke a cig.
Judge the world.
judge myself.
Think
think
think
Kids are home.
fuck
More stress.
snacks.
snacks.
snacks.
Is that all these kids do is eat and cost money?
The same Hulu Commercial drones over and over.
This shits crazy.
Like a Requiem for a Dream loop or Montage.
It's always the same.
Something stimulate me please.
Coffee?
didn't work.
Smoke a Cig.
I hate Cigs.
I'm gonna quit.
This is my last one.
Smoke another one.
"When's Dinner?"

Is that all these kids do is eat and cost money?
Kids don't appreciate shit.
They don't appreciate me.
They don't love me.
My wife doesn't actually love me.
She doesnt want me.
I feel invisible.
I just exist.
My phone rings.
Thank God, works picking up
Simultaneously
Fuck this.
I don't have the energy for this.
Works up the energy to answer
"We've been calling about your cars warranty."
Ugh.
Hangs up.
"Works never gonna pick up."
Fuck this.
I'm Bored.
Nothing interests me.
If I just vanished, would anyone notice?
Of course they would. Idiot.
Quit thinking like this.
Continues thinking like this.
I know it's all gonna fall apart soon.
They don't really love me.
They just need me.
Smoke a cig.
Fuck this homework shit.
"Do you have home work, buddy?"
"NO"
Thank God.
Stares at phone.
I wish I had chances to bond with my kids more.
(Chance comes)
I don't wanna do that.
Stare at TV.
Watch a game.

Stare at phones.
Eat dinner.
Smoke a cig.
Smoke a cig.
Smoke a cig.
Stare at phone.
I can't wait for bed.
I'm so tired.
I feel like I'm fighting off a cold.
Take dogs out.
Crate the dogs for the night.
Undress.
Lay in bed
Stare at TV.
Roll over.
Tomorrow will be better.
"Maybe"
Lay there thinking.
Fall asleep.

Repeat

My mental health was in rapid decline. The drinking was certainly not helping.

Turd Polish

"Look, if you had one shot, or one opportunity to seize everything you ever wanted—in one moment; would you capture it, or let it slip?" *Eminem, 8 Mile Soundtrack.*

What if you do capture it? What if you do take that moment and jump in with complete abandon, and rock it out of the park? What if you finally let go of everything that's ever held you back, take a massive leap of faith, and it works out better than you ever imagined?

* * *

All I can say is, be prepared. Everything that has ever held you back, whether its addiction or other mental health issues, traumas, family drama, etc. is going to be lying patiently in wait—for its perfect opportunity to strike—and trigger a downfall.

Success can do a couple things to us. It can motivate us to bigger and better things, or it can lull us into complacency. Sometimes, it can do both concurrently—at least the way I'm thinking about it right now that makes sense.

You see, ever since this whole thing started, it has all seemed like this magical, feel-good, fairy-tale type story. But I am here to tell you today, that that couldn't be any further from the truth. You just read, "Rumination," recently before this one, and that entry has been many days of my life over the last year plus.

I'm not exactly sure when it started, but things definitely got more than a little bit dark for me, and for my family. Maybe it was right around the time my brother died? No, it was for sure before that, and perhaps Josh's death was the pulling of the final Kerplunk sticks on the way to a very ugly bottoming out. I don't know. But what I have come to find out, again and again, is that I don't know shit. We don't know shit. Even the people who I consider my mentors will be the first to admit this very basic idea. But I am once again back on a journey of digging and discovering. Old story versus new story, and it has been a very interesting process.

You see, all I wanted to do was stop smoking crack, and stop shooting heroin.

I had some really powerful stories to tell to shed some light on this whole addiction thing, as I feel it still to this day, gets swept under the rug far too much.

I know what some of my gifts are. One of those gifts and passions is helping people. I still to this day absolutely love what I do in the field of intervention and volunteerism here in my community. I don't see myself stopping any time soon, but I have had to slow down quite a bit recently. Per the status quo, we can slip back so easily and effortlessly into shit.

Ya know, it's really interesting, this whole life thing. It can only be lived forward, and only truly understood backward. Looking back on the last six years of my life, and more poignantly, my successes and good fortune as an outsider and follower of my work, one might think it has just been so beautiful. There have been many beautiful moments and wonderful times, but one thing I have been learning lately is not to use "absolutes" as much as I once did. Everything is circumstantial. Not everything is good, bad, great, or horrible. Sometimes they just are what they are—and I'm reminded of Pong the Farmer as I write this.

But going back to the larger scope of thought here, understanding things backwards. It's actually a bit funny now that I laugh about this, but I used to always say, "You write one book, and people think you know what you're talking about." It's true, because, as I mentioned earlier, I don't know shit. I have never claimed to be some holier than thou, wizard, mystic, or overnight know-it-all in the field of addiction and mental health.

I share my experiences, I share my heart for helping others, and I do my best to be a good listener to those who share themselves with me. I have never claimed to be perfect. In fact, I believe that my claims of how "un perfect" I really am, have provided quite a bit of allure to so many of my readers who too, are in my shoes and like to hear from those of us who can share openly about our imperfections while all those normies and society types are going about their days like their shit don't stink.

We are all fucked up in some way. We are all hurt and wounded and trying our best to overcome something right now. Knowing that, and even more so, being able to practice that simple art form of compassion and empathy is such a powerful tool in this world, and yet it has become almost a "lost art," while we are all so consumed with self and comparing ourselves to others.

When we really listen, when we really take the time to get to know someone else, and the struggles and secret places that we all face—that's the juice. That is the one thing that truly binds us together. Our struggles. Internal and external. Some of our internal conflicts manifest themselves and spill out into the world for others to judge from their "ivory towers." Others stay buried deep inside, and no one really ever knows about them as we suffer in silence, isolating ourselves in a room full of people with a brave face on by hiding our shame and fear. I'm not exactly sure which is worse. Sometimes the latter turns into the former, when we can no longer hold it in. When we can longer pretend that we are okay. When we can no longer withstand the mounting pressures behind the damn with no means of releasing the impending explosion . . . and . . . Kaboom!

* * *

I just wanted to stop smoking crack. I just wanted to not shoot heroin. I just wanted to help people have a regular, normal life and do my best to be a good person. I had absolutely no idea where this whole thing was gonna take me. I had absolutely no idea what God was up to, or what He would have in store for me. I had no idea what I would have to endure in return for all of this; after all, every gift has its price.

As the old adage goes, "No good deed goes unpunished." (I know my therapist is going to read all this shit and want to do a whole session on it, but this is the way I'm thinking about things right now).

I didn't know that writing some book was gonna turn into all this. I didn't know that I would end up owning a successful business. I didn't know that I would be a million things or go to a million places when I got out of jail. I was just-and still am—trying to figure shit out.

Everything was so sudden. It was like a whirlwind for me. I always thought about "vigilance" as we hear it in the rooms, to typically mean looking out for danger in times of trouble, or when things are obviously getting bleak. I never in a million years thought that I had to be vigilant when things were continuously going so well. But what I'm thinking about here now, is that I wasn't truly equipped or prepared for things to go so well.

Literally, I went from: Traumatized and passed around child, who learned to detach at a very young age to not continuously feel the shame and pain, to a homeless, overdosing strung out heroin addict street person, to incarcerated inmate, facing twenty plus years, to living in a halfway house, to author, to father, step father, and husband, homeowner and company owner—seemingly in the blink of an eye. Just writing that last few sentences put me back in the space shuttle, or transcendence in my mind. It doesn't seem real.

What's all the more critical, is that I was very much involved in church, and recovery fellowships for quite some time. While all of this was manifesting, and I was succeeding at seemingly everything I touched, I was horribly neglecting myself in an area that I still didn't know existed.

It's really hard to explain and write this out, but I suppose paraphrasing a meme I saw recently would best suit it: "We set out to treat addiction, and we end up treating PTSD, Trauma, Depression, etc."

That is me, in a nutshell. At the time, early in my walk, I thought that I had a drug problem. But what I know now is that I thought that I had found a drug *solution*. For me, and for me only, it didn't matter how many times I read the Bible, it didn't matter how many fourth and fifth steps I worked, or how many amends I made—I needed to achieve atonement with myself and with my past.

You see, I was the proverbial, "turd polish," for a while. What I mean by that, is, I guess it is similar to the old adage of, "casting pearls before swine."

No I am not the swine, I am not beating up on myself—but I was still so raw and needed to heal so badly, and so deeply. Yet all of these amazing things and amazing people kept coming my way. I thought that I was really doing the damn thing, and I was, but my deep internal wounds were still festering, and the new and present world was still coming at me in full force. I lost sight of what I was supposed to be doing.

Healing as hard as I could. I was healing, but I took on so many of what seemed to be blessings concurrently, that those very things my recovery and new life were blessing me with, ended up eating me alive.

I didn't even know how to open or manage a bank account six years ago, and now all of a sudden, I'm supposed to give a keynote speech in Idaho? I'm supposed to know how to truly raise a child? Four Children? I am supposed to know how to be in a healthy relationship? I am supposed to know about opening a business? Holy crap! Everything was so much, and it had been so much. Relationships, kids, dogs. Stress, depression, death, life. Work, writing. mortgage, moving. Marriage, vacations. In laws, friends, volunteering. Somewhere along the line, all of these serendipitous and wonderful things became not so wonderful in my mind.

Somewhere along the line, everything that I had worked so hard at for so long to obtain, became such tremendous stress and struggle inside my already hurt and needing to be healed mind.

I wasn't mentally healthy enough to obtain these things, let alone maintain them. To my family, I am so sorry that I wasn't able or ready to love you the way you needed me to when we first met. I am now, and always will be a work in progress.

Only through the intense therapy that I'm doing now, can I fully grasp the absolute sickening hells and traumas that my mind endured, and then built a space ship to escape in— first with playing with friends, then baseball, then acceptance, then drugs. Now I am slowly, day by day, learning to really sit with myself and my broken mind as it heals.

Practicing these simple but effective little tricks, to snap out of my crazed bullshit upstairs like rumination and thoughts of suicide. What a bunch of irrational chaos. I know, it may be hard to grasp or understand, like how can this dude be for real right now? His life is so shitty (and scoff at the wind). It's not, that's the thing about healing from trauma. About healing from such wreckage and destruction and addiction and woe.

We addicts, we survivors of trauma have endured some of the ugliest and most depraved of situations. The only thing that has kept us going on at times, at least for me, is this inherent, built in thing called resiliency. The sad part about it all is, while we are still in the process of healing our wounds, we are gonna bleed on those who didn't cut us.

New Normal

We closed on our house, our dream home in March of 2020. The year of the COVID-19 pandemic. I am sure many of you remember, but this was right at the beginning of it all. Toilet paper was a major commodity, as was Lysol. Things were becoming more and more tense throughout the world, and businesses were shutting down left and right.

Our title company was no exception. We did the first ever, "Roadside closing" in the company's history. My wife and I in our vehicle, as the buyers, and the couple who sold us the home in their car a few parking places down from us. Downtown Valparaiso was a ghost town. Most places were, I am sure. The four of us, in two separate cars, joined by a conference call on our cells, thumbed through paperwork signing on the dotted lines as we came across them.

Our hard work was paying off. We were at the moment we had been waiting for so long. I had been holding on mentally by threads for quite some time. Stressed to the max, spread incredibly thin, mental health in rapid decline, sustaining myself and my unhealed and overwhelmed mind with IPAs every chance I got. Today was supposed to be a day of great celebration and joy—and it was. But the fear had long since settled into my mind, and my fear-based ruminating mind was here to stay.

It was hard enough before on Kinsey Street, to keep my shit together. Now, we were going to be moving into a home that was going to cost quite a bit more monthly. Yes, it was indeed our dream home, and still is, but for a couple thirty somethings who, not long ago didn't even have furniture to move into the first house, it was pretty overwhelming. For me at least. I had a hard time seeing the blessings and opportunities at this time with the head space I was in.

"Babe, everything is going to be fine. God didn't bring us this far, to only bring us this far," she would tell me.

"I know." Sounds good. It was such a majorly overwhelming flood of mixed emotions.

We finished up the curbside closing and got the keys.

Great, now we have to actually move everything into this house. Let me tell you something: you want to know who your real friends are? Ask some people to help you move. Oh yeah, and we were in the midst of an ongoing global pandemic.

Everyone was pretty much in the, "We're all gonna die" mindset at this point. That alone provided every single person we asked to help with an excuse as to why they couldn't.

"Uh, gee, yeah, we would love to come help y'all move, but, ya know, Covid. Anyway, take care and stay safe during these uncertain times, congrats on the house!"

I swear if I never hear a commercial talking about "these uncertain times" again, it will be too soon. My God how I hated that phrase. Anyway, I guess you could say we were on our own.

My wife and I, Jamie, and Connor. That was our manpower. Oh, and I had never driven a U-Haul before, so this should be fun. Somehow, I was able to maneuver the twenty-seven-foot behemoth and get it backed up to the Kinsey house. Let the moving commence. We busted our asses all day long. Box, after box. Couch, after bed, after table.

What once was an overgrown and non-livable house, now was a home that we had cherished for years —and were saying goodbye to it. We were leveling up. We were moving on to bigger and brighter things, during quite possibly the most dicey season in current world history.

How fitting. New level, new devil. Or so they say, and they are almost always right.

Well, I didn't kill anybody driving the U-Haul, so that was good. We somehow managed to move the entire house in just two trips. My back was very happy when we placed the last of the second truck load into the garage.

I couldn't believe this honestly. It was all so surreal. I was once a homeless strung-out heroin addicted street person. Now I was moved into an absolutely beautiful subdivision home in Valparaiso. I remember when I used to cut grass to get by, for eight dollars an hour. I used to be so resentful and bitter when we would visit homes and neighborhoods like the one we just moved into.

"These fucking perfect people with their great lives and wonderful jobs and childhoods. I fucking hate cutting grass for homes I'll never be able to afford."

But I had hope and something told me that if I just held on long enough, that my day would come, and here it was. I was so happy and proud. I was tired, and sore, anxious, overwhelmed, and worried. It was quite possibly the most blended emotionally that I had ever been in my life. I was still slowly losing my mind. I was still untreated, hurt, and traumatized deep down inside. It's kind of like, once the fear and rumination had begun awhile back, my mind was kind of like a giant hourglass. The sand was running every second of every day. Luckily for me, I had some cold beers to take the edge off. What a fucking wonderful idea Herb . . .

* * *

I don't exactly remember for the sake of the timeline, when the excessive drinking started. At this point, nothing had really been anything too worrisome, save for a couple nights getting a little mouthy. We just chalked it up to stress, or to being in a bad mood. Everyone has a rough go, a negative experience drinking once in a while. It was pretty much right about parallel with that. Nothing crazy.

I can look back on things now and notice that there was a very concerning connection with the decline of my mental health. The amount and frequency of my drinking, and my overall presence and likability. I had already been in a pretty consistent mental decline, and this whole new stress, plus COVID-19, was not helping. It was really hard for me to enjoy anything. It was really difficult for me to explain to anyone when I tried. I had such an amazing and wonderful life, wife, family, and home, but for some reason, I just couldn't seem to enjoy much of anything. I had been to counselors; I had tried medication. Nothing seemed to help. One of the doctors I saw diagnosed me as Bipolar and put me on Lamictal. That shit sucked. It instantly and consistently turned me into a zombie. I knew I wasn't bipolar.

What's really interesting to me, is that I wasn't always like this. I mean, when I was in drug court, the counselor I was seeing thought

I had dysthymia, or "the blues," for many of the same reasons I was complaining about now.

I believe that there is a direct link between stress, overthinking, worry, and poor mental health. I may have very well stressed, worried, and overthought myself into a depression. It sure seemed like it at the time. It was unhealed trauma. It was borderline personality disorder. It has always been the trauma. I know now it was PTSD.

Chronic and intense distress are the absolute last things that someone with PTSD needs to experience on a regular basis. Once my stress meter and distress compartments reached maximum levels, my mental health began to decline. The more I piled onto myself, the more stress I felt, the worse I became, and the more I drank. Which in turn, raised my anxiety baseline, which drove me to drink more and more. This was not good. The more stress and distress my mind endured, the more anxiety and depression I experienced, the more alcohol I consumed . . . and the closer and closer I got to a full blown "split."

Both wolves were being given food, but only one was getting fed.

We got settled into our new home really nicely. It was a dream come true. I remember how excited and proud everyone was that we had "made it." Everyone had their own space. The house even had a hot tub out back, which we took advantage of right away! It was one of the best times in our lives. Sometimes throughout the days, we would almost forget that there was a virus on the loose that was killing hundreds of thousands of people all over the world. Not really, but we tried to. Here we were, freshly moved into our dream home, and essentially quarantined right off the bat. The world was on lockdown. Earth was closed. People were dying left and right all over the world. What was going to happen? My mind went to all of the worst possible scenarios, like always. This whole pandemic thing probably took some years off of my life. I had to appear strong and stoic for the family and be their protector, but I was losing my mind. Probably worse than most. Just my luck huh, finally turn my life around, make something of myself, get married and start a family, found a company, purchase a home, and then the world fucking ends. A'int that a bitch.

* * *

Spring was turning into summer, and there was no relief in sight. There was no relief in my mind. There was no relief on the news. We own a small business whose whole mode of functionality is to meet with families, in large groups and in their homes to execute interventions. That certainly was not happening any time soon. Tiffany's work had shut down, but sometimes she could work a little bit at a time from home.

How would we pay our bills? Were we going to lose the home? How in the world could our timing be so truly bad? How was this all happening now?

More stress, more fear, more worry, more drinking.

We did our best to protect ourselves We ordered food from the food delivery services when we could, and we sprayed Lysol on everything that came into our house. There was nothing I could do however, to protect my unraveling mind. Nothing I seemed to do helped. Everything was shut down except for essential places like gas stations, grocers, and liquor stores. We had basically no money coming in and the bills were not stopping. People were not able to perform their jobs, but yet, the companies that called the shots did not cease sending bills.

"Oh we're in a global pandemic? Fuck you, pay me." God bless America.

The stress that was building inside my already fragile mind was enough to weigh an elephant down. I continued to stuff it down. I continued to gut it out as best as I could. White knuckles on the daily, I did my best to put on a normal face and carry on. I had already been carrying around old dusty boxes of compartmentalized pains, traumas, and memories for many years. I was running out of room inside my mind, and my spirit was dimming. My fire was slowly burning out—and so was I. The only thing that seemed to help was drinking. But the more I drank, the more it negatively affected me, and my family. I was spiraling, but I was doing my best to hold it together. People needed me.

Finally, some relief came in the form of the stimulus checks, and some unemployment for the self-employed, like myself. That helped ease some of the worries, but the neurological damage had already been done. I was back in emotional dysregulation. I had full blown distress intolerance. All of this had piled up and been accelerated by drinking to where I had reverted right back into my trauma brain.

It felt like I was two people. I was fully double-minded. This was dangerous as shit. Half of me was the husband, family man, homeowner, helper, lover, giver, good person. The other half of me was the man I thought I had left behind. I was angry. I was drunk. I was distant and depressed. I was edgy. I was unapproachable, I was a loose cannon. I had fully split by now. Who you got on any given day was literally a coin toss. Jekyll and Hyde had returned.

This time, I had become so volatile that my mood literally flip-flopped back and forth with little or no provocation at any given moment. Most of the time, I was out of my body. I was either back in the space shuttle, or still in the space shuttle. I was disassociating again. My wife said she could see it in my eyes when I split. I usually have blue eyes, but when I would split, they would go black. It's fucking scary, I know.

This is mental health. This is what trauma, PTSD, borderline personality disorder, addiction, and alcoholism does. It's not a fucking joke. My mind was gone.

Things seemed to somewhat level out in our space I guess. I mean, we were able to pay the bills and what not, so that was good. But we were still very much sequestered, as were millions around the world. We did our best to protect ourselves from the virus, but in spite of our best efforts, the kids still got it. This was our first brush with the virus, but not our last. It was scary. We made their meals and set them outside the bedroom doors while they quarantined in their bedrooms. We freaked out, we prayed, we worried. I drank. It seemed to be the way that so many people in the world, and in our neighborhood, handled the stress. Day drinking, night drinking, weekends, all the time. I was slipping further and further away. A bad night would happen where I was a flaming asshole, and then I would dial it back in for a while, and then again. The more I stressed, the more I drank. The more I had progressively worse anxiety, the more I drank—and the more I got ugly. It felt as though I had completely split and was watching the whole thing happen in front of me. I was in full blown "distress induced clinical impairment and cognitive distortion." I didn't even know what that meant at the time. This is a term that I wouldn't learn until later.

* * *

The summer came to an end, and the world did its best to get as close to normal as it could. Or the "new normal," another phrase I hate to this day. Virtual learning was the new thing, and work was non-existent. We hung on and hung on. I drank more and more. I was still able to maintain somehow for the most part. We were still progressing as best we could. My wife and I have always had such an amazing partnership and team mindset. She has been the eighty and I the twenty, for a vast majority of the last several years. I simply wouldn't have made it through all of this without her. Especially with what lie ahead.

* * *

School had resumed virtually, and life on earth was adapting. It was nearing the end of the summer season, August was upon us. We made do like many families did. We stuck to ourselves and enjoyed as much outside time and fresh air as we could. We had been wrapping up a very status quo day in our home when my phone rang. It was my older brother, Josh. I always loved talking with him on the phone, he always brightened my day.

"Whattttttt Upppppp boyyyyy? Whatchu doin man?"

He always began each and every phone call he made to me, and the small talk began. We talked about all the regular old stuff, all the, "how's life, how's the wife" stuff men talk about. Nothing out of the ordinary at all. Then Josh proceeded to tell me that he had been having diarrhea for several days now, which again, was nothing really out of the ordinary. Men talking about their poops that is. I never thought anything of it, and neither did he. I believe he attributed it to something he had eaten recently, and that was that. We finished up our small talk and said our, "I love you" and hung up the phone. Life went back to life.

The next week, I believe on a Monday, Josh called me again. His work had mandated that everyone in the company take COVID-19 tests. Josh was an essential worker, as he worked for the City of Peachtree. He had to be in the office because they were the ones who kept the city running. He tested positive and was sent home until he got better. When he told me this, I was utterly shaken to my core. It was one of those moments when you can feel the world stop spinning, mouth runs dry, blood runs cold type moments. I did my best to sound encouraging, and so did he. He indicated to me that he was symptom free, and other than the recent stomach issues, felt top shape. He assured me I had nothing to worry about. I believed him. I checked in on him every day and spoke with his wife as often. He was holding strong. No fevers, no cough, no issues.

His wife was nurse and had been on the front lines of this thing the whole time. She knew what she was doing, what she was looking for, and how to handle it. He was in the best and most equipped and capable hands, and those hands loved him very much, so he was double covered. She took care of him. She got him all kinds of vitamins and fluids and all the preventative measures were taken. She even had a pulse oximeter to check his vitals and oxygen. All was well, he was managing nicely. I did my best to be there for him, encouraging him and assuring him that he was gonna be fine, and he did the same for me. I was losing my mind over this, but I couldn't let him hear it in my voice. Everything was going to be fine.

About four days into it, four days after Josh testing positive, my phone rang. It was Josh's cell. He was calling to check in. It was not Josh. It was his wife. My sister-in-law, calling me to tell me that Josh's oxygen had plummeted and he was spiking fevers. He was being taken to a local hospital by ambulance to be admitted and cared for. I had no words. I had never been so scared, shocked, and paralyzed in my life up until this point. Once he got to the hospital, Josh got his phone back and assured me that this was all just precautionary.

"Shit I feel fine, Stevie. I'm good man. I don't even feel sick. Don't worry about me dude, I'm good man. I love you buddy. I talk to you soon."

He sent me a picture of himself in the hospital, with one of those oxygen hoses in his nose, duck lips out, showing the peace sign with his fingers. It was the last time we ever spoke. He was gone less than forty-eight hours later.

My big brother, my protector, my male figure. He and Carol drove from Georgia multiple times when I was in jail after being terminated from drug court, just to be at my court dates and visit me in jail. He was always my protector and best friend. He was everything to me since the day I was born. This simply could not be. My big brother. Was gone. He had lost his battle with COVID-19. A piece of me died right along with him, and my life has never been the same.

He died on August 29, 2020. My mother died on August 27, 2014. This was absolutely unreal. Why is life like this? We had so many plans and dreams. He had so much life to live, and he was snatched away from us. My mind and heart will never be the same. My, and so many others' new normal, was now to be somehow living life without the most wonderful man to walk this earth. His wife told me when he died that it was an honor to be loved by him. I know because it was an honor to be his little brother. We loved each other so much. It still doesn't seem real. More trauma, more sorrow, more woe. My heart and mind simply couldn't process this. I was in shock.

It wouldn't be long that I would once again be bottoming out. I simply could not take any more. I felt like my own life was ending. I did not handle this well at all. More and more excessive drinking, deeper and deeper into depression I dove, more splitting. I was searching for blotto and oblivion. And I was about to find it.

Invisible

To feel seen, heard, and acknowledged by the most important people in our lives is one of the most important needs and feelings in a human being's life.

Throughout my mental decline, increased drinking, downfall, and the further I dove into depression, I constantly referred to myself as, "Mr. Invisible." I am not exactly sure where this idea came from to begin with, but it was a feeling that I had a lot. Sitting here now, I think the root of it began in my childhood. I think it stemmed from the fact that I always felt so voiceless, and "in the way." I also think that it came from the fact that I had never really bonded with anyone on a deep level. I badly lacked any form of deep human or emotional connection. From the time I was old enough to comprehend most things, until recently in my life, I felt very much alone. Lonely, even in a room full of people.

I think that the way the human mind responds to things is really fascinating. When I first began this journey of mine, and my first book dropped, things were taking off for me, and I felt really acknowledged for the first time in my life. People were reaching out to congratulate me, ask me questions, and pick my brain. I felt like I mattered, I felt seen. This would actually be one of the first tumbling blocks in my mental decline. Looking back, what once was an unheard and unseen little boy, was now the same but in a grown man's body, garnering all sorts of attention and adulation. I had seemingly been shoved into the limelight. One lady at a book signing of mine told me I was, "the talk of the town." That felt really foreign and uncomfortable, because I had never really experienced the feeling of true visibility before. It was awkward, and I would just smile and say thank you.

The reason why this ultimately ended up becoming a negative force in my life, is that it left me with this need and desire for acknowledgement.

In my first book there is a chapter called, "Just say yes." It talks about how I would constantly say yes to new opportunities and new experiences that I would have previously declined. Although that was a great idea at the time, I had no comprehension of boundaries and certainly lacked the ability to enforce them; so the more I said yes for the sake of feeling needed, the emptier and emptier my "cup" grew. It wasn't long until I was basically dependent on that need to be needed for my own validation and fulfillment—and when I wasn't receiving it, it reinforced my "old story" self, that no one wanted me around.

It was kind of like this double-edged sword for me, especially once the company was up and running. I love what I do. I love helping people who struggle with addiction. I believe it is my life's work, my purpose. But I really lost my sense of true self in it all. If I wasn't working and helping, then I felt empty inside, like no one needed me, so I continued to push and push to fit myself into the front lines and stay visible. I pushed, chased, and fought tooth and nail to make this company and this new life a reality so hard and so often, that I completely neglected myself.

I became a martyr. This was my hill to die on. I did everything I could to "earn" people, my family included. I gave and gave and gave, and when I wasn't getting the feedback that I wanted or thought I should, I felt slighted. I felt invisible again. Expectations are a lot more dangerous than we give them credit for, and they can often lead to very dangerous and ugly resentments.

When I do not receive the feedback that I thought I deserved, the acknowledgement from friends, or family, it reinforced that no one actually loved or cared about me, but that people were only using me for their own gain. And though I do have much evidence to support the latter, especially professionally, it does not apply to all people. This was the way that my brain had been wired since childhood:

isolated incident + isolated incident = people and the world are bad.

I continued my quest for external validation. Even though my internal needs were growing and growing, and my own mental health required attention, there were suffering people out there who needed help and a family at home that needed me to provide for them. I could wait. I would deal with me later. As long as I took care of everyone else, I could manage. I was a full-blown people pleaser. Something that is very common with those of us who have PTSD. The feeling that I need to earn love and acceptance with my family and society. I mean, who could not understand that? I went from quite possibly the most chaotic childhood ever, to a decade plus strung out on heroin and living on the streets, where no one would care if I lived or died, to suddenly being this important success story. It was the first time in almost forty years that I actually felt like I mattered.

"For what shall it profit a man, if he shall gain the whole world, and lose his own soul?" Mark 8:36 (KJV)

I never really seemed to have any kind of authentic identity. I just kind of seemed to get along as best as I could. So, when I fell into this new world and felt like I finally had this opportunity to be someone, I went all in. I knew that I wouldn't have a chance like this again, and I sacrificed my own well-being in the process. I poured and poured from a cup that had long since been empty. The more I did this, the more my mental health declined; the more the resentments grew, the more invisible I felt. I felt taken advantage of by everyone; yet, I was the culprit all along. It was because I lacked boundaries, that I allowed myself to get eaten up like this. The more the stress grew, the less I was capable to practice boundaries, and the more I resorted to just numbing it away. One beer at a time.

The less I was able to practice boundaries, the more I felt used. The more I felt used, the more it reinforced my "old story" victim mentality. It was a very unhealthy lifestyle and feedback loop. If we live for people's acceptance, we will die by their rejection. Even the thought that I was being rejected . . . or that I was no longer needed . . . hurt me deeply. I was spiraling so badly in my head.

With all of the up and down craziness of 2020, the new home, COVID-19, Josh's death, and all of the drinking and poor mental health, I was fucked. I didn't stand a chance. I had already been hanging by a thread and losing my big brother was the final Kerplunk stick to be pulled. All the marbles came crashing down. It fully knocked me back into the old victim mentality.

It was so interesting and scary. The trauma of my entire life had now been fully reactivated. It was like I was living the entire nightmare and shittiness of my life all over again, all at once. I was once again the old story Herb. The broken, bitter victim. I was hurt all over again, and hurt people hurt people. I was very unpleasant to be around. I couldn't take another day inside my head. I was through even trying to be this success story. I had given it a solid run, but I was so exhausted and beaten down that I was ready to just finally check out. I was going to do it. I was gonna hang myself in the basement of our dream home. I had to write some letters to say my final goodbyes.

* * *

All I wanted was some relief. I don't know if it's delusional, or if it is part of this whole mental decline I was on, but I always felt like no one cared. I remember being on this hypervigilance trip where I was suspicious and paranoid about everyone. I couldn't trust a soul. I was losing my mind and growing more and more depressed by the day. In my own mind, I was already this hypocrite fraud. I had already crossed a line I shouldn't have when I started drinking, so that made me a piece of shit. I constantly felt invisible, in society, at home, with friends, and within myself. This depression I was under would not go away, and the only thing that helped was drinking and that was making it all worse. I was totally fucked. I had never in my life as an adult actually felt so lost, lonely, invisible, used, broken, afraid, and unwanted. The one person who had always been there for me my entire life no matter what had just died. Josh could always see me. He could always hear me. He always made me feel acknowledged, like I was special, and now he was gone, So what was the point?

I sat there in our dream home, day in and day out, doing my best to help people. Being a husband and father, cutting the grass, trying everything I could to make sure no one else would ever have to feel like I have my entire life—completely unhealed and completely relapsed in my mental health. I ended up causing all kinds of pain and grief, when all I wanted was to be a helper. That furthermore reinforced that I was no good. That no matter what I do or how hard I try, I was always gonna be a piece of shit, white trash, dope fiend, no good loser, that people should have written off long ago.

I started brainstorming how and when I was going to do it. I wrote out my goodbye letters to my family, and I began to muster up the courage to finally pull it off. I had decided that I was going to hang myself from the rafters in the basement ceiling with a couple of doubled up dog leashes.

I simply couldn't go on like this. I was so sick of hurting people.

No one would even miss me if I was gone.

I was invisible, right?

Subtleties

With my letters safely tucked away, now all I had to do was wait for the right time and the motivation to hit me enough to walk downstairs, drill a hole in the cross beam, install the large metal eye hook, double up the metal corded dog leashes, stand up on a five-gallon bucket, and do what needed to be done. I went about the next days of my life, ready at a moment's notice to do it—with a smile on my face for everyone I met. I saw people I knew at the gas station. I held open doors for those I crossed paths with. I greeted them all with positivity and good cheer. No one would have known if I hadn't told you what was going on inside my mind.

All I had to do, was wait for the time to be right—when the wife and kids would all be gone for a couple hours shopping or something, and I would have enough time to get this done.

I truly believe that God does for us what we cannot do for ourselves, because that moment didn't come, at least not in the time frame of my suicidal window, which was several days long. They never went anywhere for long enough, and they never all went together. At the time I was beyond frustrated. All I wanted was a few hours of time where I could just quietly check out without being disrupted, but it never came. I remember having mixed emotions about this. I was so mad that they wouldn't all leave and let this happen, but I was also relieved that they hadn't—and then I was pissed off again because now I knew I was gonna have to go on living still.

I was such a head case for a while. All I wanted to do was run, get better, or die. It wasn't really a whole big list of asks. I needed some relief. I was just too damn ego driven and prideful to just open my mouth and say, "I need some help here. Please help me." I think

I said everything on the planet but those words.

I was edgy, my moods switched from moment to moment it seemed. I was an asshole one day, and then the nicest guy in the world the next. I loved my wife so much, and then I wanted a divorce. I felt so blessed and grateful on Wednesday, and on Thursday, I wanted to sell the house or burn it down. My mind was a mess. I would spill guts in love and adoration to my family, and the next day say not one kind word. I couldn't seem to speak the words of defeat and surrender or accept the fact that I needed to. The more my mind spiraled out of control, the less in control I felt on the inside, and the more I fought for control on the outside. I didn't even have control over making enough alone time to take my own life and that made me feel really powerless and out of control. I was a festering ball of mental unwellness and the proverbial powder keg. My wife had no idea what to do with me.

What's weird, is that looking back on all of this, the writing was very much on the wall. The music I was listening to at that time was very sad sounding, with just overall negative messages about life. Sad country and bluegrass songs, rap songs about poor mental health, the movies and shows I watched were dark and ominous. My whole overall energy was just black, dark, and hostile. It's fascinating to me, how I was able to convince other people that I was okay. I certainly was not.

* * *

There wasn't any kind of an "A-ha" moment for me. There was no booming voice from the sky that appeared and convinced me not to follow through with taking my own life. There was just a long drawn out coming and going of little subtleties along the way. I would hear Connor emulate me, or ask for a meal that I showed him. Lucas would ask me to play catch with him, or Logan would volunteer to help me around the house. Tiffany would want to set some time aside for date night. My friend Doug would call just to talk. These little subtleties I noticed, and they kept me hanging on, one day at a time.

It's weird how when we are with our families, our coworkers, and friends so regularly, that things can become so hidden in plain sight. When we are around new people, or those without any types of attachment to us, things are more visible.

An old friend of mine and I were setting up a canopy and tent at a music festival one weekend. We had made a long journey by vehicle to see some of our favorite bands and drink too many margaritas. We brought everything that we would need for the weekend away, including my large speaker, on which my Spotify playlist was playing on repeat, as we set up our camp. It took about an hour and half to get everything the way we wanted it, and then we took a quick break to enjoy an IPA at our newly found home away from home.

Not long prior to this, we had met the neighbors. A group of about six dudes from Milwaukee, who had gotten there about the same time as we did. My old friend and I were sitting in our camping chairs when one of the guys from Milwaukee called me over to their site.

"Hey, Herb, right? Come here for a minute, would ya?" So I did. I like meeting new people and shooting the shit with people from different places than me.

"Hey dude, um (he motioned me to walk around the side of their tent so he could ask me something quietly, almost in secret), I heard you jammin over there man on your speaker. Some of that music man, um, I gotta ask you brother—are you okay man? Who hurt you?"

I was really taken back by this. I was also really impressed by this young man's ability to see something, say something, his empathy, and his compassion for a stranger. But of course, I had to take on a defensive type of a stance with him.

"Nah, you know man, just life brother. No big deal," or some shit is what I said.

But the moment stuck. It meant a lot to me. It also caused me to feel even more resentment towards those people in my life who supposedly saw me every day, but yet never had any kind of mention for me like this stranger had. I suppose that that was because I had spent the last year staking major dividers in between my people and me to avoid vulnerabilities and had made myself quite unapproachable Which was what I had always done to protect myself from having to feel and allow people truly in.

Something else happened to me during this chance encounter, and another one later on—but we will get to the second one later. What happened here, was that it dawned on me that people could see me. Even a passing stranger at a concert could see and hear me for what I was—a soul in intense pain. He did so, in a matter of minutes, just by listening to the music I was listening to. The little subtle things.

Little subtle messages had been trying to work on me for a while now. The messages from my wife and kids, from my buddy Doug, but nothing was really having any kind of profound impact, because I wasn't quite ready to admit defeat. I still had some kind of semblance of control, and so I held on to that with white knuckles. The more I wrestled with control, and the more out of control I got, the more spiteful I became. The whole, "I'll show you, I'll kill me" mind set. I was very volatile and ugly. I was condescending, paranoid, bitter, controlling, and it was all self-inflicted. The result is always nil until we let go absolutely.

What's interesting, is that looking back, I had subtleties of my own. I would get vulgar and snarling with people. I would get bitter and ugly. The actual words I said might have been something like, "I fucking hate you, leave me alone." What my soul was saying, what my insides were actually saying was, "Can't you see how hard I am hanging on here? Can't you feel how awful I feel on the inside?" But I just couldn't get the actual words out. My ego wouldn't let me.

I had survived the depths of hell on earth before, and I knew I was strong enough to survive this too. I was bound, set, and determined to tough it out and get through it. I would push people away and tell them I was fine, and then I would proceed to drink in the basement for days at a time and blare all kinds of sad and depressing music. I was spiteful, I was drowning in my own sorrows. All I wanted was some peace in my own mind, and I didn't know how to get it . . . because I was so god damn stubborn and so foolish as to not just surrender and open my mouth. I placed breadcrumbs of indecipherable riddles all around me indicating that I needed help, but when the topic came up, I would deny it all away. I was sick.

Pride does in fact come before the fall.

What I realized, once I had come out of my suicidal season, was that I didn't want to kill myself in whole. I wanted to kill parts of me. I wanted to kill those ugly secrets and shitty experiences, the trauma. The being molested, mistreated, being left alone, hurting all the time from its active and live presence inside my mind. That was what I wanted to kill. If I myself had to die as a result, then I would just have to be collateral damage in the process of snuffing the pain out. Since I was no longer willing to actually take my own life, I had to find a way to keep going and get through this.

One day, not long after the music festival talk with my friend from Milwaukee, I was sitting at home. I was still depressed, and I was still in the process of bottoming out and hurting people. But I decided to get up, grab those letters, grab a beer, and walk out to the back yard. I cracked the top of the beer, sat down in the camping chair, and used those letters to start myself a little bonfire. I was going to live. I was going to get through this one way or another. I knew deep down inside that there would be more suffering ahead, sure, but I was gonna live. I wasn't going to roll over and just let this thing beat me.

My wife walked outside onto the back deck, looked down at me, and was pissed that I was drinking again, and so early in the day. Which I understood, but what she didn't know at that time, was that I had just finally made the decision to not take my own life once and for all.

How could she have known?

I hadn't come out and told her. I just did my best to speak in subtleties. When we love people, oftentimes we miss those things, and oftentimes, those are the very things that keep us going, and keep us alive. Sometimes we pay attention to what people are saying, and sometimes we need to pay more attention to what people are not saying.

If you want to truly help someone, the most important thing you can do is listen to them.

Blotto

Even though I had made the decision to burn the letters and not go through with it, I was still a wreck. I just couldn't shake the rumination, fear, anxiety, depression, or alcohol. My home life was suffering. I am pretty sure that I had suffered a full-on split quite some time ago and was really feeling the effects of it. I was once a very outgoing, chipper, optimistic, and joyful person. Now I was an empty, emotionless, bitter critter.

PERSISTENT—
inability to experience positive emotions, and inability to experience happiness, satisfaction, or loving feelings.

INTENSE EPISODIC DYSPHORIA—
irritability, anxiety, transient stress-related paranoid ideation, and severe dissociative symptoms.

* * *

I had a meltdown and ended up going to see a doctor about it. I couldn't take it anymore. No matter what I seemed to do, no matter what I tried, I simply could not get out of this head space. I was suspicious of everyone, paranoid as shit, anxious all the time, and depressed. It was like I had just awoken one day in the past, in some kind of negative alternate universe. I had to go to the emergency room and talk to a mental health doctor.

I filled out their survey in the lobby and waited until they called me back. The second the lady walked in the verbal flood gates opened. I spewed everything that I was experiencing to this lady. I didn't share with her my "secret places" from my traumas because I had not yet realized the extent of what was going on. I just thought I was battling depression or something. I explained to her how I was experiencing anxiety and paranoia all the time and so on.

I think I spent a grand total of about fifteen minutes in this lady's office, and she wrote me a prescription for Zoloft. Sertaline is the actual name of the chemical, and it belongs to the class of SSRIs. I had reached a point where I was now willing to take medication again to try and get my mind under control. I was so sick of the way my mind was running everything I said and did. I was sick of ruining my marriage and home. I had to try something different. I waited until the prescription was filled at the pharmacy and took the first dose in my vehicle before heading home.

That first dose hit me like I was about to start rolling on ecstasy! It was weird as shit, but it gave me such a "geek" like I was "coming up" on some kind of speed. After the first few days, I got a little more used to it, although it did make me vomit a few times. I was rather committed to seeing how this medicine would help. I think I stayed on the Zoloft for several months, and I guess it helped a little, although I do remember it making me manic on more than one occasion.

For anyone who has experienced mania, you know, it is weird. It's almost enjoyable, but at the same time, it is very out of control; like watching yourself on meth doing everything throughout the day. Very out of body experience. So, I continued with the medicine and continued on with my life. Some days were good, some days were not so good. I suppose the Zoloft helped me maintain a little bit better, but overall, I didn't really feel any better. I just wasn't acting out on my feelings as much. For some reason, I just decided to stop taking the medicine altogether. I mean, I hadn't really noticed any major changes, so clearly it wasn't the medicine that I needed to be on. Shouldn't be a big deal at all.

* * *

The first couple days off of the medicine, I didn't feel or think any different. I suppose it had built up in my system enough that it kept working a bit, even after cessation. It was back to the drawing board I suppose, back to figuring out what the hell I was gonna do and how the hell I was gonna manage and overcome this. I guess, one thing the medicine did help me with, was that I hadn't thought about self-harm, or really had all of that rumination and paranoia for a while.

Maybe I should have stayed on it? Nah, I don't think that was the medicine. I think I have just been doing better. That's it! I got this.

I did not have this.

Right around day seven or eight of not taking the medicine, we were doing life. It was a rather typical day, all things considered. Though, typical, when you're me in the shape I had been in, can take on many different forms. It was a bright, sunny, and warm Friday afternoon from what I can recall. I had recently been on a margarita kick and had the whole set up. Shakers, limes, syrups, everything. When time would allow, I would float around in the pool and drink margaritas in my sombrero. My wife will tell you that I might be one of the most obsessive people to ever walk the planet. When I get into something, I really get into it. The margaritas were one case of this, and my wife was no longer amused. Now, I am going to do my best to put this together here, because I don't really remember—all I know is that it was definitely not good.

I guess it was around 5:00 p.m., maybe? I know that I began feeling really manic, like I had when I was taking the medicine, only way more intense. I hadn't had anything to drink that day yet, as it was still rather early in the evening for a Friday. The mania slowly started to settle in on me, and I remember feeling all hyped up and excited. Then I don't really remember anything else.

Apparently, I drove to the liquor store, purchased a bottle of tequila for my recent margarita kick, drove home, and proceeded to make some lime margaritas. I do somewhat recall, in flashes, pieces of the night. But what is interesting here, is that I began blacking out before I even took a single sip of alcohol. Then I started drinking, and it got much, much worse apparently.

I did my best to process this night with my therapist after it occurred, and from what I gathered from the session, was that I had had a full blown out of body disassociation. What's eerily interesting about this, is I can't really remember visually what happened, and I can't really remember what I was thinking either. Somehow I can remember what I was feeling throughout the night which was extreme panic and fear, intense paranoia and fright, anger, and the overall feeling that I might actually explode. It was as if I was "re-feeling" every single horror of my life all over again and all at once. It was also as if I was feeling and experiencing all of my worst possible fears all at once. I was having the first of several serious breakdowns to come.

I completely blacked out in the course of about twelve hours. Zero recollection. I didn't even remember going to the liquor store, and I did that about an hour before I even consumed any alcohol.

I woke up in jail. Waking up in a jail cell was not something I ever thought I would do again. I mean, I was a changed man, wasn't I? What was happening? How in the world had I fallen to such a place again? All of this, going back to the day we moved into our dream home felt like some kind of passing dream. A blur. Had I been checked out, and only falling deeper and deeper into some kind of abyss the entire time?

When I woke up in that jail cell, I couldn't feel anything. I was completely numb emotionally, mentally, and spiritually. What had just happened? If I had known that this was what awaited me if I stuck with my decision not to kill myself, maybe I would have made a different decision. My life was over.

What was gonna happen now? I never meant for anything like this to transpire. Why is life like this?

All I had ever known was suffering, so all I knew how to do was run from the suffering. Running created more suffering. I simply could not fathom how I had lost my mind so badly, and what made matters worse, was that I could tell I was still in the midst of the split and break down. It was going to take a while to crawl out of this abyss. More residual effects of trauma.

Thank God that nobody was seriously hurt.

I just wanted to die. The thought had just come back into my mind.

Maybe it was time to rethink that whole suicide thing.

The Wizard

As I have mentioned before, addicts, alcoholics, and those of us who suffer from mental health issues are great at the "burn down, build back" cycle. This is what I have come to know as "Comfort in Chaos." We are so good at managing this cycle, because chaos is what we have always known. It is a direct result of unresolved traumas and lack of atonement with our pasts.

Childhood traumas and really impactful negative experiences place us into nervous system and emotional dysregulation which can last a lifetime in some cases. As I have explained previously, most of my life was spent "on edge:" either experiencing traumas and traumatic stress, or dealing with and living in its after effects. As a result, it became incredibly difficult to find and enjoy contentment and serenity. Boredom, peace, contentment, normalcy, all of these can feel really abnormal to a person who has experienced prolonged and complex traumas. I lacked answers for a long time.

Maybe one day soon I would start asking the right questions.

Another way that trauma can leave a lasting mark is through the shame that it breeds. Shame and insecurity themselves can lead to serious self-sabotage. Shame can come from a multitude of sources like dysfunctional family systems, rejection, abandonment, parental examples, bullying, and betrayal. I can go ahead and check all of those boxes. Shame then leads to enormous insecurities in one's life as they grow older, and those insecurities can have terrible consequences in relationships later. Not trusting others, paranoia, fear of abandonment, questioning of a significant other, smothering. These are just a few examples of how we can self-sabotage ourselves and our relationships as a result of traumas we experienced as children.

I have pretty much been a professional self-saboteur for most of my adult life, but the interesting thing about it is that it is not intentional. I don't even realize that I am doing it most of the time. It's instinctual, like breathing air. It's almost like my brain is hard wired to subtly and slowly veer me off my path and redirect me back into self-destructive ways. That may be a bit of hyperbole there, but there certainly is something to that school of thought. It almost seems like the more turmoil, sadness, and chaos that can transpire in my life, the more I end up gravitating to it. Recently, I have begun a journey of striving for self-awareness, but I had to get there first.

I bailed out of jail after "Blotto" unfolded. I was going to be staying with my parents for a while. My dad and his new wife, as my biological mother passed in 2014. This was going to be a difficult time, taking a separation from all that I knew. This was when I really got back into therapy again. I was seeing a therapist weekly for about a year from the events of that fateful night.

Every Monday morning, I would spend chopping it up with my counselor about what was going on in my life. She was a highly touted and recommended therapist. She was in high demand with a waiting list, but a friend of mine was able to get me in with her by asking for a favor.

What a great opportunity here! If only I had possessed the capacity or felt the need to get fully-from-the-gut honest with her. But I was still very much in delusion. I was too hyper focused on saving face and maintaining some kind of image and reputation. I had reverted back into my trauma brain for quite some time, which kept me in the victim role mentality. As the saying goes, "we cannot save our faces and our asses at the same time." So, I would spend a great deal of time with this counselor spinning wheels and playing smoke and mirrors.

I am pretty sure she was able to read between many lines because she was actually the first provider I had worked with, and there have been many, who had ever brought up trauma so emphatically. I could hear her words, and I could follow her lessons, but I suppose I just hadn't had enough self-inflicted pain to finally open my ears and heart enough to begin some honest soul searching and life audits. Again, I had reverted back to the victim mentality, so everything was everyone else's fault. My life sucked, blah, blah, blah.

I continued to see this therapist pretty consistently for the course of about a year. I did my best to moderate my drinking. I ended up staying with my folks for about three weeks and then returned home.

Prior to my return, and upon my initial homecoming, it was all the same crap. Bargaining, compromising, promises, plans, etc. All the crap that comes along with loving an alcoholic, mental health partner. It's always the same with every family and with every client.

"The dance" I call it, promises, bartering, and manipulating compromises. Anything we could do to both somehow get our way on everything. But life did seem to turn around a bit for a little while. Then the barrier was broken once again, in one of our little compromises as I drank once, then twice, and then every weekend. The benders were up and roaring once again.

I had to keep a low profile though, because I had some open court cases going on, so I did my best to manage. It didn't go so well. Bender after bender, two, three, four day runs. Vanishing on my family, being a complete and utter asshole. Jekyll and Hyde were back but had never really left because at this point, I was still very much untreated. I was just continuing with therapy to make it look good and maintain some delusion of control over the situation.

Again, the less control on the inside I feel, the more I try to control on the outside. I was grasping at everything, and I was still spiraling. My poor family. I couldn't see it. With mental health and addiction issues, we witness them in first person, we hear the thoughts and the delusions in our own voice. So, even though the things I was feeling and experiencing were very much distorted and sick, I was experiencing them in real time, and in my own head. The delusions, fear, paranoia. The insecurities, ruminations, panic and dread, all seemed very real.

So, I continued to drink, and I continued to play wizard, trying to control everything because clearly everything that was going wrong was because everyone was out to get me, use me, screw me over, and take me out. My delusions, cognitive distortions, and clinical impairment were so major that I literally felt like the world was so focused on taking me out, I never wanted to leave the house. But it was my guilt, it was my shame.

How could I go out there and face the world in this kind of shape?

Then I would throw alcohol on it, and kaboom. What used to work to help keep things stuffed down and numb, was now causing all of my pains and hot buttons to bubble out. I was so full and saturated that there was nowhere to put anything anymore. Just adding the liquid solution to my body caused it all to come floating to the surface. Nothing worked, no amount of avoidance was effective anymore. The more I tried to hide from it, the more visible I became. In a bad way. This was not the attention and visibility that I wanted.

Weeks went by with little encouragement. Sure, I would feel a bit better after my therapy sessions, but it was short lived. I was reverting right back to my twisted mind and perspectives very soon after. I was treading water in blue jeans and a heavy hoodie. I was becoming more and more weighed down. In spite of my best intentions, I was acting on my poisonous thinking.

That's the cycle I had been stuck in for so long: Negative/ intrusive thoughts, negative/ugly feeling, negative/destructive behavior. It took me back to negative thoughts about myself like, "I am no good." I stayed stuck in this feedback loop constantly. So, "what's the use" became my go to, and more drinking followed. Weekend after weekend, bender after bender.

The more I struggled, the more life seemed to throw at me. Like blood in piranha-infested waters. Custody battles are ugly enough, but when a person is mentally struggling and the other party knows it, oftentimes they will do everything they can to kick you when you're down. Inflation, work stresses, deadlines, court cases, marriage problems. Everything just piled and piled on, so my mental and emotional stress grew right along with it. The pressure of it all was too much to bear. Add to the equation that deep down inside, I knew that I was a culprit here, and that brought about even more guilt, pressure, and shame.

I was breaking again.

Damage control, Herb, damage control.

But I was not going to be able to control the damage.

The more I stressed, the more I spiraled, the more my insecurities and fears grew to the point of manifesting right in front of my eyes. As if the very things I was most terrified of were happening in real time, the more I drank and acted out on those delusions. Bender after bender. More fights, more gaslighting, and blame placing. More hostage taking, more scapegoating, more stress and fear. Everything was so out of control, so I just drank to escape it all. I just wanted to drink myself to death. I couldn't handle what was going on in my life or in between my ears anymore. I didn't know what was real or imagined anymore. Life was toxic at this point. I would tell my wife that I was going for a drive to clear my head often, and I would go on drives, but not to clear my head. I would get out onto highways and take off my seat belt and search for the courage to speed up at crazy speeds and slam into a giant oak tree, or an oncoming semi.

But I just couldn't do it. I loved my family too much. I was too strong for that. I was going to make it. I knew it was gonna suck for a little while longer, but I was gonna make it.

The waters would calm at home for a while, and then things would ramp up again. This continued for a little over a year, and I would find myself back in jail, again.

It was time that I finally put my pride to the side and ask for some serious help. This was clearly something much bigger than me, and the more I wrestled with it, the stronger it got. The more I tried to maintain control, the more out of control it spun. I had seen this battle as far as I was willing to see it. The more chaos that came, the more I got swallowed up into it. I had been running on my sickened mind for long enough and had completely sabotaged my life as a result.

It was time to ask for some much needed help.

The Onion

"Hello, this is a call from . . . Herb Stepherson. An inmate
at the Porter County Jail."

I bet my folks didn't think that they were going to hear that
again, and they thought that primarily because I had convinced
them that they wouldn't. Up until this very moment, I had been
too concerned with saving face, maintaining my reputation, and
keeping up the notion that everything was okay. Up until this very
moment, I had been very much obsessed with maintaining control,
which I hadn't had in quite some time. I was still somewhat bitter
and angry, and it showed over the course of several phone calls with
my parents. Blame placing, scapegoating, focus shifting, etc. —but
I knew that all of this was square on my shoulders. I may not have
been responsible for what made me this way, but I was responsible for
the lack of effort and attention I had put into myself and my healing.
I was also responsible for allowing myself to spiral out of control so
badly.

We are not responsible for our diseases, but we are responsible
for our recoveries. We are not responsible for our traumas, but we are
responsible for our healing.

The weight of my failure to take personal responsibility was
crashing down on me. I broke a little more with each phone call. The
entire tape of my life was now available and playing in my head over
and over. I was now finally able to accept that I needed to go and get
some much needed help. I told them this over a series of phone calls
from the jail, and I called my business partner as well and told him
the same thing.

I walked out of jail to my father's vehicle which was waiting out
front. They had just bonded me out again. This time for $2,500.00,

bringing the grand total of bond money spent on me in the last fifteen months to $7,500.00. Not exactly pocket change.

I remember feeling so angry on that ride back to my dad's house. The thing is though, I was searching for someone to be angry at, and the only person I could pinpoint to be angry at was myself. Sure, I could misplace my anger easily and say that it was this person or that person, but when I tried doing so, I felt instantly convicted inside. I knew this was on me. I felt so ashamed.

How could this success story guy, this author on addiction and mental health, this intervention company owner, this husband, father, and changed man fall so hard like this?

Well, like I said before, it wasn't some overnight thing. It never is. I got to this bottom like I had all the others, one compromise at a time.

One of the most interesting and fascinating things that came out of this trip to jail was that for some reason, even though I was horribly humiliated and ashamed, those feelings were also accompanied by an intense feeling of relief. The cat was out of the bag, so to speak. I could stop pretending. I now could take a big deep cleansing breath and shift the focus back onto myself and getting myself some help. I realized, in that time, that no one expected me to be this superhuman, mighty man, except for me—and that it was okay to be human and to struggle.

The thing that was not okay, was letting it get to this point.

My wife, business partner, and parents had all gotten together and made arrangements for me to go to a treatment center out of state. Like way out of state. We were following the same exact template for success that we utilized when executing interventions ourselves. Get them out of Dodge, away from all of the people and places and things. Away from any resources, trigger zones, and away from any immediate life pressures. If we are able to preach it, we are able to practice it. This applies everywhere. I knew I couldn't beat this thing on my own, so I agreed to go. A large suitcase was packed for me, and a plane ticket booked. I spent the night at my parents' house and was off to the airport the next day.

I walked through the doors of the residential treatment center, a hot mess. I had gotten hammered on my commute to the coast and was more than a little toasty. I sat my luggage down while the tech went over some rules and expectations and welcomed me to the program. I stumbled over to the leather sectional, put the Food Network on the common area TV, and passed out for about six hours. Apparently, I was quite pleasant when I first got there. When I woke up, however, that would very much not be the case.

Apparently, this was a no cell phone facility, and we were going to be on a blackout period of one week before we could make any kind of phone calls back home. I did not like this at all, and I began to get incredibly upset. I packed my bag and threatened to leave. I asked to speak to a supervisor on the phone and demanded that I get a phone call to my parents. I personally didn't think this was too much to ask, I mean my family should at least know that I had made it there safely. They knew. I had talked to them the whole entire way—this was about control. This was about calling the shots, and I could actually feel that in this time. I could feel my control being taken away from me, and I did not like that at all. The supervisor agreed to one five-minute monitored "safe call" to let my parents know that I had made it. My attitude would not improve for many, many days.

It seemed like every day for the first week I was leaving. Fuck this place, fuck these rules, this is bullshit, blah, blah, blah. More victim shit as I wrestled with control. The very first Monday I was there, the doctor put me on three days' worth of Valium. I guess that was their, "here, this will calm his wild ass down" tactic. And it worked. I felt like a damn slug for the days I took that shit. I finally began to settle down a bit, physically and verbally, but my mind still raced. I still grappled with everything but the present moment. I was bitter and unapproachable.

I was angry and borderline rude, but I was only really mad at myself. I put me here. This was my doing, and that made me even more upset.

My first day in clinical, I met my therapist. Her name was Krystal. "Like Krystal ball, not Krystal Meth." she said.

We spent some time getting to know one another a bit in her office, and I was still very much full of "piss and vinegar" as the old saying goes.

"So, Herb, any questions, or concerns. Any input or anything you might have for me?"

"Yeah. This is fucking bullshit. I don't think this is gonna work, and I don't think it's gonna work because I am smarter than you are," was my response. What a joy I was gonna be to work with. But she handled it with such grace and understanding.

"That's okay. It may not work, but that will be on you. And you might be smarter than me, in some areas, sure, but for now I am going to need you to trust me, and trust that I might be smarter than you in some areas too."

She was so direct, assertive, and bold, but in a very calm and kind way. She just bucked right back up to me. Interesting. She had my attention.

* * *

I remember when I finally mentally and emotionally settled in. We all had to attend a meeting every single day at local AA and NA (Narcotics Anonymous) clubhouses there in town.

This old man was sharing, and he said something like, "If I can't get out of this, I might as well get into this."

In that moment, he was speaking to me. I had been wrestling with this whole vulnerability and openness thing for about the last thirty-seven and a half years, and it finally dawned on me what an opportunity this was.

So yes, Krystal, it was going to be on me. I would get out of this what I put into this. Up until this trip to treatment, I was still very much untreated. I had done all the AA/NA, church stuff, and the CD&A (Comprehensive Diagnostic & Assessment) programs back home, but this was my chance to really open up and do some research on myself. I knew that I was ready to go to treatment, but up until that moment, I wasn't ready to actually dig in, probe my life, and do the dirty, difficult work of healing. This was going to require a lot of processing with my therapist. That old man who shared that that day, may have very well saved my life and doesn't even know it. It was time to get to work.

* * *

Once I honestly and seriously made the decision to dig in and do the work, it was like a light had turned on inside of me. I was gonna share it all. I was gonna tell the whole story. Not the story I would share when giving a talk, but the real one. The gritty, ugly, sad truths of my life. I was going to air it all out with my therapist, and we were gonna process it together. What did I have to lose? Worst case scenario was that I wouldn't get anywhere, and some stranger across the country would know my whole real story. I could live with that.

So, we started at the beginning, as you have read—"Starting with 1985 and we moved on from there. Man, I opened up to this lady like she was Barbara Walters. It's kind of like, once I broke that barrier with her, once I realized that I could trust her, and once I realized that this healing thing was on me, a massive sense of motivation and urgency came over me. This was life or death. I had to peel the layers back, and she was going to show me how. We spent about twenty full hours together in individual sessions. She also facilitated some of the process groups which was cool. She had this really unbelievable ability to break stuff down and explain it in both addict and therapist terms. She was in recovery too, and I have always said that addicts make the best therapists.

One day during a session, I was going on and on about some shit. I was upset. I was sad. I was feeling it all.

She looked at me dead ass in the eyes and asked me, "So, Herbert, what the fuck else would you like to try and control—and drive yourself crazy in the process?"

I didn't know what to say.

"Yeah," she continued, "You're a control freak, and it's because your entire life has been spent living in such uncontrollable conditions, constantly traumatized and victimized. Though not your fault, it has led you to dying on the hill of control and living in a victim mindset."

She had my full attention. No one had ever called me out on the carpet like this before, and she was right. I had never really examined my life like this before. I had never known how to. I had never fully considered how all of the events that unfolded in my life actually went into making me who I was today. For the longest time, I just thought I was faulty. I thought I had depression, anxiety, bipolar, or maybe I was just a hopeless addict and a drunk. It had never fully occurred to me that all of this addiction and alcohol stuff actually had a real, tangible source. A root cause. Things were starting to make sense.

* * *

Onward we marched. We talked about everything. Fears, insecurities, parenting, relationships, successes, failures, communication, and boundaries; I am pretty sure we covered everything possible in the clinical world, and most of the DSM (Diagnostic and Statistical Manual of Mental Disorders). It was like I had finally realized that this was some kind of moment I had been waiting for my entire life.

Those of you who know me, and those of you who have read my stuff in the past, know that I had tried to get into treatment many times, but never could. It was only through my work in the field, interventions, etc. that I was able to attend a program now.

I am still in that, "We make too much for Medicaid but not enough for private insurance" demographic. My wife, business partner, and parents had to call in a favor with some people in the industry to make this a reality. I could sense that this was a really important opportunity and privilege to finally connect some dots. We were peeling back layers.

I think in the session we had gotten to the point in my life to where I had started using drugs to begin with. We left off for the day, and I was in the group room doing whatever the exercise and processing the group was doing. I was an active participant. I was eating this shit up. I love the human mind. I love talking about philosophy, people, and relationships. I was on fire to learn as much as I could.

About midway through the group session, the door to the group room opened, and Krystal's head popped in. She gave me her classic "pointer finger curl" to come here. I met her in her office, and she closed the door. She proceeded to read off a long extensive list of criteria from a computer screen to which I rattled off a series of "yes" to each and every one. When she completed the list, she flipped her screen around and showed me what she was reciting the criteria for Post Traumatic Stress Disorder. I didn't really know how to respond. It was too simple of an explanation. I thought war vets were the ones who had PTSD, not me. This was mind blowing. But there was no fighting it. I knew this to be accurate. I knew she was right. I could just feel it. I had spent fifteen years trying to find answers, but I hadn't been asking the right questions. I hadn't been peeling back the right layers. When she shared this with me, it was like a door unlocked inside my mind. We were getting somewhere.

* * *

About a week or so later, I was again, sitting in group. We hadn't done any individual sessions yet this week, but it was only about Tuesday. Krystal, again, pulled me out of group, and I met her in her office and closed the door.

"Just a quick question here, Herb. Do you ever think about killing yourself?"

I didn't really know how to respond. This was out of the blue and took me by surprise. So, I just answered it honestly. "I mean, doesn't everyone think about blowing their head off from time to time?"

She stared at me with understanding and a touch of pity, shook her head, and in a hushed tone replied, "No."

I could see that she felt great sadness for me. She then proceeded to go down another list of criteria, to which I responded "yes" to every single one. Again, she flipped the screen around to reveal another Diagnostic Criteria page. This time it was for Borderline Personality Disorder (BPD), which stemmed directly out of the trauma and PTSD.

This one made me squirm a little bit, not gonna lie.

"It's one of the weird ones," I said, as I judged myself, and in that moment, experienced what so many of us who suffer like this feel on a daily basis—stigma. Again, I knew she was right.

My wife had also been right about this. She had been conducting her own research about my mental conditions for a while, and both diagnoses I had just received were on my wife's radar, and it all made sense too. The splitting, mood changes, fear of abandonment, the delusion. The anger, anxiety, depression, the risky use and abuse of alcohol—all of it was me to a T. Another door had unlocked in my mind. I was getting answers.

Upon receiving the new diagnosis of BPD, I really began to ponder my life. I know that we had done lots of processing, both individually and in groups, but I was in rehab, and this was going to be a full-time job for me. Even in the free time we had, I studied myself. I journaled, prayed, and practiced breathing and meditation techniques. I probed my life and looked deep within myself. I really began to study how my current relationships, current interactions with other humans, my behaviors, the way I talk, the way I felt, and my overall outlook on life were impacted by things that had taken place over twenty-five years ago.

It's actually quite fascinating. It all began making sense.

One example that comes to mind is fear. Fear takes on many forms. There are healthy fears and unhealthy fears. Most people have instinct when it comes to healthy fears. One would not just run out and do push-ups in the middle of an expressway, because you would get hit by a car. That's a healthy fear, but I was so full of unhealthy fears.

* * *

I laid there on my bed on Christmas morning, pondering what my fears were, and where they came from. When I was done meditating on the life cycles of my fears, I took the time and wrote them down. Three full pages of fears. Everything from fear of heights, to fear of rejection, abandonment, dying alone, fear of failure, fear of success, fear of doing nothing, and so on and so on . . . I walked that list out to the bonfire pit and talked to God about these fears, and where they came from. I released every single one of them, lit them on fire, and started a roaring bonfire with my list.

It was about so much more than the fears though. In this moment, I was letting go. I was letting go of all of it. I was letting go of my hurts, trauma, betrayals, and all the times I had been rejected, and turned away, all of my failures. I was finding forgiveness.

Forgiveness is something that I didn't know that I had struggled with until I got to treatment. It's almost like, all of the things that I had been through created within me a hostile heart, full of resentment. Resentment is in fact, a coping mechanism. That coping mechanism of resentment allowed me to maintain the illusion of control, and those resentments also fed into my delusions of reality. When my heart is full of resentment, then it clouds my mind, and my perception of life, reality, and of people.

I was done being angry. I was done being hurt. I was done holding people hostage in my heart. I went through my life's tape right there as the bonfire burned away my fears. I allowed forgiveness to flow to anyone and everyone that I had once held a grudge toward. I allowed forgiveness to anyone and everyone who ever hurt or wronged me. Then I got to the most important person of all to forgive, myself.

Silent heavy tears rolled down my face, as I looked at all of the places throughout my life where we had done each other wrong.

Where I was wronged, I forgave. When I did wrong, I forgave.

It was like watching the movie of my life in real time, allowing myself to finally examine it, feel it, know it, understand it, accept it, and then let it all go. I no longer had any animosity or hostility inside of me. I could literally feel it all just washing away.

I could feel those dusty old boxes that I had been carrying with me for decades burn up in the bonfire flames. I could feel all the gray matter in my brain freeing up, and taking deep cleansing breaths, no longer clustered and crowded by compartmentalization. I could feel my heart open again, accepting what was, feeling what is, and making way for what was to come.

This was one of the most important moments of my entire life, and in the lives of so many.

I had finally peeled it all back to the core. I was free.

Forgiveness is to set a captive free, and then realizing it was us who were captive all along.

I didn't have to be afraid anymore.

I was safe.

How to Peel an Onion

First, we have to identify the negative actions, then discover the thoughts that drive those actions.

Next, discover the core beliefs that drive our thoughts, uncover the events and experiences we had that implanted those core beliefs inside of us.

We start with the outside layer, and gently pull it back, revealing another and slightly softer and more vulnerable layer.

We continue this process until only the most tender and vulnerable portion of the onion is left, the core.

We then examine and study the core until we fully understand what it is, and why it is important in the later development of the outside layers.

Repeat this process as many times as needed, until we no longer cry when doing so.

Visible

I collected myself after my little bonfire ceremony and headed back to my room for some coffee. I immediately hit my knees in my room and leaned against my bed to pray. I was not asking for a single thing. In spite of everything that had happened in my life, especially recently, I was grateful. I was making sure that God knew that.

Maybe I am/was sicker than most, maybe its normal, maybe it isn't, but in spite of everything that had transpired in my life over the last couple years—in this moment—I was grateful. I knew that I was safe and was in the midst of healing. I could feel it. No matter what it took to get here, no matter how ugly the past was, it brought me to this exact moment, kneeling against my bed in a rehab center thanking my creator.

I knew that my journey was again just beginning, but I also knew that now, I would have a shot. I was still in the game. I didn't deserve to be. Truth be told, looking back on all of my life, it's miraculous that I am still alive quite frankly. That meant I had a chance. This would be chance number 48,397 or some shit. God has been gracious to me. This much I knew.

I finished up my prayer, got myself together, poured a cup of coffee, and headed on over to the main house of the center. As I was making my way in through the screened in porch, I passed a friend of mine that I had made there.

We were both finishing up a smoke, and I decided to share with him my little ceremony at the fire pit, the burning of my fears.

He took a drag off of his cigarette, blew it out, and then looked at me quizzically. "What do you have to be afraid of, Herb?"

I then gave him a short list, but a list of some of the more significant fears that I had.

"Do you have any evidence of this?" was his only response.

In that moment, I was provided such tremendous confirmation that I had indeed let those fears go. His response, although simple and direct, really worked its way into my mind and stuck. The timing was perfect because I had just cleared so much space in my mind and heart, that now my friend's simple basic rationale had plenty of room to sow. He had just planted a very simple seed in my mind.

When the student is ready, the teacher appears indeed.

* * *

The following weeks were intense. Coming off of the powerful weeks before, and event next to the bonfire, I was hungry for more. Groups, groups, groups. I had already filled up one entire notebook and was now working on filling up the second.

Life was like I was seeing in color for the first time. I was able to really absorb so many things now. I honestly believe that things we carry around in our minds, even subconsciously, take up physical and real space. It's as if I had just, "Marked as read, send to the trash can" icon, and then proceeded to "empty trash bin."

My ears were open. Toward the end of the week, as we were on a break between groups, Krystal pulled me aside to check in for a minute. She asked me a very simple arbitrary question, it would seem.

"So, how are you feeling, Herb?"

I didn't answer the question directly at first but proceeded to tell her about the bonfire, forgiveness, and my prayer at my bed instead. She followed along as I told her all about it in pretty specific detail, and then she asked me again, but this time, she included the word *now*.

"So, Herb, how are you feeling, now?" she insisted.

I took a moment to formulate an answer that could possibly encapsulate how I was actually feeling.

"Naked," was my response. Just that one word at first, and then I went on to elaborate.

What I meant when I said that I had felt naked, was that for the first time ever, I finally felt fully seen. I had laid it all out on the table for full examination, "warts and all," as they say. All the good parts, and all the ugly parts. Full blown, hold nothing back real-life vulnerability. I felt validated and liberated. It's almost like for the first time in my entire life, someone was actually willing to listen to the full story, but no, for the first time in my entire history, I was ready to let it be heard.

It was very validating to me, and I knew that I wasn't just some victim. It was so much more than just, "I have had a rough life."

I had witnessed, experienced, and felt so many things that impacted and flat out changed me on so many levels. I had always been scared to share them all in detail for many reasons. The top reasons that came to mind were: no one would care enough to hear it all, and someone would tell me that it wasn't that bad. I was so used to dealing with fake and inadequate friends throughout my life that I kind of just developed the mentality that:

No one cares anyway, and those who do listen, can't be trusted with the information I am going to share with them, so what's the use?"

Most people would probably just tell me to suck it up, man up anyway.

* * *

So, there I stood, next to my therapist in a treatment center. It was January of 2023. I felt naked as a jaybird, having finally found a safe place after all of these years to unload all of the horrific, heartbreaking, scary, joyous, happy, vulnerable secret places of mine, that I had been forced to hide in those dusty old boxes for all these years.

I had just shared some things with this lady that I had never had the courage, or ability, to share with someone in her profession in my entire lifetime. I felt visible. I felt seen. I felt heard. I felt like someone finally understood me. I felt light as a feather. It hadn't occurred to me to even consider what this therapist of mine might be thinking about me, after all of the shit I had just unloaded on her—and for the first time in my life, I didn't care.

I knew in that moment, and in the days following, why I had felt invisible for all of those years going back to childhood. I had somehow, in the process of all this therapy, gained some priceless perspective on my life. The past had in fact, changed.

I had a new and profound understanding of myself. I could see me. The reason why I had always felt so invisible, was because I was essentially trained to be invisible. Kids are to be "seen and not heard" philosophy crap, except I *never* felt seen or heard. I never, until the last seven or so years, even knew of a human being that I could fully trust enough with the kind of things I had to share.

I was trained to lie to CPS. I was taught to *shut the fuck up or I'll give you something to cry about.* I was constantly shuffled around like an unwanted dog from relative to relative. I was totally invalidated and denied the very few times I did try to speak up for myself. I was violated, used, beaten, and was made to feel insignificant for so much of my life. This is not a victim stance at all.

If anyone thinks that I would be happy to recommend a therapist for you, I think you might need one.

This is factual hard data of my life. What I have learned throughout all of this, is that how we speak to our children, how we validate or invalidate them, how we build them up or tear them down, becomes their image and their inner voice. If someone grows up feeling invisible, and unheard, there is a very real chance that they will carry that with them for a very long time.

Because I never had the opportunity to fully unload all of the shit that was making me who I was, I carried it around with me, in those dusty old boxes. I had that shit inside of me for so long that it had become my identity. It was like ever where I went I had those words tattooed all over me: loser, failure, molested, shame, drug addict, white trash, *insignificant.*

When I got clean and wrote the first book, I received some recognition for the first time in my life, and I latched on to that identity. I was things. I was labels. I had no clue who I really was, or what I was capable of. I just shape shifted through life trying to make it as best I could, and I was always so raw from dragging it all with me, that it ate me alive.

I should have done this first. I should have done the treatment thing first, gotten this portion of my life out first, but it wasn't an option for me at the time. All of this sensitive and vulnerability that I have shared with you all, and with my therapist, is the "why." They are the things, events, traumas, and driving forces that took me to drug addiction to begin with. I have so many answers to questions I didn't know I needed to ask.

I hope this is all making sense because I can see it all right now.

* * *

I was dealt a really shitty hand. My life was truly awful for a very long time. I have been beaten, molested, addicted, robbed at gun point, jailed, abandoned, homeless, neglected, and violated on many different levels over the course of about thirty years. There was a time when my only meals came out of garbage cans, and I am here to tell you today, that those things are not who I am.

I am here to tell myself that those things are not who I am. I am not what has happened to me—I am what I do about it. I am a survivor, and so are you! And likewise, your pains, your traumas, your past, your secret places are not who you are. Those things do not define you. You are so much more than the wounds that you carry.

Life can be so very cruel and is to so many people out there. It can chew us up and turn us into people we swore we would never become. Just because I have forgiven myself, and I have gained new perspective on my life, does not mean that I get some kind of free pass in this world. Just like my past is not an excuse, enlightenment is not an automatic pardon. There will still be people out there who don't like me or want me around, and that's okay. Because for the first time in a very long time, I want me around. I like me.

I have stumbled into something over the last month and a half here, in my life—self-awareness. This is something that I am not going to relinquish without a fight. If you look at some of the great minds throughout history—those with seemingly infinite practical wisdom—they all have something in common: Self-awareness. I believe that the harder we can all work on ourselves, the better this world will become.

It's interesting to me that when I had had my profound spiritual experience at the great banquet, I was blown away. I was blown away at the magnitude of God, and during this time of spiritual growth, I was adding something to my life, and being accepted for just who I was in God's eyes.

During this time of therapy and treatment, I was subtracting and reducing myself down to the barest of minimums. I was examining exactly who I was and what exactly made me the way that I am. I got naked, I got vulnerable, and I spoke my core truths. I peeled those layers back one by one, with the guidance of a professional. It was the greatest thing I have ever done for myself.

It was the first time in my entire life that I had felt fully and totally visible.

I understood myself, only after I destroyed myself. It was in the process of putting myself back together that I discovered who I really was.

I thought that my therapist was going to judge me when I started the whole treatment journey. But as I was preparing to leave that place, she pulled me aside once more, and simply said to me, "Herb, it was an honor to hear your story."

Jesus replied, "You may not realize now what I am doing, but later you will understand." John 13:7 (NIV)

I may not have done what you've done, or been where you've been, but at one point or another, I have felt what you've felt.

To Heal

I have had a couple of what I would refer to as, profound experiences in my life since beginning this journey of mine almost eight years ago. The first one, as I have talked about before was the Indiana Dunes Great Banquet. During this experience, I witnessed what was referred to as a "crash course in Christianity." It was truly beautiful. I heard testimonies, and stories from other men who had struggled in their own lives. I experienced true fellowship, felt real mature acceptance, and I experienced grace as I have come to understand it. When it comes to grace, we all experience it in different ways. I am sure if we were all to look back on our lives, we could easily point out moments and even seasons when we received grace. Remember, justice is getting what we deserve, mercy is not getting what we deserve, and grace is getting what we don't deserve.

During this four-day retreat, that is the Great Banquet, I remember really being blown away at how flawed and faulty all of us are, and how open some of us are and admit it. I remember as the weekend progressed, this overwhelmingly full feeling, like spiritually full. The whole "my cup runneth over feeling." It was magical. I felt accepted, cared, and provided for, and I felt loved, just the way that I was. I experienced forgiveness from God, as I understand him, and I experienced what I can only describe as pardon. It was a truly powerful experience for me because I had some serious baggage and bondage. It was a beautiful experience in my life.

* * *

What does the word "recover" actually mean? The first definition I found when Googling this word is this: "Return to a normal state of health, mind, or strength."

Sounds good, right? Looking at my own life journey, what was normal for me, if to recover was to return to a normal state of health, mind, or strength? In my opinion, "normal" as I understood it was not good. In here lies a conundrum, for if "to recover" were to return me back to "normal," then that would mean to return back to what was normal for me.

Follow me here, I am going somewhere. I know *my* definition of normal is not the same as "John Q. Public's." I get that.

So, take away the using, and what was normal for me: Trauma? Chaos? Jail? Turmoil?

I read somewhere in some recovery literature, that, "We are not simply looking to 'recover' our lives back to how they were, before using drugs took over," because for many of us, that would be just as ugly as our lives were when we were all strung out living like crazy people. I know for me it would. Take away the chemicals, and I am still a trauma riddled, broken spirited, ill minded, scarred, and faulty human being. I don't know if it is "recovery" so much that many of us have been after all along. Perhaps that is why so many of us, myself included, have relapsed many times over.

So, if it's not "to recover," is it "to restore?" To restore back to a prior state? No, that is too similar to "to recover."

You see, throughout all of this, I have been striving to fully and finally conquer "this thing," but what was it that I was really trying to conquer? Drugs? Alcohol? No. I have been striving to conquer the thing or things that drove me back to the drugs and alcohol time and time again.

I think that's why people relapse with so much sobriety time under their belts. Their "thing" hasn't been discovered, addressed, confronted, and conquered. When we are still unhealed, our mind is still capable of functioning on the harmful patterns and pathways that have always been there. Sure, we may have a great support system, we may go to meetings, we may have lots of reasons to stay sober, but if those pathways in our minds are still open for traffic, and the right set of circumstances occur, it is all the easier to "divert traffic" back into those pathways that were once used to protect us. To provide relief, ease pain, increase pleasure. Does this make sense?

Think about it as a short cut through the woods, as a child. If that short cut is still available as a quicker way to get to our destination of relief and it starts to rain while we are out playing, are we going to take the long way home, or hop on the short cut?

I use this example, "short cut through the woods when we are children" because that's exactly when we start to develop our paths, techniques, and our survival skills—as children. Unknowingly, subconsciously, however it happens, that is when they begin. We rely on these same skill sets and mechanisms, whether we want to admit it or not, right on through our adult lives.

"Can't teach an old dog new tricks," as the old adage goes. But what if we can? Teach old dogs new tricks, that is.

We find our paths, skills, and mechanisms early in life. They work, and then we rely on them for decades to come. What once used to be a barely visible deer path through the woods behind our house, is now a full-blown dirt road, rutted out and cleared enough for us to fly through it as fast as we can on our Huffy bike to beat the rain. We can hop on that path with very little effort. We know each and every bump and hump, twist and turn. We have it memorized. We have used it a thousand times. We use it so much that we begin using it even when it's not raining out, just because its faster and more convenient. This is the same thing we do with our brains, from an early age, without even knowing it.

So, if the shortcuts, pathways, operating systems, and mechanisms in our brains from an early age are what made us into addicts/alcoholics to begin with, then why would we be longing to simply "recover" ourselves back to such a place?

Is this making sense?

I think what we are actually longing for, at least I was, to heal, unlearn, and recreate myself. To make new, like never before. To progress and heal in such a way that it was as if those old pathways never existed, closing them for traffic once and for all.

To heal, what? To unlearn what? To recreate how?

To heal for me meant to fully examine my life with the guidance of a professional. To unearth those ugly, shameful, horrible secret places inside of me. Risking complete vulnerability and throwing myself all the way out there.

"To get naked" I call it. To go through my childhood, upbringing, relationships, examples that were set, and so on. To identify major events, to identify and recognize harmful patterns, and to connect the dots and data points in my current life and relationships with others and myself—back to the time the precedent for these thinking, feeling, and behavior patterns were set.

It was during this time of digging up and examining of what makes me tick, think, feel, and act the way I do, that I was able to point out the positive/negative patterns and mechanisms that were still in my employ today. It was also during this time that there were some things that really needed to be addressed: resentment, anger, bitterness, victim mentality, spite, insecurities, shame, guilt, fear, and traumas. All of these things went into my brain's chemical makeup, which then led me to seeing the world through these lenses. In turn, it brought about more pain and led me to living life with a hostile heart. I had brick walls built up around me ten miles high. Throughout this process, we took them down, brick by brick. I was slowly able to find something that I didn't know I was looking for: *Forgiveness.*

Once the digging, unearthing, and examination portion was complete, it was time to perform a professional audit on those findings. What about these things was constructive, destructive, useful, practical, positive, or negative? We now had cause, effect, and practicalities. We were reverse engineering my life, taking everything about me apart, to find out how we could put me back together in a more beneficial way. We were looking at "what we have, what we haven't got, what we needed, and what needed to go," as Father Martin Ashley puts it. It was in this process that the "unlearning" took place.

I realized that certain ideas, beliefs, thoughts, feelings, and behaviors were causing unmanageability in my life—and causing pain and distress in the lives around me. Once we established and understood my "blueprint," we were able to make corrections and revisions, make updates if you will. We put together something that would be more beneficial in my life and in my relationships. In order to learn new, we had to unlearn old.

It was in these two processes, that we found the most effective replacements for old harmful thoughts, feelings, and behaviors. We were then able to slowly implement and practice new insights, perspectives, and beliefs. It was kind of like trying on clothes, challenging myself to think, feel, believe, and behave in new ways.

To see how this might be a benefit for myself and my loved ones.

This is something that I have come to know as *Dialectical behavior therapy* (DBT). The more challenges I went through, the more my mind opened, and the more growth and healing took place. I was indeed putting myself back together, bit by bit. I was healing, and I was recreating myself. I was learning that the old ways of thinking were not the only ways of thinking. Not only did those old beliefs, thoughts, and feelings get me to a point of misery, they were also obsolete and outdated. I was hitting "ctrl + alt + delete" on my mind, my core beliefs, and my spirit. Just because I had come from a really ugly place, didn't mean I had to return there.

That was my second profound experience since beginning my journey. The sharp laser cut with clarity that I do not have to be who the world, my traumas, and my pains made me to be. That I do have a tremendous power in this world. The power of choice. By stripping myself down completely, I was able to find out what I was really made of, and what to do about it. I was freeing up, I was slowing down. I was allowing myself some space to be re-planted in more fertile soil.

One of things that I realized throughout that process, was that on a very deep, subtle, and almost subconscious level, I was actively choosing my hostile heart, my anger, resentment, bitterness, and my victim mentality. Those things gave me some semblance of control. When you grow up in a world full of chaos, a world that is so out of control, to hold on to anything that gives you a sense of manageability, brings something like peace. I had held on long enough. It was no longer serving me. I was now able to let it all go. I had never felt more refreshed, replenished, light, or quenched in my life.

Dig. Examine. Audit. Relinquish.

This was how my healing commenced.

I didn't want to "recover" something lost or "recover" a previously existing state of being or frame of mind. I wanted to recreate, renew, and re-start.

"And I've got love to fill me in, I've got family to help me re-begin." *Old Barns*, by Greensky Bluegrass

* * *

The first twenty-nine years of my life were spent in the ugliest, most hate filled, trauma riddled, disgusting parts of humanity that I can honestly imagine. I witnessed very little, but hate, loss, racism, backstabbing, condemnation, vengeance, violence, violation, abuse, neglect, abandonment, greed, utter chaos, and uncertainties. So, it was natural that those exposures left quite the lasting impression on me. They went into the programming of my mind—my heart's blueprint.

As I went through a thorough audit of my life examining who I really am, I was able to see how each and every type of experience that I had was impacting me and my relationships today. I had finally come to a point in my life where I was free, willing, and able to fully determine what was going to have meaning in my life moving forward.

I no longer had to be who the world made me to be. I was going through a major shedding and unlearning of some pretty heavy and ugly vestiges that had been implanted into my heart from very early on. I was rewriting my code. I was no longer willing or able to continue to experience life through the lenses of pain, hurt, trauma, and sadness.

It was high time to fully heal my inner child and begin to see the world through Stevie's eyes once again. To be pure. To be fully healed, soft and loving. To let it all go and walk in love and soft heartedness once again. It was finally safe to do so. I was healing.

As a child goes throughout their life, they are going to encounter various intermittent or ongoing negative events in their lives. We call these negative events when there is significant enough trauma. Though their lives will also contain many positive events, typically children don't necessarily require tremendous mentorship or processing for the positive events in their lives. It is the negative events in our lives that we encounter that usually require mentorship, love, bonding, and processing. If we do not have those as children, then we are left kind of navigating life essentially from trauma to trauma in our own little bubble.

Trauma is a noun. It is a thing, like a stapler. Meaning it exists, and when it enters our mind, it sticks. As we navigate our childhood and mature, our individuality and identity are being formed within us. If we have high levels of trauma impacting our minds, then we are subject to those altering our sense of self.

Bad things keep happening to me, and I don't know why, so it must be because of me. I am bad. I am the problem.

The more we experience trauma without adequate processing, the more it negatively impacts our self-esteem and our self-worth. The more trauma we hold onto, the lower our self-image falls. Low self-esteem and low self-worth equals low standards of living, and poor boundaries. Why would a person say no to drugs, if they don't feel that they are worthy of a higher standard of living? This is what they mean when they say, *if you don't stand for something, you will fall for anything.*

* * *

When a child endures chronic and significant trauma throughout their life, it has lasting and sometimes permanent effects on them later on. Trauma becomes the lens we see the world through. It becomes our inner voice, it becomes the way we experience other humans, and it greatly impacts our moral compass later on. If we do not have a healthy sense of self, self-respect and self-love, then we will also not have healthy boundaries and self-discipline later on in life. Our minds are constantly being shaped, and the way we experience the world depends on how we experience the relationships closest to us, early on in life.

When an adolescent child uses drugs to feel good or fit in, they unknowingly self-medicate their underlying and unhealed trauma. They simply cannot fathom this at the time of initial chemical intake. They just think that it feels good to be under the influence.

For so many out there, this is probably the first time that they have felt good, accepted, or celebrated in a long time—as their friends encourage them to try something new and exciting. Thus, they are stuck chasing chemical escape for many years to come. They end up always searching for something to shut the pain and the noise off, but there is no chemical solution for unresolved trauma. Using chemicals to cover up or mask unresolved trauma is like putting a band aid on a broken leg. It just won't work.

Drugs and alcohol have always just been a symptom for me, of something deep-seated and underlying. It took me years and countless tries at recovering to realize this. When I went to treatment for the first time and took an honest look at my life from start to present, I found some answers I had been searching for, for a very long time. My catalyst, my "why."

The "why" I began and continued to use drugs for as long as I did was trauma. I was attempting to numb and muffle the screaming inner child deep within. To ease his pain.

Special note:

Trauma may be a reason that one acts out in certain ways. It may be a "why" for you, but it is not an excuse to continue doing so. Having unresolved trauma in your life is not a free pass to keep living life in negative ways. The negative behaviors should be a reason to confront your trauma and begin your healing journey. It might be time, if you are anything like me, to begin "unlearning" some stuff that was programmed into you many years ago . . . find some "why's" in your life and begin living life according to your truest self. I know that it may be difficult, and even scary to dig. You might feel like you are betraying people in your life, betraying people in your past for examining your life through a scope to find trauma. You are not.

Pinpointing trauma in your life is not about finding out that your parents, grandparents, other relatives etc. were or are bad people. It is about examining how negative and painful experiences impacted you, and to understand how that made you think, feel, believe, and experience life today.

It is also a pathway to great forgiveness, and to truly forgive is to be truly free.

Dear Stevie,

I just want you to know that I am okay. I know you're scared right now, and you feel invisible and unheard, but I see you, I hear you, right here and right now. It may seem like no one cares, but I do. I just want you to know that even though you're surrounded by sick people and dysfunction, you make it out!

Oh, how lonely, scared and exhausted you will be at times but do not give up! You and I know the heart you have, and one day not far off, you will find forgiveness. Sure, it's gonna be awful at times, and you're gonna suffer and have to unlearn so much, but you are going to learn so very much too!

I know it's not fair, Stevie. You don't deserve this. You don't deserve all the things that happened to you. I wish I could say it is going to get easier right away, but it's not. In fact, it is going to be tough for a long time. But I promise you, it will all work out. It is going to actually get better than you can even imagine right now. Your suffering will not be in vain. You know that you are a good person, and a champion deep down inside. Oh, the battles that you are going to fight, and win!

If only people could even understand the things that you will face, the struggles that you'll endure, and the triumphs you will find.

I am so very proud of you. You are a great human being. Good people and good love are in store for you one day. God has His hands on you and will not leave your side. Some days it will feel like you are all alone, and other days it will feel as if you simply do not have the strength to endure. But you will persevere. You will rise, and fall, and rise, and fall again.

It is not some simple task to overcome what is ahead for you. But you will. With that heart of yours, that spirit of understanding and empathy, you will go on to help so many people just by being your authentic self.

You are perfect just the way you are, and one day not too far off, you will find peace, forgiveness, and atonement. I wish that I could tell you not to do something, or to change something in your life to alter your life's trajectory, but I can't. For without everything happening just the way it did, I wouldn't be here to write you this letter. It all makes for one helluva a story to tell.

So, buckle up, keep your faith, and hope alive.

I'll be right here waiting.

Stay true to yourself kid,

Herb.

Dear Dad,

I just wanted to write you a little something and let you know how truly special to me you are. I know that life has been hard for us at times, and that there may be parts of you that feel like you have failed in some areas. But I am here to tell you, right here and right now, that I am so very proud that you are my father.

I do not feel or believe that you have failed me, or Lucas in any way. Sure, you made mistakes along the way, big deal. We all do. When we are born, when you were born, no one gave us a manual that detailed how to handle each and every situation and interaction as they arose. I think you did more than great with my brother and me. We, the Three Musketeers, are all still here! We are the last one's standing. I bet nobody saw that coming. You impacted me in so many ways that I don't even think you realize. You never left my side, you never walked away from me, and you have always had my back through the thickest and the thinnest.

No one has ever advocated for, defended, and protected me like you. No matter what ever transpired in my life, even in the bad times, I could always count on you dad. I love you more than you will ever know.

When I was in treatment on Fridays, we did guided meditation. One Friday, the instructor was walking us through meditation and directed us to take our minds to our happy places. I just want you to know, that at thirty-seven-years-old, laying on the floor of a rehab one of my happy places throughout the entire course of my lifetime, was playing catch with you! After all these years, after all that has unfolded in our lives, it was still so effortless to transcend my mind back to playing catch with my best friend, my father.

I have always admired you. I have always looked up to you and loved you tremendously. Even though we didn't have a lot, we always had enough, and we always had each other. You showed me what "all for one and one for all" really means. You have always stood by me, to this day.

I just want you to know, that there is absolutely nothing that I think you should hang your head about, feel guilty for, or beat yourself up about.

I made it, Lucas made it, and we are all still here together! I am a father too, and I know the pains and conviction that can come along with feeling our errors and shortcomings. I also know that we have and always will do our best.

I still believe in you, and I still love, admire, and respect you so very much. You've done good dad. Thanks for never giving up on me.

"You see, Daddy's don't just love their children every now and then, it's a love without end, Amen." George Strait.

I am so proud to bear your name,
Love you dad.

Stevie.

Tiffany

Almost seven years ago, a woman took a chance on a guy living in a halfway house named Herb. He didn't have anything. No phone, no home of his own, no car, I believe at the time they met he was cutting grass to make ends meet. He was fresh off a decade long battle with drug addiction and was fighting just to be able to see his son. Herb didn't know much about who he was, or where his life would take him. For some reason though, she saw something in him. Upon their meeting, it was as if they had known each other forever. They were kindred spirits. They had this immediate connection.

She was a single mother of three, working long hours to support herself and her children. They spent as much time together as they could. It felt right. It felt like they had been searching for each other for a very long time. They did everything together. For Herb, he knew she was the one, almost right away. He could feel it in his bones. They were best friends. These two worked their asses off, with grit and dedication to put a life together that they could all be proud of! It certainly was not easy. They climbed up from an empty house with zero furniture, to milestone after milestone. They were making this family life work!

When their relationship became serious, Herb had begun telling Tiffany his story. He told her about all of the drug addiction, the poverty. He told her everything. He also told her that even though he was on a path of growth, healing, and recovery, that setbacks may in fact be in his future; for there is no cure to what lies inside of him.

Together they made a promise to never give up on one another, no matter what life threw at them. They have stuck to that promise to this very day.

* * *

Well, as you all have read by now, there were tremendous setbacks for Herb. His life, and his mind have never quite been what most people experience. Things got so dark for Herb that he often contemplated taking his own life, but Tiffany never left his side. She never gave up on him, even when she considered that he may not make it himself.

She was his wife, best friend, counselor, confidant, hand holder, outlet. She was his cornerstone throughout all of his life. In spite of Herb's personal struggles, they remained dedicated to one another, and as a result, they climbed and climbed. No matter how bad things seemed to get internally for Herb, she never left his side. They made a promise, they swore a vow to one another, "Through sickness, and in health as long as they both shall live."

And Herb had gotten sick again. She stuck by him as if he were battling cancer. She was there praying with and for him. When his brother died, she held his hands and dried his tears as he sobbed in tremendous grief. She was there when his mental health was declining. She knew that what was happening in his mind was illness and not some kind of moral failing. She saw him like no one else could. He was her special man, and she was his sweet girl.

As the battles waged on inside of him, she was there to guard and protect him. She was there many nights to hold his hand, hug his neck; assuring him that he was safe, and that everything was going to be alright. The more she held close, often, the more he would push away. He had never known love, he had never known trust, and he had never known true friendship. She was showing him all of these things and more, now. It required him to let her, and he was trying his best, in spite of the ongoing war in his head. He spiraled and spiraled—and she persisted with his aid. She was not going to lose the love of her life to himself. She was standing in the gap for him. He would do it for her. They were all that each other had, and more. They were soulmates, destined to be, and they had each other's back.

Herb eventually began to bottom out, losing his internal war. Tiffany was there every step of the way, to help him pick up the pieces, and help him reconcile. Though she wanted to give up and walk away at times, they loved each other too much to quit. They made a promise to each other in front of God, their families, and to the world. They were home to one another.

Eventually Herb finally admitted defeat, and asked for some help with his mental struggles, and Tiffany was there every step of the way. She made arrangements with his family and company for him to go to treatment. She looked after Lucas for him while he was there. She walked his struggles out with him, as if they were her own. She never left him, betrayed him, and never doubted him for a second. She has been the only one who could ever really see him, all this time—even when he could not see himself.

He knew she was the one the first time he laid eyes on her, and she still is to this very day. She is it. She is his very best friend, soulmate and twin flame. They are best friends, they are a power couple, and they are unstoppable. They belong together.

Throughout all of this bittersweet, up and down, success and failure alike, one constant has remained. Them. Herb and Tiffany. In all of this beautiful and tragic world, with so much wonder and awe, nothing compares in his eyes to his sweet girl. She is all that he sees. She is it.

I will forever be in debt to her, with such tremendous gratitude, because she never gave up on me; even when NO ONE would have blamed her for walking away. She was all I had at times, and she knew I needed her. She has saved my life more times than I can count. She is a hundred reasons why I am still alive. If you see me, I see her.

"All I'm worth is just this promise that I made to you, to stand beside you just like you have stood beside me."

All my Love,
Herb

Unconditional Love

Born into chaos,
Trauma from the start.
Abused and abandoned,
Fear weighed down his tiny heart.
Always felt alone,
Searching for connection.
Wanting only to fit in,
But never having a best friend.
Unseen and unheard,
He felt like a ghost.
No one to step up,
When he needed them the most.
From a lost little boy,
To a trauma laden teen.
He began to find relief,
In a bottle, in some weed.
As he grew up,
He searched for a purpose.
Anything with a meaning,
Something to make him feel worth it.
At home he found no hope,
Drug addicted parents set the precedent.
Mom would run, dad would chase
He became a burden and irrelevant.

A massive void in his world,
Caused by the lack of safety and love.
But then he found relief,
In the harder type of drugs.
A headfirst dive into oblivion,
Became a cherished reprieve.
But this gift he thought amazing,
Turned and beat him to his knees.
Fast forward to adulthood,
Never experiencing real love
No hope or ambition,
No real faith in God above.
Programmed by his past,
But he wanted to be better.
Still comfortable in that chaos
Emotions bursting from the pressure.
Stress and fear held him down,
"Playing the cards life handed me."
Lashing out and causing pain,
To myself and my family.
Wanting to be sober,
To find a better path,
But unable to shake free,
Of the bondage of his past.

Began to find some hope,
Put together some good things.
Took the steps needed to grow,
Things slowly began to change.
Made some good decisions,
Life began to improve.
Found some joy in this life,
But still had more pain to pursue.
Fell off one more time,
This one a different type of bottom.
Kept the outside things together,
But inside his spirit rotted.
Fast forward to today,
I found another chance.
And I'm so grateful for the gift,
And have taken a new stance.
I have unconditional love,
From my wife and my kids.
You'll give me reason to fight,
You'll give me a reason to live.
So grateful for you my sweet girl,
For not giving up on me.
I will give this chance my all,
To become the man you need.

I have learned a lot about myself,
And I am healing from my trauma.
I will learn to live without the chaos,
Give up the fight and constant drama.
I love my life today,
And I am happy for this chance.
I will work hard to back these words with action,
To become my best version of a man.
The future looks so bright,
And my past no longer pulls me down
I thank God for this gift
For this blessing that I've found
I am a work in progress,
It won't happen overnight.
But I will strive daily for atonement,
For our family I will fight.
Staying sober and committed,
To this new path of mine.
If I do this every day,
I know that I'll be fine.

Hypocrite

Fraud, phony, two faced, deceiver, lip-server, fake, liar. Go ahead and insert whatever other synonym you wish here. I have heard them all.

You see, I have never, not once, not ever, said, proclaimed, touted, announced, or declared how perfect I am. I have never once stood out on "the stump" and talked myself up like I was some kind of answer, like I had it all together, or that I was somehow "cured" or some kind of exception to a rule.

I struggle. I fail. I fall. I own it. You see, from the very beginning, when I started trying to piece some kind of life together for myself, I had thirty years of intense wreckage and trauma to clean up. I was all alone. I had no one to carry me, no one to guide me. I had no one to enable me or make this any easier. I knew that there would be struggles and setbacks of course. I vowed to be 100% authentic through it all, and I believe that I still am.

All I did was write some books, stop shooting heroin, turn my life around, and founded a company whose entire purpose is helping people who struggle. I married my best friend. I have raised her/our children and my own son to the best of my human ability. I have done my absolute best to give back to this community in every way possible. We donate to charities, we volunteer, and for the most part, we keep to ourselves. I have spent the last almost eight full years, day in and day out, pouring every single shred of everything that I have into my family, career, company, our community, helping others, and doing the absolute best that I can to make a life for myself.

Yes, I began to unravel. Yes, I fell and struggled. Yes, I am humiliated and embarrassed. But I own it. I am human. Does this mean that I am a hypocrite? A fraud? I will leave that up to the court of public opinion on this one. But I believe in my heart the answer is no.

Love and tolerance is my code, and always will be. I have been somehow placed in the light of notoriety because I wrote a book. Big deal. I am still a human being, and I will succeed with humility, and I will fail with grace. But I will never cease striving to be the best possible version of myself, and I will never cease my authenticity.

Believe it or not, I have always tried to live my life with the utmost integrity, honor, and valor.

The point that I am trying to carve out here, is that all I have ever tried to do while on this planet is find myself, improve myself, love everyone equally, and leave this world better than I found it.

Was it by definition hypocritical of me to go on helping people in my work, while struggling mentally and struggling with alcohol myself? Yes.

Does that make ME a hypocrite? NO.

It makes me human. In fact, I read somewhere that when someone helps you, and they struggle themselves, that's not help, that's love, and I will second that. You see, even though, I was struggling myself for a time there, I couldn't turn my back to anyone who was suffering. I simply do not have the heart to do such a thing. I poured every single piece of everything that I am into this new life of mine, and my failure lied in ceasing self-care. That's when I lost myself, and that is what led me to the bottoming out that I endured. I own that. That was my mistake. It is not one that I will repeat because I make new mistakes nowadays. Life is a non-stop process of learning, growth, and development. Given where I came from, and what I have endured, I am pretty damn proud of the man I am today.

As I go from here on to indeed make new mistakes, I am sure; there is much to atone for. There is much to clean up. It is my mess, and I will clean it up. I will bounce back higher than I ever have before.

I know who I am, and I know whose I am. I know that this walk of mine, this appointment of mine, will not be easy, and I may struggle again. But when God calls us to our missions, He has already factored in our foolishness. He does not call the qualified, He qualifies the called.

I will always be here to help anyone in any way I can.

I have a family. I have a beautiful and wonderful wife. I have a loving and amazing home. I have an incredible life that I thank God for every day. I have a few actual friends.

I have a company that is dedicated to helping other human beings end their sufferings and turn their lives around. This very company was instrumental in helping me as well, I have so very much to be grateful for.

I will make mistakes in the future and am not sure what exactly lies ahead, but I am walking into it with an open heart of acceptance, and with renewed curiosity and vigor.

To all of those who have been supportive, encouraging, and loving, I see you too, and I am incredibly grateful for your love and prayers.

Very sincerely yours,
The Hypocrite

The Man in the Arena

"It is not the critic who counts; not the man who points out how the strong man stumbles, or where the doer of deeds could have done them better. The credit belongs to the man who is actually in the arena, whose face is marred by dust and sweat and blood; who strives valiantly; who errs, who comes short again and again, because there is no effort without error and shortcoming; but who does actually strive to do the deeds; who knows great enthusiasms, the great devotions; who spends himself in a worthy cause; who at the best knows in the end the triumph of high achievement, and who at the worst, if he fails, at least fails while daring greatly, so that his place shall never be with those cold and timid souls who neither know victory nor defeat."

–Teddy Roosevelt, The Man in the Arena

War Time

Life can be and oftentimes is an ongoing battle, especially for those of us with mental health issues. Depression, Anxiety, PTSD, BPD, Addiction, etc. make going through our days all the more difficult and turbulent at times.

When I first got clean and was living at the halfway house, I got a tattoo on my chest. A full chest plate image of an eagle holding a quiver of arrows in one claw and olive branches in the other. The image is strikingly similar to the eagle on the back of a one-dollar bill. It is almost identical. The difference between the two is on the dollar, the eagle's head faces the olive branches. The eagle's head on my chest faces the arrows.

An eagle whose head faces the olive branches is known as a, "Peace Time Eagle," which symbolizes a time of great harmony, joy, and peace.

Mine is known as a, "War Time Eagle," which symbolizes exactly what you may be thinking, a time for war. War with and within myself, war with the world, and war with my past and future. I knew it was going to be a very long and painful pilgrimage ahead. I didn't know what might happen or where it would take me, but I was here for it. And I was ready to start fighting.

* * *

Before soldiers head for battle, they prepare and strategize. The ways of preparations have evolved throughout history, but typically those who emerge victorious are the ones who had planned best and showed up most equipped. This is not always the case, but usually the more advanced a side is, the better the outcome is for them.

Typically, from the little I know about actual war, the generals and leaders devise their plans of attack and defense, and then pass those plans down to the soldiers to execute. The soldiers, I imagine, prepare in much different ways: prayer, hyping themselves up, making sure their weapons are functioning properly, and of course, suiting up into their outfits of protection.

These pieces of protection that are described in the Bible, "The Armor of God," are as follows: loins girt with truth (belt of truth), breastplate of righteousness, shoes with the preparation of the gospel of peace (peace), shield of faith, helmet of salvation, and the sword of the spirit/word of God.

Now, you may not be a person of Christian faith, or have never read the Bible, that's okay. I really like the description here, and it is one that is very widely known. So, humor me even if it doesn't particularly speak to your faith.

So what do we have in all of this War Ready Ensemble? A belt, probably not a leather belt from Walmart with holes in it to help hold out pants up. More than likely a heavy steel belt, very wide in breadth to protect our midsection and lower torso. Just above this belt begins the breast plate, a large and heavy fortified shell of sorts which protects us from swords and arrows that could be hurled at us. Shoes more than likely heavy boots outfitted with steel to protect our base. A very sturdy shield, emblazoned with the insignia of whom we are fighting for. A very sturdy metal helmet for obvious reasons. A massive sword, or in modern day instances, a very high-powered, high-capacity rifle. Hopefully you can get the imagery. I can see it now, and when I think of armor, I think of the British soldiers in the movie *Braveheart*, with the chain mail and the heavy metal swords.

As the armor is described in the Bible, what is significant about each and every piece? What do they all have in common? What is missing? Notice that "The Armor of God" does not include or describe any pieces of protection for our backs. The backs of our legs, the backs of our necks, or funnily enough, our asses, or rear ends. What do all of the pieces have in common? They are all front-facing pieces. They all fit and protect the front facing portions of the soldiers.

I wonder why that is? Well, I believe it is because we cannot win a battle that we are running from. If we are getting hit in the back, then we are not facing the "enemies." In order for the armor to serve its purpose, we must go in face first. We must march directly into our adversaries, with courage and bravery, and trust that the armor is going to do its job.

Now I know that this is a bit metaphorical here, especially as it pertains to mental health. I can see the connection though. I have felt the effects of both running from my issues and confronting them head on. They are stark in contrast to one another and have dramatically different results.

For years I thought that me getting better was *just* about not drinking or using, and for a time, it was. This was also an excuse of sorts for me not to boldly and fearlessly confront the actual reasons that brought me to using to begin with.

"Hey, I'm clean/sober so I must be doing something right," and I was. But that was just the very beginning for me, and many of us out there. It was also a defense piece for me. It was a piece of my "armor" so to speak. It was my shield of arrogance. I held it with me everywhere I went. Any time I felt something threatening an old vulnerability of mine, I would hoist that shield and display my own insignia: "Clean and sober." Or I would hide behind humor and deflect it away. But, as with all armor, no matter how modern it is, there are always weak points.

It took me really spiraling out . . . once I finally had something and someone to lose . . . to finally be ready to take a step back and objectively look at myself and say, "I am missing something here." And that I believe is one of the most fascinating things about trauma. It hides within us. It literally hides. We don't always think about it; in fact, I hardly ever did. It is so subtle too, oftentimes we don't even realize that we are having a trauma response or acting out on our mental health issues until after the fact.

You see, I honestly thought that I was a changed man when I began spiraling out, and I was. But I still had so much to explore and confront in order to achieve the level of significant healing that I was really striving for. Unfortunately, with unhealed parts of us, we don't even realize that they are there until they flare up or rear their ugly heads, often with dramatic consequences and leaving us again auditing what the hell just happened. This is what they mean when they say, "We don't know what we don't know." I believe this very much.

We simply do not and cannot know or understand how much an

event, a season, a loss, an addiction, etc. has truly affected us if we do not examine it. I believe that really truly processing things beginning at an early age is critical, before harmful events and seasons become traumas. If this is not possible, as is the case with far too many in this world due to lack of access to adequate mental health services, then as soon as we are able, we must initiate the process of processing.

Even if we believe that we are well adjusted, well rounded, mature, and mentally healthy adults, we should attend some kind of therapy. I always say that everyone on this planet would benefit from going to rehab at least once, even if they have never done a drug in their life.

You see, this is important because we may not know how something has and is actually affecting us now. Remember, we are used to our own "normal," and what we interpret as normal, may be anything but. It is in those subtle unexposed "isms" inside of us that we could be living, acting, thinking, and believing in maladaptive and corrupt ways. I suppose, in keeping up with the armor/battle metaphor, this would be the binoculars of new perspective or the spyglass of a fresh vantage points. We cannot simply rely on our own first-person perspective and our own thinking to solve our own problems and survive our own troubles. It is critical that at some point in our lives, we all find a therapist, pastor, mentor, counselor, or just someone who we truly trust, and tell them the whole story. It is imperative that we learn from ourselves and from our own life stories and actions. This is how we learn self-awareness and grow past the hidden things that are holding us back and causing us to act against our character.

You see, I didn't even know that the vulnerabilities, wounds, and traumas existed inside of me the way they did—until I again and again acted out on them, messed my life up, and was essentially forced to take a good long honest look at my life in total.

I didn't know about them because I am me and they live inside of me. I had always been using my own thinking, beliefs, and perspective to interpret the very life that gave me those things. That doesn't work. We must be willing and able to confront those messy parts of ourselves and learn how they went into creating who we are today.

We don't have to and shouldn't be made to feel weak or ashamed for embarking on such a journey of self-discovery and healing.

Getting vulnerable and being open about my most sensitive parts of my life story was the most courageous I have ever felt in my entire life. It provided me with new armor, quite possibly the most valuable piece of them all: wisdom, knowledge, understanding, insight, and self-awareness. It helped me identify the places that I had been "weak" in the past or "more vulnerable to attack," if you will. A fool knows how strong he is, and a genius knows how weak he is—and where he is weak.

We gotta do it. We gotta armor up and walk into the battle with ourselves and with our own stories. That is how we learn the most valuable knowledge we will ever hold, and that is the knowledge of ourselves.

We cannot change what we refuse to confront. What we resist, persists. All of the armor listed above makes no mention of protecting us from behind so if we refuse to walk boldly into it, and we choose to run away, we die.

The armor we slip on as we prepare for battle is all designed so that we can face the enemy, not run away. Please be bold enough and brave enough to face those dark and scary parts of yourself and your story. Your life may depend on it.

As the old saying goes, "If you want peace, prepare for war."

Bittersweet

Once upon a time, in the Ancient Farmlands of rural China, lived an old cattle farmer named Pong. Pong was a fifth-generation farmer who was tilling the land and growing crops to earn a living and provide for his small family. That was all that he knew. I say small family because Pong and his wife, Wi, only had one child, a young man in his late teens named Pong Jr. They didn't have much land, but it was all that they needed. One strong horse to till and plow their land each year which would provide enough harvest to sustain their family and pay their bills. It wasn't much, but it was an honest living.

One day, Pong and his son were getting ready for the day's work of plowing and preparing the land. They had their morning tea and headed to the barn to get the horse ready for the day's work. Upon their arrival at the stable, the pair could tell that the horse was acting a little out of sorts but couldn't figure out why. Against their better judgement, they proceeded to lead the horse out of the barn and toward the fields to work. As soon as the three made clearance into the fields, the horse bucked, jumped, and got loose from its lead rope and ran away, leaving Pong and his son devastated.

How could they work now? They certainly couldn't afford a new horse on their modest living. What were they to do?

Once news of the runaway horse made its way around town, neighbors would come to Pong voicing their concerns, and concern for themselves, as Pong's harvest always yielded to the local markets and helped feed the community.

"Pong, Pong, what will you do now!? How will we all eat?! Isn't this such a terrible thing?!" they would ask.

Pong, being a man of great wisdom and insight, replied, "Well,

I don't know if this is a good or a bad thing, but what I do know is that I don't have a horse now."

The townspeople were shocked that a man, a farmer and a town staple, was not as crazed over the loss of his prized work horse as they were. Although internally he was incredibly stressed out, he continued in his faith and his mission. The fields were not waiting. They had to be plowed. So, Pong strapped on his shoulder the plow and spent his days dragging the fields himself—and the evenings looking for his horse, all to no avail on the latter. Long grueling days went by. Loads of extra work, still no horse.

About two weeks later, just before sunrise, Pong awoke to the sound of what appeared to be playful neighing and hoof stomps out in the barn yard. Was he dreaming? He rushed outside into the morning chill and noticed that not only had his beloved horse returned, but he had returned with a mate! His prized horse had returned with a female wild mustang! They would later find out the horses had mated, and Pong and his family would soon have THREE HORSES!

When the townspeople found out, they were so excited for Pong and his family and were so happy for themselves, for this meant that Pong would soon be able to get three times the harvest in the same amount of time!

"Pong, Pong, isn't this such a great thing?! You will soon have three horses and be able to feed the town three times as much!" they cried.

Pong, being a man of great wisdom, replied, "Well, friends, I don't know if this is a good thing or a bad thing, but what I do know, is that very soon I will have three horses."

First came the challenge of breaking the wild mustang and teaching her to farm. This would not be an easy task, as horses are fickle creatures, and a pregnant horse is particularly difficult to break. But the fields were not waiting, and this needed to be done.

So, Pong and his son would spend hours with their trusted stud horse plowing and tilling the fields, and the evening hours working with the new addition to their team. She certainly seemed to be doing well for a while. About three weeks into their training, Pong was riding the stud out into the fields, leading the female being ridden by his son, when suddenly a snake slithered out into the path of the female horse. She bucked back in fright, throwing Pong's son off of her back. She then bucked back and forth and stomped down on Pong's son's leg, shattering it in two places.

Pong Sr. was able to corral the female and get her stabled, and it was decided that they would wait until after the female gave birth to try and break her again. But now, Pong and his family were faced with a new dilemma. Pong Jr.'s leg was horribly mangled.

When the townspeople learned of this, they were heart broken, as Pong Jr. was Pong's right-hand man, and now their harvest and provisions were again in jeopardy.

"Pong, Pong, what are we gonna do? Your son is now lame, and now you will only be able to produce half of your yearly crop! What are we going to do? Isn't this such a bad thing?" they cried.

Pong, being a man of great faith and insight, replied, "Well, I do not know if this is a good thing, or a bad thing, but what I do know, is that my son has a broken leg and cannot work the fields now."

Being that this was Ancient China, and medical care was not what it is today, the care and rehabilitation for Pong Jr.'s leg was primitive. Sure, they would be able to get him walking again, but they would not be able to get him anywhere near his former shape, and Pong Jr. was a very strong and durable farm hand. He would be bedridden for months on the mend.

Pong Sr. was a very old man, but he too, was a very experienced and durable farm hand, and he knew that the fields were not waiting, and that winter was coming. So, he would arise early and work late. Working for two so to speak, while his son got better. He was finally able to get his fields tilled, planted, maintained, and he would yield a very fruitful harvest! He was feeling very blessed and fortunate that he was able to overcome such adversities and still pull together a harvest. He would finally be able to rest and enjoy some down time.

During the beginning of the cold winter months, a terrible and vengeful civil war broke out with the dynasty to the west. The town and territory, or dynasty that Pong and his family lived in, and its leaders and Generals went door to door, not requesting but ordering that all men aged ten years to fifty were required to show up for battles. The only exception would be those who were not fit for battle. Being that Pong Jr. was still healing from the horse accident, and Pong Sr. was sixty-two-years-old, his family was spared.

The rest of the town was not so lucky.

As luck, or God, or fate would have it, not one home in Pong's town had a boy younger than ten years old. Every single male in the town was sent off to war, and they were all lost in battle. Ultimately Pong's community had to surrender to the dominant forces of the opposition, and not one single male from his town returned home from war. It was truly devastating for everyone.

As the dust settled, and the smoke cleared, Pong Jr.'s leg healed enough for him to work, and life went back to normal. As normal as it could be in a post war era. Pong and his son were finally able to get the female mustang under control, break her, and train her to farm the land. As time passed, the female gave birth, and this young male pony was assisting with the farm work too! As for Pong and his family, although they were very saddened for the rest of the community, they were very happy to have survived and still have each other.

Eventually, the town was withering with low population, as all of the males were killed in battle, and the older males who were not called to war were dying off. Though this was very sad for so many, this made Pong Jr. a very important young man. Not only were they the main providers in the community, but now he was the only healthy male left to help the community continue to repopulate and multiply. Though selfishly, this made Pong Jr. glow with male bravado as he knew he would be a VERY busy man, it also carried with it a very large amount of responsibility. Pong and Pong Jr. knew this.

The women in town would cry out to Pong Sr., "Pong, Pong, you still have your son, you still have your land, and if you will allow your son to marry my daughter, we will divide our land with you, and crown you and your son as royalty. We will donate half of our earnings to you and your family, and you will be a very important person for years to come. Isn't this such a great thing?"

Pong, being a man of great wisdom, took a deep breath, and said, "Well, after all these years, I suppose it was a good thing after all, that my horse ran away."

* * *

It has been said that justice is getting what we deserve, mercy is not getting what we deserve, and grace is getting what we do not deserve.

Looking back on your life, in what ways have you received

justice, mercy, and grace? Looking back on your life, what events took place that you just didn't or couldn't understand? What horrible pain have you experienced? What loss? Grief? Trauma? In what way can you look back at it now, and what grace can you pull from it? Are you able to reflect back on events in your life that were once terrible and uncertain times, and pull something precious from them?

In what ways has God, the universe, fate, or whatever you believe in, used your suffering for good? In what ways has the justice you have experienced actually been mercy and grace? Is there a grey area between these three ideas?

How can you relate to Pong, the farmer in this story, and apply it to your own life? Is everything good, or bad; or is it just what it is, for now?

After some time has passed, were you able to look back on the current circumstances you faced with and discern the lesson from all of the todays, as they compile and form a life catalogue in your heart.

How can God use your current circumstances today for good? For the good of you and for the good of the world? How can you utilize this pain, this triumph, this lesson, this blessing, or this loss, or victory, to benefit the good of your community? Is that even possible? Do you even know? How can you use the justice you have been served, to then serve mercy? Can that even happen? I believe that it can.

Pong was a very wise and insightful man, and it was because he had learned to grow through what he went through, and he knew that even though a situation may seem utterly awful right here and right now, eventually time would pass, and he would then have an opportunity to look back on the past circumstances and pull some goodness from what seemed dire before.

Oftentimes, we see rejection, but it is really redirection.

Sometimes we see loss, but it is really opportunity.

We may feel pain, but it is really growth.

All we have is the right here and right now. There will be tomorrow for some of us, and for some of us not. But for those of us who are fortunate enough to continue on in time, opportunities will continue to present themselves, to utilize our past and reflect, to make a more important choice with our future tomorrows so we can make the world a better place for others.

Life itself is bittersweet. Sometimes life just sucks and sometimes it seems like we're on a winning streak like no other . . . and then it sucks again. Sometimes life doesn't illicit anything at all, it kind of just is, and I believe that's where the notion of the pursuit of happiness comes from. Those fleeting moments of bliss and joy that tickle our stomachs with butterflies and amusement. Those pure sweet happy times. I also think that this is the way it is supposed to happen. We cannot enjoy the bliss and the joy without the sorrow and pain. Just like we cannot enjoy springtime as much without the dead cold snaps of winter.

This is more of Herb's psychobabble, but I think it makes sense.

I have said it for years and asked the question more like this: "Why does God allow suffering?"

I believe it is first so that we can draw nearer to him and power up our relationship and dependence upon him. Second, so that we can overcome our sorrows, and then in turn use our experiences to help the next one in line who is suffering in a season that we just overcame.

The most powerful thing that we can share with each other is not facts, or sciences, or opinions, or beliefs. The most important thing that we can share with each other is our own experiences.

For everyone and everything: is either a lesson, or a blessin'; and life itself, is bittersweet.

The Silversmith

Have you ever endured a substantial trial in your life? Of course, you have. Have you ever endured an incredibly difficult season? Of course, you have. Perhaps the substantial trial or season in your life was something or many things that seemed to be unrelentingly happening to you; or perhaps there was an era in your life where you/I/we just couldn't seem to get out of the rut that we ourselves created or brought upon ourselves. Either way or both, I'm sure we can all relate to this.

Some of us may be here right now. Nothing seems to go right or go our way. Even with the purest of intentions, it just seems to constantly be one step forward and two, five, eight, or ten steps back. We find ourselves stuck in the "what's the use" mindset, or worse—"I give up," or "fuck it" mindsets. All three of those mindsets are incredibly dangerous places to dwell, addict or not, and can lead us to some pretty dark places and serious bottoms.

What I have come to believe is that every season, and every trial has its purpose. I didn't always feel this way or believe this, but I most certainly do now. We grow through what we go through, and it all leads us to exactly where we are, right now.

* * *

My Grandmother is the sweetest lady to ever walk the planet. Am I biased in this statement? Absolutely. Am I also right? Absolutely. She was, is, and always will be my biggest fan, supporter, prayer warrior, and guardian angel. I gave this woman absolute hell in return for her efforts of trying to raise me and guide me while my dad was in prison, and I was strung out on just about everything. Even though I was so busy not listening to her, much of the tutelage and inspiration did in fact stick. Case in point, this whole damn entry here.

Gramma was always there for me, no matter what. She enabled in some ways, and in others, she did not. I think she only bonded me out of jail one time, and that was a result of the pressures from my dad to get me out of Cook County jail.

She was always there to help mold, mentor, lecture, and guide me, even though it seemed to go in one ear and out the other a lot of the time. It didn't. It just seemed that way I'm sure. She was always very patient with me, dedicated, and kind.

She was always the very first name I would put on my visitation cards when I was spending time away in the local county jails or in prison. Sure as shit, she was always the very first one to come and visit me, without fail, no matter what. I understand that that may kind of sound like enabling, and to some degree it might be, but she never came to baby me, or anything like that. I truly believe that she understood all along how very sick I was and could sympathize with how bad I was struggling. She would come and see me, twice a week, every week, to pray with me, and yes, to lecture me. I would just listen, and "uh-huh" and nod my head yes. But what I really know now, is through all of this . . . through all the years and relapses, and using, and jail, and sleepless nights for her . . . I'm sure she was ministering to me. Something that is very near and dear to her heart—sharing her incredibly devout faith with others who will listen. And Gramma can spit game too. She is not a novice by any stretch of the imagination.

She's a spiritual gangster as anyone in any fellowship. She's just never been an addict, but she understands suffering like no one I've ever known. And isn't that really the whole juice to it? Empathy and suffering? Aren't those two of the most powerful things that could ever bind us flawed humans together? Not suffering in a trauma bond type scenario, but don't we just have this innate drive to want to feel, understand, and help others who are less fortunate or hurting? I think so.

But anyway, Gramma got it. She is locked in, man. One of "Gramma's greatest hits" or "Gramma's On—Repeat" for us Spotify users, was the parable of the Silversmith.

* * *

I would be in jail. Again. Gramma was my only visitor. Again. She would come with such grace, understanding, compassion, and kindness, but she would also come with a very subtle "listen here, motherfucker." (Although my Gramma didn't even come close to swearing) Her type of delivery just demanded to be digested at times. She would talk to me about how when we "face these fires," she is reminded of the Silversmith.

Now, as I understand it, the Silversmith back in the day would start with what I can only imagine as a giant lump or ball of very rough and contaminated silver. I'm not a geologist, but I would imagine it's a very crude process at first, especially in the Biblical time frame in which my Gramma was referring to.

The silversmith would take the lump of crude silver and stick it into the flames of the forging fires until it was glowing hot and molten. Once it was a liquid, they would remove it from the fires, allow it to cool just a bit, and use a special tool to remove the "slag," or obvious contaminants in the precious metal, and then return the silver back into the fires. They would repeat this process over and over and over again, until the metal worker was satisfied with his or her work. Each time, refining the precious silver more and more. More diligence, more precise tools, and each and every time the metal was cool and cleaned, less and less slag or debris was removed, as the metal would become cleaner and cleaner. And the most experienced silversmiths, who had been in practice at this craft for many, many years, could tell that the silver was truly pure when they could see their reflections looking back at them in cooled and polished bars and coins.

I don't know why I felt so led to share this with all of you today, but it was put on my heart last night and I woke up and it was still there—so that's usually a pretty good sign that I should share it. But what's the point?

I suppose the point is, we all face fires, we all face trials and tribulations. We all have "slag" and "debris" that need to be removed, and we all need refining. Regardless of specific religion or dogma, we all have a "smith." We all have someone or many people who we reflect. As I have always said, we are the average of the five people we associate with or depend on most. As the fires of our lives hit us, and the slag is removed, and we are polished, we will begin to reflect the smiths who are pushing and pulling us in and out of the fires.

The whole double edge to this idea here is 1: Fire burns. The fires of life are never comfortable, they're painful and difficult, and scary. Sometimes they're humiliating and embarrassing. Sometimes we think we will never get out of them alive. And 2: Be mindful of your "smiths." We can go from the fire into the frying pan, real quick. We must be careful and discerning about who we are trusting to refine us, to help us remove our slag, and to help us polish. Otherwise, all of our firings can in fact, be for naught.

Who are your smiths? Who are you depending on? Who is helping you shine and polish? And are they shining you up for your own brightness, or to trade you off in barter for something for themselves?

My Gramma would tell me, and you, "God is the Silversmith, and he makes all things work together for our good. So that we can have our slag removed, so that we can then help forge, and shine others who need it." I believe her 100%, with all my heart.

* * *

A wise man has many councils.

It is in the fires of life that we are refined and polished, but we must learn to reflect the smiths who got us here. Then in turn, use our skills to help others shine. That's the mission.

That's why God allows suffering. 1: So we can realize our dependence upon him; and 2: So that we can be refined, we can have our "Slag"(fears, doubts, insecurities, addictions, shortcomings, etc.) removed, and then help the next one in line to do the same.

Reflect on who made ya.

The Starfish

"Once upon a time, there was an old man who used to go to the ocean for exercise.

One day, the old man was walking along a beach littered with thousands of starfish that had washed ashore with the tide. As he walked, he came upon a young boy who was eagerly throwing the starfish back into the ocean, one by one.

Puzzled, the man looked at the boy and asked what he was doing.

The young boy paused, looked up, and replied, "Throwing starfish into the ocean. The tide has washed them up onto the beach, and they can't return to the sea by themselves. When the sun gets high, they will die, unless I throw them back into the water."

The old man replied, "But there must be tens, of thousands of starfish on this beach. I'm afraid you won't really be able to make much of a difference."

The boy bent down, picked up yet another starfish, and threw it as far as he could into the ocean. Then he turned, smiled, and said, "It made a difference to that one!"

Adapted from *The Star Thrower*, by Loren Eiseley (1907—1977)

Acknowledgments

I just want to take a moment and recognize some people who have made an impact on my life. It is the people in our lives who make it worth living, and I have some people to thank, who I love and cherish very much. I will forever be grateful to each and every one of you. Thank you all from the bottom of my heart for loving me and for believing in me, even when I didn't believe in myself.

First and foremost, I must thank God. I pray that my life and my work in this world will be pleasing to God and bring Him glory and joy. I know that I have fallen short time and time again, but God has never left me or forsaken me. There were times when I couldn't go on, and it was God's love, grace, and mercy shown through the people closest to me that got me through my most difficult times.

Of course, I must include my amazing wife Tiffany, and our children Jamie, Logan, Connor, and Lucas. You five are quite possibly the reasons that I am still here. You all will never in a thousand lifetimes ever know the love, adoration, and admiration that I have for each and every one of you. To be a part of your lives, and to get to participate in life with you is my greatest joy. It is an honor to be loved by you all. I am so proud of each and every one of you! My sweet girl, my shining star, and my three little bears. I love you all more than you will ever know!

To my parents, Dad and Gail. Thank you for always having my back and for taking care of me when I was at my lowest. Gail, thank you for taking care of my dad. It is so sweet to see you two so in love. You are two of the real ones in this world. I appreciate and cherish you both more than you will ever know. Thanks for never giving up on me!

To my little brother Lucas, I am so incredibly proud of the man you have and continue to become. I admire and look up to you more than you may realize. It has been such a distinct honor and privilege, experiencing life with you. I hope you know how much precious love I hold inside my heart for you little brother! Mom and Josh would be so proud of the man you are today! You inspire me 'Dood'!

To my dear friend Brian Hero, thank you. Since our first days working together in Lowell, you have always been a real friend who has always guided me and mentored me in positive directions. You were instrumental in helping me get my life back, and I will never forget that. I will forever hold a special place in my heart for you.

For Mitch Peters, Ken Elwood, Steve Pribyl, Sheriff Dave Reynolds, Judge Roger Bradford, and Gary Germann. Thank you, gentlemen. None of you owed me anything, and yet each and every one of you went out of your way, above and beyond fashion to stand up for me, defend me, and give me multiple chances at a decent life. I know that I am still and always will be a work in progress, but because of each and every one of you, I still have an opportunity at life.

Dan Ball and Dave Mangel, De Colores my brothers. I love you both with my whole heart and hope you both know how much I respect and honor your friendships. Thank you for being the strong Christian men in my life and for always doing your best to keep me accountable and growing in the right directions.

The Mundy family and Carol Doughty, I love each and every one of you more than you will ever know. Thank you all for believing in me and supporting me throughout the course of my lifetime.

The Crawford family, the Penick family, and Gramma. Thank you all for the love you have shown me, the seeds you have planted in my heart and for all the support, prayers, and patience as I tried to put my life together. I love each and every one of you.

Debbie, and the entire Mockler family, Ken and Lisa Morton. I love, respect, and appreciate every single one of you. I hope you all know that I would be there for each and every one of you at any moment's notice. Near or far, I will always have nothing but love for each and every one of you.

Lita Peters, Debbie and Tracy Sandoval, Todd Willis, Scott Hamilton; Thank you all for always being my friends, and for believing in me. I know that I have been a knucklehead for most of my life, and each and every one of you have always seen something in me and made me feel valuable. I love you all. Thank you!

Bob and Sue Rohweder and Rich Norton, Thank you all from the bottom of my heart for being my friends, for believing in me, and for helping me succeed! I will always hold a special place in my heart for you three. I love you all!

Thank you John Paul Owles and Joshua Tree Publishing for believing in me all this time. It has been a blessing to work with you and learn so much from you. Thank you for helping me tell my story.

To my therapists in treatment, Krystal Derr, Michelle Woodside, and Alex Lind; You all saved my life. I mean that. Thank you all from the bottom of my heart for everything you have done and everything you will do for people like me. I know without a doubt that you three will continue to go on and save countless lives. I am forever grateful. I love you all tremendously.

To my Treatment Crew: Bobby J, Ryan M, John A, Tim P, Jake D, Lanny B, D.C., and Josh L. Thanks to each and every one of you for the tremendous impact you all had on my life. I will forever hold a special place in my heart for you. You all inspired and moved me in ways I cannot express. Thank you for helping me get my spark for life back. Keep on widlin' / G.O.F.R.M / L.F.D.

"When 'We' replaces 'I', even illness becomes wellness"

I owe my life to these people.

About the Author

Herb Stepherson was born in Clayton County, Georgia. He is thirty-seven years old and married to his beautiful wife, Tiffany. They have four children and currently reside in Valparaiso, Indiana.

Together they founded Genesis of Recovery, an intervention firm that helps any and all who suffer from the disease of addiction. Since beginning his recovery and healing journey, Herb has published two books, given a TEDx talk, founded an intervention company, given his heart to God, written bills to become laws, and founded a domestic non-profit organization.

Though he will undoubtedly struggle with mental health issues for the rest of his life, he and his wife have made it their mission to make this world a better place. Serving their community in the battles against addiction, advocating for a multitude of reforms, and making recovery a reality for all and inspire change on many different levels. They work together hand in hand, hoping to inspire as many people as they can to heal, recover, and live life most abundantly.

Their intervention and recovery assistance company, Genesis of Recovery can be found at: www.genesisofrecovery.com. You can also connect with Herb at www.Junkboxdiaries.com.

"It is in sharing our struggles and vulnerabilities that we connect with others and inspire change in them. Empathy and experience are some of our most powerful connecting points, and by offering my own personal struggles, I hope to let others know that they are not alone, and that there is always hope, even in the darkest of times. No one should ever feel ashamed for struggling mentally. Going to therapy for mental health should be as normal as going to a doctor for a broken leg. No one is a lost cause, and no one should ever be made to feel that way. Each and every human being on this planet should be given the opportunity to experience love and be given opportunities to turn their lives around." -Herb Stepherson